Reviews

Barry Triller, Executive Vice-President, Clarica

"Rocket-Man is an entertaining and thoughtful book on the challenges, woes and opportunities of being in the dynamic business of sales. It presents the key topics of being successful and sustaining success in a story-telling manner that is easy to relate to for anyone who works in sales or with sales people. The concepts are sound and tested via real life experiences of the author. It will be of assistance to currently successful sales and marketing people, as well as to those who are currently experiencing less than peak performance."

Carmen Gray, Prophet Consulting

"Rocket-Man offers tangible, user-friendly advice on the art of sales through a refreshingly easy-to-read, seemingly real-life tale. But more than that, Rocket-Man is inspiring and pertinent for everyday life - how we are interacting with our kids, our spouse... Through the experiences of 'Bob', the author presents ways we can reflect and potentially enhance satisfaction with relationships at home and at work. I recommend Rocket-Man for anyone who has reached a plateau personally or professionally."

Sheldon Dyck, VP – Business Financial Services – Alberta Treasury Branches

"Rocket-Man delivers a very powerful message about the need to consistently be 'brilliant at the basics'. Perhaps of even greater importance is that it does so in a light, easy to read, and entertaining way that all sales folk will be able to relate to and identify with. Rocket-Man is a must read for the new salesperson learning the craft or the seasoned veteran who is attempting to return to greatness."

Rocket-Man: The Resurrection!

Featuring Brilliant at the Basics

Brian D. Kjenner

Canadian Cataloguing in Publication Data

Kjenner, Brian D. (Brian David), 1958-
  Rocket-man, the resurrection

  Includes bibliographical references.
  ISBN 0-9688189-0-0

  1. Selling. 2. Customer relations. I. Semchuk, Joel. II. Title.
HF5438.25.K48 2000   658.85   C00-911423-8

Edited by: Joel Semchuk

Cover Design: Shawn Christenson
                  Mediashaker

Published by: Selling Solutions Inc.
                  Edmonton, Alberta
                  Printed in Canada

To Allyson, Daniel, Kelvin, and Alexa, who represent my greatest source of pride. Thank you for your patience and support!

To Blair, who believed in my ability to deliver Rocket-Man from the first passage on.

Chapters

Chapter 1
Introducing Rocket-Man!

*A*s I make my way back to the office, I turn down one of the residential streets. Not because it's a faster way to the office, but more because it isn't. It is early afternoon, and I'm returning from another sales call... and they didn't buy again.

The houses on the street are small, close together, and old. The thing I love about this street is the trees along the boulevard; in the middle of summer, it's like driving through a tunnel. It reminds me so much of the neighbourhood I grew up in.

It's fall now, and most of the leaves are on the ground. I slow down as I see an interesting sight: an old man is cleaning up his front yard with several bags neatly bundled all around. The man is wrestling with a stepladder as he tries to position it beside one of the trees that has lost all but a few dangling leaves.

I bring the car to a complete stop, and I look back to see what will happen next. Once the ladder is positioned, the old man reaches for the rake that is lying on the ground. I watch as he cautiously climbs one step at a time, one hand on the ladder, the other hand dragging the rake up behind him. He stops three steps from the top and slowly raises the rake over his head with both hands. Once it is in position, he reaches back down with one hand grasping the ladder to steady himself. Slowly he starts flailing with the rake in an attempt to knock the remaining leaves to

1

the ground. It occurs to me at that instant that this is a man who has very little to do with his time. Although, even sadder yet, neither do I.

I think to myself, what a great setting for a retirement planning commercial. I can see it vividly. The caption would read, "So what do you have planned for your retirement?"

At first, the thought is funny, but then a chill goes through me. To think this could be me one day—if I can't find any new clients.

With depression setting in, I release the brake and begin rolling slowly down the street. I have to get back to the office; I am already late for our divisional meeting. Today they are introducing yet another new manager. We have seen so many new managers over the past few years that it is hard to keep track of them all.

This is a story about me, Bob Stephens. I'm a salesman. A good salesman... or at least, I used to be. I am now 40 years old, and I feel like I have passed my prime. Is that even possible at 40 years old? I have been selling for the same company for the last fifteen years. That's a long time with one company... especially these days.

As I wind in and out of the residential streets, I reflect back to when I first started. I was just out of university. Within a few years, I was lighting the world on fire. In fact, that's how I got my nickname 'Rocket-Man'!

I had only been working for my company for a couple of years, and things had been going well for me. I was the new kid on the block, and it hadn't taken me long to rise up to the top; over those first few years, I was the one winning all of the awards.

I'll never forget the day... there I was, in my car, driving into the parking lot. I had just come back from another great sale, and I was on top of the world. Back then, the sales came a lot easier. I had Rocket-Man blasting, and I was singing at the top of my lungs. Little did I know that a couple of my co-workers, Teddie and Sarah, were in the parking lot as I drove in. How was I supposed to know they could hear me singing so clearly? I turned a little red when I finally noticed them, but I could tell by their expressions that it was too late. "They are just jealous!" I told myself. Jealous of my success.

I got out of my car and modestly tried to slip by them. We exchanged our polite "good mornings" before I ducked into my office. "Maybe they didn't hear me after all," I prayed.

First thing that morning was our monthly sales meeting. It was a command performance... everyone was there. I was pressed to get there on time because I wanted to sign the contract with my newest client before the meeting started. Back then, I loved starting the day with a sale.

As I walked into the meeting, Teddie and Sarah chuckled, but I chose to ignore them. I was more focused on the fact that I was about to get a little 'token' of appreciation from the boss, John Andrews, for another great month. I was hoping that the token this month would be cash. Since I was a newlywed, it was nice to earn a little fun money that only I knew about. I also loved it when John came up to me after the meeting and gave me another 'atta boy!' It seems childish, but for some reason, it really felt good.

John was always very entertaining when he did the monthly sales meeting. He loved to do the 'countdown' for the top salespeople, just to keep everyone in suspense. He would start at the 5th, then the 4th, the 3rd, and so on. I didn't care if I came in 1st every time as long as I could stay ahead of Teddie and Sarah.

That morning, Ralph got out of the chute early with the 5th spot. Then it was Chris in the 4th and Teddie at 3rd. I figured that left Sarah and myself. When John announced Sarah's name, it took everything in my power to not jump out of my seat with glee.

Before mentioning my name, John started building to a crescendo, listing off all my accomplishments over the past year or so. Everyone at the meeting knew John was referring to me, but it was kind of a nice effect.

When he finally got around to saying, "... and the salesperson of the month is Bob Stephens!", those clowns - Teddie and Sarah - jumped up and started singing 'Rocket-Man'! As I walked to the front of the room, I could have died; I was so embarrassed.

The nickname Rocket-Man stuck with me for years... or at least it did for as long as my results were coming in. Now that my results have slipped, Rocket-Man is only a painful reminder of how things used to be. In fact, the new salespeople don't even know Rocket-Man exists. Some of them don't even know my real name.

As I approach my office building, I once again feel the frustration; I know I am a good salesperson. After all, you can't achieve what I've achieved without being good... damn good! My problem is that I just can't put my finger on what has changed. As far as I can tell, I am doing everything the same, but for some reason, the results just don't seem to come anymore.

In the past, I could always talk to John Andrews about these kinds of things, but he retired several years ago. Consequently, I lost touch with him and every other manager that has paraded through since. John Andrews was so good for me. He knew what buttons to push to get me back on track. Maybe that's the problem, I thought; I need another 'John Andrews' in my life.

All of the managers since John Andrews have been focused on one thing and one thing alone: numbers! If they are not talking about sales, they are talking about budgets and how, for whatever reason, we are always behind. It seems to me that the managers in our company have lost touch with the one important thing needed to produce those numbers: the people!

I pull into my stall, grab the reminders of another sales meeting gone badly, and casually make my way up to the office. I am late for the meeting but now it doesn't seem to matter. When John Andrews was here, the meeting room was always packed... now it is only half full. I walk calmly past the dignitaries and grab a chair in the back row beside Teddie and Sarah. We stick together, the three of us, because we now represent the 'Old Guard' of the division.

Sitting with my friends makes me feel better, and I lean over to Teddie and whisper, "Should I bother remembering this manager's name, or will he be gone soon, too?" Teddie frowns and shakes his head.

Throughout the discussion of targets and goals - most of which will never be reached anyway - the three of us exchange witty one-liners under our breath.

I can see the new manager sitting in the front row. I assume he is the new manager; he is the only one not saying anything. And moreover, he has the look of someone who is about to be inducted into the Hall of Fame.

"We'd like to introduce you to Jeff Townes!" the woman from head office says and then pauses, as if we are supposed to applaud. Jeff Townes makes his way to the front of the room and stands beside her. When no applause takes place, the woman from head office proceeds to spew on about Jeff's history with the company. The only notable comment I pluck out of them all is that this is Jeff's first assignment as a manager.

"Oh great," Sarah replies, "a brand new manager. Just what I always wanted!" The people a couple of rows up hear her comment and turn around with a smile, as if to agree.

Now it is Jeff Townes's turn to talk. Boy, is this guy pumped! He goes on and on about how happy he is to be here and how anxious he is to get to know each of us, blah, blah, blah. During his talk, he never stops pacing as he constantly thrashes his arms around. It is as if he is on fire.

I lean across to both Teddie and Sarah and comment, "There should be a warning label on his jacket that reads, 'Do not place near flammable liquids!'.

Before the end of the meeting, Teddie and Sarah and I dub Jeff Townes 'Sparky'. I am not sure which one of us actually came up with the handle, but it sure seemed to fit. We walked out early because we had another engagement we needed to attend: coffee time!

Over the next six months, Jeff Townes continued pounding up and down the halls. Office by office, he tried fruitlessly to break ground with the existing sales team. The sales team, on the other hand, continued to slip month after month, with me leading the way. Now there is even less excitement when we have our regular sales meeting, particularly from those of us who are no longer recognized.

On a couple of occasions over those six months, Jeff and I actually spent some time together. While Jeff and I talked, all I could think about was the two of us being "buddy-buddy": him calling me Rocket-Man, me calling him Sparky. Sparky and Rocket-Man... rather has a ring to it! Fortunately, Jeff doesn't know me as Rocket-Man; I am not sure I am quite up to explaining the origins of that!

Whenever Jeff came into my office, I'd make sure the door was closed quickly behind him. I didn't need Teddie and Sarah ribbing me about sucking up to the new manager. Those two wouldn't understand; it's as though shunning the manager is part of the dues required to being a member of our club.

The thing that bothers me the most is that every time Jeff and I talk, he asks me to come and join the training classes he holds for the new salespeople. Can you imagine that? He tells me he wants me to talk to them about what it takes to be successful, but based on my results, I know it's just a ploy to get me to go back to boot camp. When I decline, Jeff always replies, "Come on Bob, I'd like you to get to know them. And them to get to know you."

How could I tell Jeff that for years the 'Old Guard' hasn't really spent a lot of time getting to know the new salespeople? What was the point? They start and, within a few months, they were gone. We even have a name for them... we call them "WMI's." Every time someone new starts, the 'Old Guard', in our generally unscientific manner, sizes him or her up, and if they don't fit our mould, they become labelled WMI (Won't make it). Salespeople really can be vultures.

To Jeff's credit, he has managed to hire this one new crackerjack. At every opportunity, he holds her up like a trophy as if to say, "See, this is how you are supposed to do it!" At first, I was moderately happy for her, but the more Jeff brags about how great she is, the less I like her. The truth is, I've never even talked to her.

As I sit at my desk dwelling on my past, I catch a glimpse of the monthly sales statement. My thoughts immediately switch from a cocky attitude about Jeff to an insecure feeling about my future. I know what the numbers in the statements look like, and I begin to feel a knot forming in my stomach.

Curiously, I have this great list of prospects that I have been working on of which probably a dozen or more are "that close" to signing contracts. That's it! That's my problem! I need to get better at closing the sale! Maybe I have just lost that 'killer instinct'.

Then I shake my head. No... that doesn't make sense either. I know I am in the business of helping people - the business of building relationships. Forcing someone to buy something they don't want isn't a great way to start any relationship. It just doesn't make sense.

All these problems haven't helped things at home either, I muse. My wife, Sandy, has always been the one to pick me up and dust me off when things aren't going well. But lately, her endeavours have not been working.

Sandy and I decided, long before we had our kids, that we wanted her to be able to stay at home with them. And now, although the kids are getting a little older and a little more independent, it is still nice to have Sandy at home to keep our family life a priority.

I realize that if my income keeps dropping like it has over the past few years, I am either going to have to look for a better paying job or else Sandy is going to have to go back to work. How can I get a better paying job at this point? Anyone who would consider hiring me is going to want to look at my results. Results don't lie.

However, I can't imagine Sandy going back to work, either. It's so great for the kids to have her there when they leave for school and when they arrive home. No, it's not that Sandy couldn't get a great job. She has a good education, she is a hard worker, and she is so good with people. Maybe she should go sell, and I should stay home.

This thinking isn't getting me anywhere, I realize.

I try to get some actual work done, but after glancing over the papers on my desk and at my computer I realize that I just cannot concentrate. All I can seem to focus on is my future and the fact that my sales record has to improve if I want to still be here.

I find that when I get to this point where I fear for my future... there's always golf! I love golf. The only good thing about my decline in business is I have been able to make more time for golf. Every couple of weeks or so, I go out with my "professional group"... at least that's what we call ourselves. We even have a name for each member of our threesome: the Butcher, the Baker, and the Candlestick Maker. Eddie is a lawyer and specializes in contract law, so seeing that he is always cutting up everyone else's contracts, it seemed appropriate that he is the Butcher. Brian is a partner in an accounting firm, so we thought, since he works with bread, we'll make him the Baker. One time, I opened my big mouth about my nickname, and so I became the Candlestick Maker - I guess that's better than being called Rocket-Man!

We had this bright idea that we would get together every once in a while and exchange leads; we told ourselves that would be the admission price. It worked so well, we stopped doing it. Anyway, they're a great couple of guys, and although the 'lead thing' fell apart, our friendship didn't.

When we first started golfing together, I was always the top player and had to give the guys strokes. I used to shoot in the eighties, but over the last few years, my game has slipped to the point where I have lost all pride and I now have to ask Brian and Eddie for strokes. It was either ask for strokes or lose both my money and my pride for the rest of all time. I have to get my golf game back!

At least with golf, I know what I need to do: take a lesson or two, and then get back to practicing. I sure wish figuring out what is wrong with my 'sales' game was that easy. As my thoughts switch back to sales, I look around my office and become aware of the dull pain in the pit of my stomach.

I give myself a shake... realizing that this 'stinking thinking' isn't getting me anywhere! Instead of focusing on what's wrong, I need to start focusing on what I can do to turn things around. I have to be decisive! I know... I am going to book a golf lesson!

"It may not solve my sales woes," I convince myself, "but at least it's a decision!" Men have such a great way of justifying their irrational decisions.

I rack my brain, wondering where can I get a golf lesson. The problem with golf pros these days is all they want to do is change your swing. This one time I went for this lesson; I wasn't there five minutes, and this golf pro had me doing everything different. Don't get me wrong; I am all for change if I can see the results. Nevertheless, I need to find a place where I can get a lesson from someone who really knows the game; someone who is really interested in helping *me* get better.

I thumb through the yellow pages looking at golf course after golf course. I didn't realize there were so many golf courses around! How am I ever going to pick one? Then I find one... Canyon Meadows. Sounds like a nice name for a golf course.

I dial the number and listen to the phone ring. I count four rings... I'm hanging up on five, I tell myself. Finally, someone answers. "Canyon Meadows, how can I help you?"

It sounds like an older man to me, I think to myself. "I want to take some golf lessons. Do you provide golf lessons at Canyon Meadows?"

"What do you think? We're a golf course!" the man chuckles. I really don't see the humour, particularly given the mood I am in.

"OK, what packages do you have available?" I ask as the man's chuckling subsides.

"Well, you just missed out on some group lessons we started a couple of weeks ago, but if you're interested, I would be willing to give you a break on some private lessons."

This is an old guy with a bad sense of humour and he wants me to pay for private lessons! "How much?" I ask, as it seems to be the best way to end this call and get on to the next.

"Well... " he starts and then pauses, "... why don't you come out and meet with me and we'll see if we can work out a fair price. I'd like to meet you to see if we're playing on the same fairway."

I don't understand his analogy, so naturally I can't think of a good reason to say "No." "OK," I answer, "when do you want me to come out?"

"Right now!" he almost shouts.

Exactly how busy is this golf course anyway? Before hanging up, I ask a few details about the easiest way to get to the course; at least it isn't too far out of the way. This is a good time to go anyway, I convince myself. Sandy told me this morning before I left that she was going to be late with the kids. I think they are preparing for an upcoming school play but, quite frankly, most of the conversation is a blur.

Once I am in the car, I notice that the knot in my stomach is going away. It feels good to be thinking about something other than my job. As I pull out of the parking lot, my thoughts focus on my upcoming meeting with this 'so-called' golf pro. How much is this going to cost? I wonder. Sandy is going to kill me if I come home and tell her I have spent a gazillion dollars on golf lessons. Although it won't actually cost a gazillion dollars, that won't matter much to her. She keeps a pretty good tab on what I spend these days.

Driving along, I question what I am doing. I start to think of exactly how I am going to say "No" to him. This is unbelievable. Here I am on my way to meet someone to discuss golf lessons, and all I can think about is how I am going to say "No". He seemed like such a nice guy... that will make it even harder. Then I realize that it's probably going to be easier to say "No" to him, whatever his name is, than it will be explaining to Sandy that I signed up for *private* golf lessons.

As I pull into the golf course, I accuse myself of thinking too much. "This should be fun," I say to myself. I love golf! I decide to leave my clubs in the car so that I am not forced into taking a lesson today. That way, if this 'pro' doesn't like the way I say "No", it will be easier to run to my car. And there I go, thinking too much again!

Chapter 2
The Answer Shall Appear

*A*s I walk toward the pro shop, my thoughts slow to the point where I notice my surroundings. I see all of the parking stalls I could have taken instead of the one near the back where I ended up. As illogical as it is, there's always that temptation to run back and move the car one hundred yards closer to the door ... but today I leave my car where I parked it.

Closer to the pro shop, I start taking note of the cars: a Porsche, then a Mercedes, a Lexus, and a BMW. I look over my shoulder and see that the rest of the cars are pretty plain... mine included. Is it my imagination or are the nicest cars at these golf clubs always parked in the best spots? It's almost as if there were a pecking order for cars, and they know it.

I glance down at my watch to see it is just about 4:00 pm, and I know that Sandy and the kids are going to be home by 7:30. That should give me lots of time to meet with this guy and then get home before my family. After all, I am not going to be buying anything today anyway; I have already convinced myself of that.

Approaching the entrance of the pro shop, I can pick out the same chuckle I heard earlier on the phone. Presently I see two gentlemen in their sixties standing at the counter, having a visit. I don't want to interrupt, so I start browsing around the pro shop; I find the merchandise always looks so great in these places. The sweaters are folded perfectly with a wide range of colors available.

I wander over to the assortment of golf clubs on the other side of the small shop, thinking that maybe I just need a new driver. I convince myself that can't be the problem after I check the price tags.

Across the room, I hear the gentleman behind the counter speak up. "Can I help you?"

"Yes, my name is Bob Stephens. I talked to you a while ago about arranging a golf lesson; you suggested that I come in to meet you," I say as I make my way to the counter. The other gentleman has now strolled out of the pro shop, leaving the two of us alone.

The remaining man sticks out his hand. "I sure did. My name is Russ Atkens; I'm one of the pros here at Canyon Meadows. It's nice to meet you, Bob."

As we shake hands, I look him in the eyes and notice that although he is obviously over sixty, he is still in very good shape. He stands about 5' 9" with a slight build, and still has a full head of wavy gray hair. He looks like a golfer.

"So you want to take some golf lessons, do you Bob? Why is that?"

Seems unusual to have a golf pro ask me why I want to take golf lessons. "Well, I guess it's because I am not happy with my score these days. I used to hit pretty consistently in the eighties, but for the past year or so, I haven't broke ninety once."

"Any idea what changed?" Russ inquires, calmly.

Much like my problems selling lately, I can't really put my finger on the problem. "No," I answer, "I really haven't noticed anything I am doing differently. There is one thing though... nowadays, when I hit the ball, I find I am standing a lot closer to it when it lands than before!" I say this with a smirk; I want Russ to know I have a sense of humour, too!

A broad smile comes across his face, exposing wrinkles acquired from too many days in the sun. "Well, we're definitely going to have to do something about that, aren't we?"

Just then a nicely dressed middle-aged woman walks into the pro shop. "Thanks for keeping an eye on things, Russ."

Russ smiles and nods at her. Before she makes it to the counter, Russ asks me, "Would you mind if we slipped over to the club house for a coffee?"

"Sounds good to me," I say, even though I really wasn't in to having coffee at 4:00 in the afternoon. Russ glances over to the lady and says, "Bob and I are going over to the club house. Can you take a message if anyone calls for me?"

"Anything for you Russ," she says in a sweet but somewhat sarcastic tone. She watches Russ until he is completely out of the pro shop.

When we get to the clubhouse, it is half full with golfers enjoying the 19th hole. Many of the golfers smile or otherwise acknowledge Russ as we wade through the tables.

By the time we sit down, a young waiter is already there with the coffee pot and cups. Obviously, I realize, I am not the only one who goes for coffee with Russ.

Once we are settled, Russ asks, "So what do you do, Bob?"

"About what?" I ask, confused.

"What line of work are you in?"

"Oh, I'm in sales with a company here in the city. I've been doing it now for fifteen years."

"Bob, I used to be in sales, and I loved it.... You sales guys; you've got the life. Write your own check; work your own hours. Must be nice. Half the men and women out here during the day are in sales." Russ gives me a wink and then focuses on his cup for a sip of coffee.

"They must be in a different line of sales than I am. The last check I wrote myself bounced!" We both laugh politely at my poor joke.

Then Russ's tone changes. He looks at me straight in the eye and asks, "Bob, what do you really want out of golf?" Before I can answer, Russ continues. "By the time you finish these golf lessons, what do you want to have achieved?"

I am a little surprised at how serious Russ has gotten about both me and my golf game.

"Eighties," I say, talking slowly, "I want to be shooting in the eighties."

"That's it?" he questions. "You want to shoot in the eighties?" Russ continues to stare at me.

"Well, no. I want to shoot in the eighties consistently..." I think for a moment and then continue, "... and I want to have fun! I want to be able to go and play a round, shoot well, be confident in my game, and myself and I want to have fun doing it. Oh yeah, and most important, I want to beat the Butcher and the Baker!"

"Who are the Butcher and the Baker?" Russ asks with a smile.

"Oh, it's these two guys that I golf with every couple of weeks. I have been golfing with them for years. They used to beg me for strokes... but now the tables have turned."

Russ smiles and nods, and then his serious tone returns. "How bad do you want this?"

He still hasn't broken eye contact. I am now feeling a little uncomfortable with how serious he is. I try to break the ice. "Well I'm here, aren't I?"

He doesn't reply. He looks at me silently, waiting for me to answer.

"I want it pretty bad," I continue, my voice gaining excitement, "I've got a young family so I can't afford to be out here all the time, but I am serious about improving my game. I want to get back to the golf game I used to play, and I am prepared to put in the effort."

Russ finally breaks eye contact. I guess that's the answer he was looking for. "That's the key, Bob, but you need to know that I can't get your golf score back to the eighties."

Now I'm confused. This is the strangest conversation I have ever had with a pro! "Russ, if you can't help me get back to consistently shooting eighties... what am I doing here?"

"I can help you master the fundamentals of the game once again; you had a grip on them before when you were shooting in the eighties. While we'll work together at bringing those basics back, you'll be responsible for investing the time and effort into practice. That's what's going to bring your score down! Does that sound fair?"

I nod my head in agreement, thinking to myself that this is a pretty powerful message from someone who doesn't have one cent of my money yet!

Russ continues. "Bob, I want you to think of what makes a great golfer great! Do you follow professional golf at all?"

Russ doesn't know me that well but he sure seems to know what my hot buttons are. "Russ," I say, "I love watching golf! For years, I have been following the greats from tournament to tournament."

Russ leans forward. "So, what makes those 'great' golfers great?"

I think for a moment and reply, "It's a bunch of things; they have a perfect swing, they practice endlessly, they're confident, they're competitive, they know to bounce back from adversity... "

Russ continues to make strong eye contact. "You are exactly right. Did they get there on their own?"

It doesn't take me long to figure that out. "No. Every one of them that I know of has a coach or a mentor they rely on."

Russ asks, rhetorically, "If they are the greatest golfers in the world, why do they need a coach?"

I think for a moment. In some ways, it's a good question. "Well, I guess they need a coach to provide them with feedback on how they can improve their game. Their coach is probably someone whom they trust immensely - someone whom they respect. I assume the coach helps them keep their game sharp and helps them bounce back quicker when things go wrong." I figure that was everything, but Russ does not break his eye contact so I try to think of more and suddenly it hits me.

"From a professional golfer's perspective," I tell him, "it would be difficult to have an objective opinion on how to get better when you are only seeing things from the inside out."

Russ looks me square in the eye. "Bob, you and I are on the same fairway! If you're willing to put in the effort, I want to apply to be your coach. What do you think?"

I was stymied. How could I say no? I was looking for a golf pro who was really interested in helping me get better... someone who cared about me and what I wanted, and here was just what I needed. Besides, maybe I could learn a thing or two about improving my selling game; this guy is a great salesman! I put out my hand to Russ. "Russ, I would love to have you as my coach." He grabs my hand firmly, and we shake hands.

Even before we finish shaking hands, reality sets in. How much are private lessons going to cost? I realize that I've already told Russ I want him as my coach, and we haven't discussed price. I start feeling uncomfortable thinking about bringing up the cost now, so I decide I might just as well blurt it out. "Russ, I have to admit I am a little concerned about cost. How much are your lessons anyway?"

Russ looks straight at me, but with a warm smile on his face. "Bob, I understand. I charge $75 for a one-hour lesson. You can take as many as you want. After you have taken a couple, I would be happy to drop the price a little. It's really up to you."

While $75 is more than I was thinking of spending, I really feel Russ is sincere about helping me. Besides, he has already spent a fair amount of time with me and hasn't charged anything. There goes my male justification process. "Russ, that sounds fair. When do you want to get started?"

"Why don't you and I take a walk back to the clubhouse and book a time with Leslie?"

We both get up and make our way through the tables and out of the clubhouse. On the way back to the pro shop, my curiosity is peaked and I ask, "Russ, how long have you been at Canyon Meadows?"

He smiles and looks at me. "This is my first year."

I'm paying $75 a lesson from a new golf pro? I think to myself.

"I'm pretty much retired now," Russ explains, "although my wife would disagree."

"What did you do before Canyon Meadows?" I ask, hoping the answer has something to do with golf.

"I was on the pro tour," he says, looking straight ahead. I lock my eyes on Russ with a certain amount of shock on my face.

He chuckles again. "Sorry Bob, I should explain. I didn't actually play on the pro tour. I was a coach for some of those greats you've watched on TV. I really enjoyed it over the years, but the schedule got to be too gruelling; all that travelling from tournament to tournament."

All of a sudden, the $75 seems like a bargain, and I guess it is. I know Sandy isn't going to be too happy about me taking private lessons, but I know she's pretty understanding. I might not be able to sell my customers, but I'm still not too bad at selling her on what I want. Besides, like the saying goes, "It's better to beg for forgiveness than to ask for permission!" Whoever came up with that saying obviously spent a fair amount of time on their knees.

"Russ, I thought you said you used to be in sales?"

Russ looks up at me. "I was in sales, Bob... way back when I was a struggling golfer trying to make a name for myself! That was how I paid my way to get into the right clubs, meet the right people, and learn the game. I loved sales... but I loved golf more!"

"Russ, we really do have a lot in common... I love golf more too!" These days, that couldn't be truer.

We walk into the pro shop to see Leslie standing behind the counter working on the books or something. She looks up and sees both of us, but her attention moves directly to Russ. Before we even get close to the counter, she says, "Russ, Dave Mathews just called, and he's stranded on the highway. He called me on his cell phone apologizing profusely."

"That's OK Leslie," Russ calls back, "I know Marge wouldn't mind if I got home for supper anyway. Leslie, I'd like to introduce Bob Stephens. He would like a golf lesson with me. Can you book an appointment that is convenient for him?"

She nods and smiles, but it is apparent she is still not happy about the unexpected cancellation.

Russ turns to me and shakes my hand. "Bob, I think we are going to work well together," he says before making his way out of the pro shop.

Leslie pulls out a weather-beaten book from under the counter and starts flipping through page after page. "How did you manage to get an appointment with Russ anyway?" she asks without looking up. Then she pauses slightly, only raising her eyes. "Were you referred?"

"I wasn't referred. I just found your golf course in the phone book, called, and Russ answered the phone. I talked to him, and he told me to come out."

Leslies drops her eyes to the book and mumbles, "We've got to get him to stop answering the phone." Then she says without looking up, "I don't have any times available for the next couple of weeks. Were you thinking of a weekday or weekend appointment?"

It is becoming apparent Russ is in demand. " I was hoping for early on the weekend," I say expectedly.

"The next weekend appointment I have is in three weeks," she says with an 'I'm sorry' kind of smile.

"Russ said that you would book an appointment at my convenience," I say, getting a little annoyed.

"You mean three weeks from now isn't convenient?" she asks and looks back down at the appointment schedule. I stand there, refusing to answer the question. Then her face brightens, and she looks up. "Why don't you take Dave's time?"

"I thought Russ wanted to get home for supper?"

"Oh, he never gets supper at home anyway. I'll make sure the kitchen takes good care of him."

"Well, I'm here, and I do have my clubs in the car." I look down at the suit I am wearing and cringe.

Leslie notices my attire. "Don't worry about that." She walks over to the small change room and grabs a Canyon Meadows golf shirt hanging on a hanger from inside. "Here," she tosses it over to me, "put this on."

I slip inside the change room, and in an instant, take off my jacket, shirt, and tie, and slip on the golf shirt as if it is a race. "It actually fits," I call out.

"Just leave your shirt and jacket there. I'll make sure no one touches them. "Where are your clubs?" Leslie asks as I make my way out of the cubicle.

"They're in the car," I answer, buttoning the last of the buttons on the golf shirt.

"You run and get them, and I'll go talk to Russ," she orders. We both walk out the door and split off in different directions.

Now it doesn't seem so illogical to have moved the car closer to the pro shop. On my way to the car, I contemplate driving it back with me but then decide, a second time, not to.

Once I am at the car, I open the trunk lid and sit on the edge to put on my golf shoes. Tying up my shoes, I can picture the black mark across my butt from the dust on the rubber. I grab my golf clubs and, in a half run, half walk pace, try to wipe off dust that I can only see in my mind. I drop my clubs carelessly in the rack and bolt back into the pro shop.

Leslie has made it back behind the counter, and she looks up at the clock as soon as she sees me. "Russ is down by the driving range waiting for you. I'll get your bill ready; you make sure you stop by and pay it on your way out. I'm going to hold your clothes for ransom."

"I will. I promise," and then I am out the door. I grab my clubs and make a run for the driving range. The banging of my clubs against each other sounds like Santa's reindeer in full flight, so I switch to a quick walk.

I can see the line of golfers at the range, driving one ball after another. Russ is sitting quietly at a table, watching. I'm not sure if it is a coincidence, but more of the golfers are in the spots directly in front of Russ... with a scattering of openings at either end.

As I get closer, Russ turns his head over his shoulder to see me coming, "I didn't expect to see you again so soon, Bob." He gets up and turns to meet me.

"I hope I'm not taking you away from your supper with your wife," I say apologetically.

"Don't worry about it. Marge wasn't expecting me home until later anyway."

Standing there with my golf bag still hung on my shoulder, I ask, "Did you want to head over to one of those empty spots so I can show you my swing?" I realize that I'm talking like an eager puppy ready to play.

"No, Bob. First the mind, then the body. Have a seat."

This is not what I was expecting for a $75 lesson. I set my clubs down and grab a seat beside Russ. We are now both positioned looking at all the golfers in front of us.

"Bob, when we were in the clubhouse, you talked about what you wanted out of golf. What was that again?" he quizzes me, as if he didn't remember.

"I want to consistently shoot in the eighties, I want to be confident with my game, and I want to have fun."

"Great. That's what I thought. I want to start by talking about the basics of the game... in particular, the swing. Take a look at these golfers. What do you notice about them?"

I look at them, one after the other. Some are good golfers, it appears, and some are not as good. I search for an answer that isn't so obvious. "They are all right handed?"

Russ smiles and pans across the whole group, checking to see if I am right. He laughs. "I guess they are, but that wasn't what I was thinking of. You see, Bob, they are all hitting differently: They have all taken the universal golf swing and they have adapted it to their body and their mind. Over the years, many, many books have been written on the 'perfect golf swing', but the reality is that although there is a 'perfect golf swing', it varies with each person who picks up a club. Would you agree?"

"I guess that makes sense," I reply.

"I want you to remember that, Bob. The fundamentals of the basic swing are exactly the same for everyone, but everyone will adapt those fundamentals to their body and mind. Next point, why is the golf swing so important?"

"I guess, uh, because the essential swing doesn't change from shot to shot?"

"You're right. Can you imagine how difficult the game of golf would be if every time you walked up to a ball, you used a totally different swing for each situation? Once you master the steps of the golf swing, those

16

fundamentals will be there for every shot. The swing is tweaked based on the situation, but the fundamentals are always the same." Before I can respond, Russ continues. "Bob, you said you're in sales, right?"

"I am."

"Let's talk salesman to salesman. Do you create a totally new sales presentation for each new prospect you meet?"

The obvious answer he is looking for is "No", but the truth is, my sales presentation does seem to change a lot with each prospect. So, I give him the answer he is looking for. "No Russ, the presentation is basically the same, but I adapt it for each client."

Russ slaps his hand on the table. "Exactly! Golf is no different."

I nod my head in agreement. It actually does make sense.

"Next, Bob, remember when we were talking about the great golfers? When a great golfer is walking up to a ball one hundred and seventy-five yards out from the hole, is he or she thinking about the many steps of the golf swing - head down, left arm straight, you've heard it all - or are they totally focused on the shot they are about to make?"

The answer is obvious. "They're focused on their shot."

"You're right. The great golfer engrains the necessities of the swing through practice and repetition. When their game is on, their swing is unconscious. All they think about is the shot they are about to make." He pauses for a moment. "When you go see that new client for the first time, are you thinking about your sales presentation or are you focusing your attention on the client?"

I am surprised at his persistence with the analogy. Again, I give him the answer he is looking for. "I concentrate on the client."

"Right again! If you had to focus on what you were saying, how could you be focusing on what they are saying? Have you ever seen one of those great golfers you watch on TV lose their concentration?"

I nod, but I can't think of any specific examples.

"Sometimes what happens is their swing stops working right in the middle of a game. Instead of concentrating on the shot they are about to make, they think about their swing and try to pinpoint what is going wrong. Usually a recipe for disaster, wouldn't you agree?"

"Definitely," I say with a smile.

"So Bob, we're going to start by taking you back to the essential golf swing. We are going to bring that swing to the conscious state where we can fine-tune it. I haven't seen your swing yet, but I might suggest you tweak your swing if the basics have slipped. Is that OK?"

"Of course," I answer, "that's why I'm here."

"No Bob, you're here because you want to be shooting consistently in the eighties, you want to be confident with your game, and you want to have fun. Tweaking your swing is just a small step in that direction. Right?" Russ nods.

"Right."

"If we change your swing slightly, how do you think that will feel?"

I think back to all the other golf pros that have asked me to change my swing in the past. "It's going to feel awkward. You see, Russ, I want to improve my swing, but I don't want to change it. Too many times in the past I've had golf pros try to teach me a new swing, and I just get muddled up."

Russ pauses, nodding sympathetically. "You're right about that, Bob; it will feel awkward to change your swing. But... I'm not giving you some new technique or some fancy way of hitting the ball... I'm only asking that you make a commitment to learning the very basic essentials of the swing."

Despite myself, I am nodding to Russ's logic. It has been years since I thought about what makes up the perfect golf swing; I was just out there getting frustrated!

Russ continues. "We need to train the brain, and that will take your time and effort. In other words, you are going to have to practice, practice, practice! Are you prepared to invest all that time before we meet again?"

"I am, Russ," I answer, without really thinking of how I am going to fit so much practicing into my familial and professional life.

Then he reaches around and pulls out a palm-sized, laminated card from his pocket and hands it to me. "These are the basics of the golf swing you are going to re-learn and master, Bob. I want you to keep this card. Every time you go out to practice, I want you to move your swing to the conscious and then focus on the basic steps that are drawn here. I want you to concentrate on each of these steps until they are second nature. When it's time to play in the real game though, I want you to put the card away and just forget about it. The middle of a game is not the place to be analyzing and adjusting your swing. Agreed?"

"Agreed." I look over the points on the card and slip it in my shirt pocket.

Then, for the next forty-five minutes, Russ watches me hit ball after ball. I hit some well and others not so well. Russ is always complimentary, even when I hit bad shots. From time to time, he gets up, comes over, and asks me for the card. He then draws my attention to one point or another, recommends a change, and then returns to his seat.

Even though I can't actually see him when I am hitting the balls, I know he is studying my every move. I find myself looking forward to his praise as well as his suggestions. After the golf lesson is over, we walk together up to the pro shop. "Bob, you really do have a great swing. But, like most things in life, there is always some room for improvement. How did the changes I recommended feel today?"

"A little awkward, but there's nothing new. I can see that over time I had forgotten a few of the things you've pointed out."

"Change is usually awkward at first, but that's OK. With practice, the changes will become a natural part of your swing in no time. Before our next golf lesson, I want you to make sure you make some time to practice the basic steps we've discussed."

"I will, Russ," I slip the card half way out of my pocket and back in again to show I still have it, and then I turn left to go back into the pro shop and Russ turns right towards the clubhouse. I have my wallet out and my credit card in hand when I walk up to Leslie. "Here you go!"

"How was the golf lesson?" she asks, smiling.

"Russ is very good. I've never had a lesson quite like that before," I laugh, "I'm not used to spending half my time sitting down talking about the game. "

"Russ is good. Did you want to make another appointment with him?" Leslie is already reaching for the appointment book.

I think about what Sandy might say about me taking golf lessons - about my lack of success in sales - and I respond with the first thing that comes to my mind: "You betcha!" A guy has to reward himself now and then!

"You won't regret it, Bob!" Leslie says as if she knows what I am thinking. "Are you available during the day at all? I don't have another opening until Thursday the 20th, from 3:30 to 4:30."

After my lesson with Russ - and now to know how in demand he is - I'm not going to let the opportunity pass by. "I'll take it!" I cry.

"Great. How do you spell your name?" Leslie looks down and places a pen on the open spot of the page.

"Bob - Bob Stephens. That's with a 'ph'."

"Please mark the appointment in your schedule and if, for whatever reason, you need to cancel or rebook, we would appreciate it if you could give us at least twenty-four hours notice. There are lots of people who want to get in to see Russ, and we don't like cancellations. Is that fair?" she asks, looking straight at me.

"Fair enough. I won't be cancelling," I answer, trying to convince both her and myself. I feel a twinge in my stomach as I think about the fact that I haven't even talked to Sandy about this yet.

It is now 7:10 pm, and I race for the car. It is always that way lately... running behind.

I think about my conversation with Russ as I head towards home. What an interesting man! As I reflect on his approach, I definitely see why he is in high demand. Having been through a lot of golf lessons in my time, I have never had anyone actually ask if they can apply for the job as my coach. Wow, is that powerful! Russ really made me feel important. I think that with his knowledge and experience, and my desire to get better, I really can be a great golfer again - well, I muse, maybe not great... but at least good.

"Good would be nice!" I declare.

It is now 7:30, and the traffic has died down. I get closer to my home, and I am soon back in familiar territory, doing my usual weaving in and out of streets, trying to cut precious minutes off the trip. Sandy, and pretty well everyone else who rides with me through this maze, thinks I am crazy and they don't actually believe it saves any time. It probably doesn't, but I do it anyway.

I roll up into the driveway, and all of the lights are on in the house, and I mean all of the lights! Maybe it's because my sales and my income have been down that I am particularly sensitive about wasting money. Oh, I realize, this is a great line of thinking! I can just picture it: In one breath, I am ranting and raving about leaving the lights on, and in the next, I am telling Sandy how I committed to private golf lessons during the day while I should be working. At least I catch this contradiction prior to walking into the house. Maybe, I decide, I'll just stroll through and turn off the lights myself... this time, at least.

When I get in the back door, I call out, "Hello, I'm home." At various points throughout the house, I can hear the kids yelling "Dad's home!" in unison, followed by a stampede of footsteps.

It's great to have my kids come running to see me when I get home at the end of the day. Especially these days! David and Amanda reach me at the same time. Our youngest, David, is nine, and he is a little bundle of energy. Amanda is twelve, and she is turning into a little lady, or at least she is at times. The questions and statements of the day's events start flying.

"Hi Dad. Can we go swimming tonight? Can we, can we, please?" David persists.

Amanda pushes for equal time. "Dad, I need your help with my lines."

I try my best to reply to both of them at the same time. "David, I think swimming tonight would be fun. Amanda, what do you mean you need help with your lines?"

"Dad, don't you remember?" she scolds me, "I'm in the play at school. Mom and I told you about it this morning!"

"I do remember, dear, but would you refresh my memory, please?"

"Sure you do, Dad! Remember? I told you I get to be the hero!"

I was going to correct her - females are heroines - but I know she doesn't care, and I know it doesn't matter. "That's right!" I say, "How

20

could I forget? You'll be a great hero. You've already got experience - you're my hero!" and I give her a hug. Fortunately, she is still young enough to appreciate my corny humour.

"Daaaaad," she draws out for extra effect. "I need to practice my lines, and I need you to help me."

"I'd be happy to help you, Amanda. Before we do anything though, I need to talk to your mom to see what the schedule is for tonight."

I kneel down to talk to David. "Give me a hug, big guy!" After a quick squeeze, David is running off to some other interest. Before they are out of sight, I call, "Where's Mom?"

Amanda yells, "She's on the phone!" before disappearing around a corner.

Walking toward our bedroom, I notice the house is a little out of order. This isn't a problem for me, but it is for Sandy. I click off light after light, counting them for future reference - of course. As I turn off the light in the living room, I see Sandy talking and laughing on the phone. It must be one of her friends. "Sorry about that," I flick the lights back on and continue on to the bedroom.

I pull off my tie, drop my shirt in the basket, and hang up my suit. Sandy's voice is ringing in my mind as I stand there in my underwear. "Bob, make sure you check your pockets." I have this bad habit of stuffing papers, credit cards, and especially money in my pockets, only to have the remnants strewn through the washer and dryer. I pick up my shirt to find the receipts from Canyon Meadows inside. Maybe Sandy has a good point!

I look around for the clothes I wore yesterday. There they are - beside the bed on the floor right where I left them. A little wrinkled, but that's OK... they're comfortable, and I'm not going out tonight anyway, other than perhaps to the pool.

As I walk back into the kitchen, Sandy is just walking in from the living room, saying her good-byes on the cordless phone.

"How was your day?" I ask, moving in for my 'hello' hug.

"It was busy. I basically ran around all day and finished off at the school helping out with this play. Why are you so late?"

That didn't take long, I think; I was hoping to ease into this conversation on my own terms and timing, but now I see that isn't going to be the case. "Oh," I stammer, "I dropped into Canyon Meadows Golf Course on the way home tonight and met with the golf pro there," I speak confidently, but maybe not convincingly.

"Oh sure... you were golfing, weren't you?"

"No, really, I just had a coffee with the golf pro. I'm thinking about taking some golf lessons." I surely can't tell her I have already had my first lesson quite yet.

"How much is this going to cost? Seems to me that you're already worried about the lights being left on, and now you're thinking about taking golf lessons?" she says as tension rises.

I jump back. "I never said anything about the lights being on!" Now I am particularly glad I caught this in advance. I pause for a moment and then continue more calmly.
"I'm not even sure if I'm even going to take them yet."

Now I am trying to figure out exactly how I am going to deal with this. Sandy speaks before I can. "Why do you need golf lessons anyway? You know our finances are tight."

"Sandy, you know I've been going through hell at work trying to get my sales back up. I need a distraction - something to help me get my mind off what's wrong." Sandy knows I am stressed about selling and our future.

"You're a good salesman, honey, and you've been through this before. It will come back. I'm just not sure going golfing is the answer. How much does it cost?" She is talking in an understanding voice, and for a moment, I relax.

"Before I talk about the cost, let me tell you about this golf pro. I phoned this golf course called Canyon Meadows... ."

She interrupts. "Where's that?"

"It's about forty minutes from here; just north of that new mall going up. Anyway, this old guy answers the phone, and it ends up he's the golf pro. After we talk for a bit, he tells me to come straight there. I'm thinking you and the kids will be late tonight so I might as well." It's good to build in my excuses early, I always believe. "I get there, and he takes me for a coffee. He wants to know why I want to take golf lessons."

Sandy cuts in. "Him too!"

I give her that 'give me a break' look, and go on cutting the story short where I can. "He really got inside my head, this guy. He asked me what I wanted out of golf, and I said that I wanted to shoot in the eighties. He wouldn't leave it alone, asking 'What do you really want out of golf?', and I started telling him. He talked about great golfers, and how, even though they're great, they still need a coach to help them stay on top of their game. Then, he leaned across the table and asked if he could apply for the job as my coach. I was really taken back. This guy is good."

The entire statement seems to roll right over my wife. "How much is this going to cost, Bob?"

I realize she doesn't have enough information to really understand how good of a deal this is. "Hang on, hang on. It ends up Russ - that's his name - was on the pro tour coaching professional golfers, but now

22

he's retired and is teaching at Canyon Meadows. I can't believe how lucky I was to get a lesson with him! Isn't that unbelievable?"

She catches my minor slip, and her eyes burst open. "You've already taken a lesson!" She pauses. "No, Bob, *it* isn't unbelievable... you're unbelievable! How much was it?" she demands.

"Sandy, calm down. It's really reasonable. It's only, well, $75..."

She interrupts again, almost shouting. "You jerk! Do you realize how little money we have in our account?" She shakes her head, pauses for a moment, and then continues. "How many lessons do you get for seventy-five bucks, anyway?"

Knowing I am in trouble, I decide to come clean. "Well, that's per lesson...."

Sandy comes unglued. "Seventy-five dollars a lesson! Are you crazy?"

I try to calm her. "I know it sounds like a lot, but this guy is very, very good. He also told me he would drop the price the more lessons I take."

She turns away. "This guy is not only a good golf pro... he's a saint, too. No wonder you went for it!"

"Sandy, I'll find a way to make the extra money to pay for the golf lessons," I say, looking for ways to sell her.

She looks at me scornfully. "What are you going to do Bob, deliver papers?"

I stop; she has hit me below the belt. I stand there, staring at her without saying a word. In an instant the tension builds in my head. A thousand cutting comebacks race to the front of my mind, but I restrain myself. I know that saying any of those things won't solve anything; Sandy and I have been down that road before, and it does nothing other than make both of us feel awful... sometimes for days. My feelings swing between anger, frustration, and hurt. After what seems like an eternity, I break my stare and walk out of the kitchen without saying a word.

In the hall, I stop to take a deep breath. I am sure the kids have heard us, and I don't want to upset them, so I work to calm myself back down. It's at times like this that I think Sandy doesn't know how good she has it... although lately, that argument is far weaker than it used to be. She stays at home with the kids while I kill myself to try to provide for the family. What wouldn't I give to switch spots with her, to be able to stay at home taking care of my family!

From her perspective, Sandy probably thinks she has sacrificed her career, her future, and her independence to stay at home with the kids. She's constantly reminding us that nobody appreciates her... and maybe that's true sometimes. It's like we're in the same room, but we're separated by glass. I can see her world and she can see mine, but we can't actually get inside each other's space to truly understand the other's perspective. "Maybe it's better that way," I try to convince myself.

I finally calm myself to the point where I can face the kids, and I search for the nearest TV, convinced I will find them there. This is another one of those times where being with the kids feels particularly good. Sure enough, they are both in the family room glued to the set. Judging by their trance on the TV, I feel a sense of relief that maybe, just maybe, they didn't hear their mom and me fighting over stupid golf lessons. I can feel the tension build again as I begin to re-live the moment. So, trying to break both their concentration and mine, I step in front of the screen.

"Did you kids want to go swimming?"

The word 'swimming' is enough to launch David from a sitting position to about six inches off the floor directly in front of my face. Amanda is a little slower to react, but she is excited all the same. "Yeah Dad!" they yell together.

The expression on their faces and the excitement in the air helps to take my mind off my troubles. "OK, you need to get your bathing suits and towels. Did you have supper yet?" I ask, as I remember I haven't taken time to eat.

"Mom took us out for hamburgers and fries before the play," Sarah says with a big grin.

With both kids running in different directions through the house, I make my way back to the kitchen. I don't have the energy to deal with Sandy right now, but I also don't want to start building a huge wall between us that we will only have to dismantle later. Sandy is still there with her back to me, busy with something.

"Sandy, I'm going to take the kids swimming," I say in a monotone voice.

"That's great, Bob. They'll really enjoy that. Did you want anything to eat before you go?" I can sense in her tone she knows she has hurt me. She isn't saying sorry and neither am I, but I know we will have this resolved sometime tonight. Actually, I feel a sense of relief flow over me.

"That's OK. I'll have something when we get home," I say, closing the door behind me.

It is a kid's swim night, so I elect to watch from the stands. I need some time to think anyway. The kids run into the change rooms and I make my way to the observation area to find a seat. Within minutes, they emerge wet from the shower, clutching themselves for warmth. While David waves both arms, when he spots me, Amanda gives me a concealed one-handed wave... just in case any of her friends are watching.

Sitting there, I think back to my conversation with Russ. In particular, I remember our discussion about "What makes a great golfer

24

great?" I attempt to recreate the list in my mind. They have a great swing, they practice hard, they're competitive, and they know how to deal with adversity. I can picture Russ's face, as if he were sitting next to me, asking, "Did they get there on their own?"

The answer is "No." Even though they are great, every golfer on the pro tour has someone they rely on to help them keep their game sharp.

But why is that? They're already great golfers. I guess they need someone like a 'Russ' who not only knows the game, but perhaps more important, knows them. They need a coach who they trust, someone who can bring an objective, 'external' perspective. These coaches are no doubt particularly valuable when things aren't going well. They help the once-great golfer identify what's gone wrong, figure out how to correct it, and implement the change into their game.

At that moment, it is like a bright light goes on in my head. I need a coach who can help me get my sales game back! I know I can be good again, but I just need to find someone who I trust... someone who cares about me. I know that different people need different coaches. For me, I need a coach who understands the sales game, will celebrate the wins with me, and will 'pick me up and dust me off' when I fall down. Perhaps most important, I need someone who believes in me maybe when I don't believe in myself.

I realize, keeping an eye on the kids, that when I first started out in sales, I had John Andrews. John always cared about me whether I was up or down. It didn't matter how low I felt when I walked into John's office, I always walked out feeling like I was ready to take on the world again.

Over the years, John was always there for me. Too bad that after he retired, I just couldn't bring myself to let the other managers into my world.

I try to think of a solution. What about Jeff Townes? He's eager, without a doubt, but I have a difficult time relating to him, so I mentally cross him off my list. Who else could I approach to be my coach? I think of all of the other people in our division... definitely not Teddie or Sarah; they would laugh me right out of the office.

I wonder if maybe all I need is someone who knows the basics, and again Jeff's name comes back to mind. Perhaps he does know enough about the basics to help me, I try to convince myself. I find myself searching for all of Jeff's positive points to support my thinking.

Although he is new to our division, I muse, he apparently has been around the company for quite a few years. If I am not mistaken, when he was introduced, the woman from head office did talk about some of the successes Jeff enjoyed when he was in sales. This thinking starts to build confidence in my choice. Jeff has made a gallant effort to get to know me, but I realize that it is probably my fault it's never gone past a few superficial meetings. He's very friendly - in a 'Sparky', kind of way - and he hasn't pushed himself on me since the first few times after he arrived. I catch myself talking out loud, and I check both ways to make sure no one is looking at me.

Heck, he can't be too bad... I noticed Sarah was in his office the other day. At the time, I credited it to Sarah sucking up to the new boss, but now that I think about it... Sarah has been doing better than she used to.

That's what I am going to do, I decide. I am going to talk to Jeff, and I am going to do it first thing tomorrow! I don't know if he is interested in working with me, but I need to take that first step. I need to find a coach!

Sitting alone, a smile stretches across my face. It occurs to me that if you are seeking the answers to your problems, that maybe, just maybe, the best place to look for the answers isn't always the most obvious. I went for a golf lesson, and found wisdom in the words of Russ Atkens. Perhaps the answers to our problems are all around us. Maybe it is just a case of paying attention and 'the answer shall appear'!

I am brought back to the moment when the buzzer sounds to signal swimming is over, and I look through the sea of kids trying to locate David and Amanda. Amanda is at the side drying off, but I don't see David. I stand up and start walking over closer to get a better look. I start kicking myself for not watching the kids closer. They're both good swimmers, and there are lots of lifeguards, I tell myself, as if I am building a case.

I feel a sigh of relief when I spot David in the far corner of the pool being coaxed out by one of the lifeguards. 'First in, last out' is obviously his motto. When I finally get the kids' attention, I tell them to hurry up; I want to get home to talk to Sandy.

Chapter 3

The Coach

$\mathcal{W}$hen I drive up, I notice that most of the lights are out. This means that either Sandy has gone to bed early - a bad sign - or she has taken heed of my advice on conserving energy - a good sign. I hope for the latter. I am starting to build excitement about my revelation, and I don't want to return to the argument about golf lessons. In fact, right up until this moment, I had forgotten about our 'little' altercation. Between Sandy and the kids, they are my godsend, particularly when I have had a bad day... which seems to happen more often than not. There have been some nights when I have lain awake fearing for my future - our future - and I can't sleep. The more I try to think my way out of it, the more restless and wide-awake I get. Over the years though, I have found one thing that seems to work.

I go to one of the kids' rooms, and while they are sleeping, I lay down with them and brush the hair back away from their faces. There is nothing more peaceful than the beauty of a sleeping child. When I do this, I tell myself that this is what life is all about, not sales, not money, not even golf! In the end, regardless of either success or failure in my career, if I can be a great husband and dad, I will die a happy man. It's like this 'calm' comes over me, and within minutes I am usually sleeping.

I am caught up in my thoughts as the garage door closes, and the kids bolt out of the car towards the house. I yell out the window, "It's time to get ready for bed!" I am not sure if they even hear me, seeing as how the door to the house slammed right in the middle of the word 'bed'. Besides, I just noticed the window that I am attempting to yell out of is closed. Why is it I always seem to be communicating with my kids this way these days?

I sit in the car collecting my thoughts. It dawns on me that I have a plan! I really do want to take the golf lessons with Russ, and I really do want to get my income back up. I decide that I'll make a deal with Sandy: I'll take one more lesson with Russ, and I'll also figure out a way to increase my sales and my income. If I don't see an improvement in both my golf game and my sales, I won't take any more lessons.

After I think about it - it's a plan, not a great plan, but a plan - I jump out of the car and walk into the house and find Sandy standing in the kitchen. We struggle to make eye contact and conversation, and after an awkward moment, Sandy breaks the silence. "I made a sandwich for you."

"Thanks, hon. Where did the kids run off to?"

"I sent them off to get ready for bed. Amanda still wants to practice her lines with you, and we need to read with David." The look on her face tells me we're not over this yet, and then it comes out. "Bob, I checked the account today, and we don't have a lot of money left before payday."

Now I am starting to understand why she reacted the way she did about my golf lessons. While I am the worrier about my career, Sandy is the worrier about our money. We're quite a team!

"Look, Sandy, how would it be if I took one more lesson? I am really impressed with this guy, and I do need something to get my mind off sales."

"Whatever, Bob," she says, as if she has given up fighting about the money.

Now for my plan - that will make her feel better. "When I was at the pool, I thought more about my conversation with Russ. I figured out I need to find a coach to help me with sales. I really need to find someone like a 'Russ' who can help me get my sales back up. I have decided I am going to go meet with Jeff Townes to talk about this."

"Who is Jeff Townes?" she asks, puzzled.

"Don't you remember? That guy I called 'Sparky'; the new manager I told you about. His name is Jeff Townes."

"Yeah... you haven't had too many great things to say about him as I recall."

I curse silently; this is a problem I have had before. I come home frustrated and say something about someone to Sandy, and naturally she takes my side - perhaps because of my slanted version of the event or the person. The problem is, while my frustration with the situation fades, Sandy ends up with a one-sided opinion of that person that she carries forward even though she doesn't really know them. It happens to her... and it happens to me.

"Actually," I continue, "Jeff is a good manager. He started out a little over-zealous, but he has definitely improved over the last six months. As I was saying, I'll take one more lesson to start, but if I can improve both my golf game *and* our income, I get to take more lessons. Deal?"

"OK," she agrees, reluctantly.

I go over to Sandy, and we kiss to seal the deal; shaking hands is far too sterile when you're making up. We celebrate overcoming another obstacle in our marriage by getting to bed early, but for two hours, I toss and turn trying to go to sleep. This time, at least, it is different. I am getting excited about the idea of increasing my sales numbers again. I realize that Jeff may not be the perfect coach, but perhaps we can work together. I look over at the clock: 12:37 am. So much for going to bed early!

Finally I manage to fall asleep, but all too soon, the alarm clock blasts off. Lying there as the alarm wails, I struggle to gain enough coordination to shut it off. Then, in the morning silence, I reflect on my decision; what had seemed to be a great plan last night now scares me a little. Now it is reality, and I am facing a new day - a day when I am going to approach Jeff, a manager I have ridiculed in the past, to be my coach. Lying there, all I can see is everything that can possibly go wrong. These thoughts make me question whether I am doing the right thing.

I roll over to give Sandy a kiss and notice she is already up and out of bed. Down the hall, I can see the lights are on in the kitchen. I sigh, gather my courage, and force myself out of bed and shuffle to the bathroom to get ready for the day. Standing in the shower, confidence in my plan starts to rebuild; I know I am doing the right thing, I tell myself.

When I get out of the bathroom, I go to the closet to pick my clothes for the day, flipping through my slim assortment of suits. At one time, I bought two or three new suits every year, but with my income dropping, it has been a while since I wandered into my favorite clothing store. I look through my closet and pick my best old suit. Then I grab a shirt and a tie to match, slip on my shoes, and I'm ready.

When I get to the kitchen, Sandy is already enjoying her first cup of coffee. I walk over and give her a kiss good morning. "How did you sleep?" I ask.

"Pretty good," Sandy looks me over. "Bob you really need to get some new suits... and that tie has a stain on it. I hope you don't have to meet any clients today... "

"No, dear. Don't you remember? I'm going to talk to Jeff." I stare seriously at her. "Sandy, I really am serious about getting my sales back up."

She barely even blinks. "Make sure you have some breakfast. And don't forget the mouthwash!"

I don't have time for breakfast this morning. I fill up my mug with coffee and grab a banana and a couple of bagels. Sandy takes note as I move around the kitchen. "Don't forget your lunch!" she says. Then comes the one-minute lecture. "If you took your lunch every day, you could pay for those golf lessons in no time."

I search through the fridge in silence, determined not to go there again. With my lunch in hand, I head for the door, but Sandy jumps to her feet to block my way. "Don't forget to say good-bye to the kids."

I do a 'one-eighty' and start searching for David and Amanda. Amanda is in the bathroom first - a bad sign for David. I find David still in bed trying to muster the energy to get up. I kneel down and give him a quick kiss. "Have a great day, David."

"You too, Dad. See you tonight!"

Then I bang on the bathroom door. On the other side comes this loud "Whaaat?" I assume she thinks it is David, or at least I hope so. I call through the door, "Hi honey, I have to head to work early. Have a great day!"

I hear "Bye Dad!" and I am on my way to the door. I stop to give Sandy a kiss good-bye. Sandy had heard on some talk show that couples that kiss each other good-bye everyday make more money. At this point, I can't imagine making less money, but I do it anyway.

Then, once free of my house, I jump in the car, and, within minutes, I am weaving back and forth through the different side streets. I picture my conversation with Jeff... trying to imagine what I will say and how he will respond. This isn't going to be easy, I conclude, considering I haven't given him the time of day since he arrived.

When I pull into the parking lot, I am disappointed to see Jeff's stall vacant; I was hoping I could get in to see him before the rest of the salespeople arrived. Wondering how to approach my new manager, I walk through the office and exchange the usual 'good mornings' with the staff.

As I grab my second coffee of the day, I notice how Sarah is already busy in her office, on the phone. This is perfect; I can talk to Sarah and get the scoop on Jeff before he gets in. Before I do that, though, I decide to find out what Jeff's schedule is for today.

Jeff's assistant, Bruce, is working away when I get there. At first I had a hard time thinking of Bruce as one of the staff. But then, the world is changing, and I guess Bruce seems to be doing a good job. But then again, what do I know? I've never even taken the time to talk to him before.

"Hi Bob," Bruce says, "how are you this morning?"

I am a little surprised that he even knows my name... although how hard is 'Bob' to remember? "Good morning, Bruce. I'm OK. How are you doing?" I ask the questions, but I don't really care what the answers are. I want to make an appointment with Jeff and get back to Sarah before she gets on to other things.

"I'm doing well. Is there something I can help you with?"

"Actually Bruce, I want to talk to Jeff. Do you know what his schedule is for today?"

Bruce answers in a sympathetic tone. "I know he has a training class between 9:00 to 10:30. Then he is out of the office on several sales calls with the new people for the rest of the day."

This is not the answer I want to hear. I have gone from, "If it's Jeff calling, tell him I'm not in." to "Jeff is the answer to my prayers." in less than 24 hours.

"Can you tell Jeff I'd like to see him for a few minutes when he comes in? What time does he get in, Bruce?"

"He's usually here about ten to nine. I know he has to get ready for the meeting, but if you like, I'll let him know you want to talk to him."

"Hey... tell him it's something good, will you?" I know I can be accused of only talking to Jeff when there is a problem, and I don't want him avoiding me because he doesn't want to face a problem this early in the day. I look at my watch... it's now 8:30 and I want to get back to talk to Sarah. In the hall, I meet all of the new salespeople arriving for the day. Some of these people I don't even recognize, although I assume that since they're here, they must work with us. As we approach and pass one another, the heads drop down to avoid eye contact, or worse yet, conversation. Some mumble "good morning" but by the time I hear it, it's too late to reply anyway.

As I walk up, I notice that Sarah is talking to someone. Rats! This isn't what I wanted. The someone is Karen Timber: one of the new salespeople. I recognize her because she is Jeff's only shining star.

Sarah notices me standing there. "It's Rocket-Man," she says with a smile, "how are you doing?"

I instantly go red; I hate it when Sarah does that. Karen looks at me with a surprised expression and then looks back to Sarah. "Rocket-Man?" Karen asks.

Sarah starts to answer, but before she can, I jump back in to avoid the embarrassing explanation. "Hi, my name is Bob Stephens. Your name is... " I say as if I don't know her name. I don't want to give her that satisfaction.

She looks me straight in the eye and shakes my hand firmly. "Hi Bob. I'm Karen Timber. I've heard a lot about you."

Now it is my turn to be surprised. Based on my attitude and results over the last couple of years, I can't imagine this woman has heard anything too positive. "I'm sure that if you have heard it from Sarah, it can't be good!"

Karen smiles, gets up out of her seat, and waits for me to move out of the doorway so that she can leave. I turn my attention to Sarah. "Don't be calling me 'Rocket-Man' to the new lads!" I say in my best Irish accent. "They don't care about our old war stories." Sarah has Irish somewhere in her ancestry and she is proud of it.

With Karen gone, the two of us look at each other. Sarah looks particularly attractive today; she is in her mid 40's and is now divorced. She had a really tough time when her husband left her, but I must say she hasn't looked better in years.

I instantly think of my wife. Sandy isn't a jealous person, but she definitely doesn't like it when I talk about Sarah. You see, about a year after Sarah split up with her husband, she and I went out for a beer after work to talk. The talking went on throughout the night, and so did the beer. We ended up back at her place until some ridiculous hour, and probably went a lot further than we should have. It was a stupid thing to do, and Sandy has never let me forget it.

Sarah speaks first. "What brings you to the office so early, Bob?"

"Well, Sarah... " I settle into the empty chair. It is still warm from Karen's presence.

She cuts me off with, "Bob, it's 8:35 and I am speaking at the training meeting. It starts at 9:00 sharp."

I am a little taken aback that she has cut me off so quickly. Then reality sets in. Between Sarah, Teddie, and myself, we have wasted many hours of many days talking about the way it used to be, the way it should be, or the way it could be. The funny thing is, nothing ever came of those discussions. We weren't looking to solve our problems; we were looking for others who shared our gripes, and we shunned those who didn't. We didn't need any optimists raining on our pity party. Quite frankly, and now quite understandably, most of the good salespeople have learned to steer clear of us.

"That's OK, Sarah. I only need you for a few minutes." I have to cut to the chase. "Sarah, I know you have been meeting with Jeff a few times. What's he like?"

A strange looks comes over her face. "Are you feeling OK, Bob?"

"I feel just fine, but thanks for asking. So tell me, what's he like?"

"Why do you ask?"

I am sure it must sound very weird to hear me interested in knowing more about Jeff, particularly with some of the things I have said about him over the last six months. "Sarah, I'd love to sit down with you and have a long-winded conversation about 'why' - and I am prepared to do that - but neither you nor I have time for that right now."

"You're right Bob, we don't," she gives in. "I'm not sure what to say about Jeff." Then she leans forward. "I'll tell you something, but you have to promise to keep it a secret."

I move up with anticipation. I love secrets, although around this office 'secret' is a loosely held term. "I promise I'll keep it a secret." Promises are loosely held too!

"You better!" she threatens with her finger. "The other day, Jeff asked if I would help him out. He's frustrated with the sales of the division, but more so, he's frustrated by the lack of support from the salespeople here, people like you."

"Me? What about you?" I cry, trying to defend myself. I can clearly see Jeff's strategy now: divide and conquer!

"Actually, Jeff did say he was frustrated with both Teddie and myself as well," Sarah confesses.

"That's more like it! So what do you know about him?"

"He's actually a very good guy... and he knows his stuff. He's been around the company for a long time, but he is new in management and he needs a little help. After meeting him a couple of times, I actually started to feel sorry for the guy. He asked me to talk to the new people this morning, so I said I would. Now Bob, you have to tell me why you're asking about Jeff. Are you planning a mutiny?" she asks with a smile.

I am a little taken aback by her accusations, especially since I have been working hard to change my perspective on Jeff... at least over the last twelve hours or so. "Not at all. Actually, I'd like to help Jeff, too."

"Give me a break, Bob; you've got something planned. I know you better than that!"

"OK, OK," I pause, taking a deep breath. "You know that for the past few years, both my attitude and my sales have been in the toilet. I have been doing some soul searching, and I've decided I want to turn my situation around; I want to get my sales back up. I figure the best place to start is to find out if Jeff can help me. I'm a little skeptical... but at least it's worth a try."

"Don't you think this is going to affect your golf game?" she says without even blinking.

I almost laugh; opening my soul to Sarah is like handing her a stick and asking her not to hit me, so I give a quick, "Don't you have to go to a meeting?" before I leave. Walking out the door, I say over my shoulder, "I don't want you to say a word about this to anyone - especially Teddie!"

She holds up her finger to her lips, "Mum's the word." I know she won't say anything. She may not be able to keep other people's secrets, but she keeps mine. After all, I know way too much about her, and she knows it.

Walking to my office, I think back to my conversation with Russ, when we talked about the importance of having a coach. I'm not looking for a babysitter, I thought, but it would be nice to be able to talk to someone now and then - someone who is interested in me and who is willing to help me get my sales back up.

I think about Jeff, and his challenges as a new manager in a tough division. Maybe we can help each other. Maybe there are some things Jeff could do for me and some things I could do for him. I had my head down as I was thinking, so I didn't even see Jeff coming and his voice interrupted my thoughts.

"Good morning, Bob. I hear you are looking for me?" Jeff says in his usual 'plugged-in' way.

Jeff is a little younger than me: he is six foot, athletic, and fairly good-looking. The only consolation is that Jeff is balding and I am not - at least not yet. He's a squash player - a very good squash player, or so I have heard. It's funny; when we first met he talked about his squash game and asked if I played.

"I haven't played in years," I said, "although I do still have my trusty racquet in the basement." I am not sure why I called it 'trusty' – 'rusty' would have been far more appropriate. I guess Jeff was just trying to get to know me when he asked me to play with him. I remember how I reached around and patted my lower back. "Geez Jeff," I whined, "that would be great... but I've got a bad back." It wasn't true, but I thought I would save us both the embarrassment.

So now, with Jeff standing right next to me, I stand there lost for words: I hate being caught off-guard. "Yes, Jeff," I stammer, "I was. I understand you have a training meeting this morning. How's your schedule for the rest of the day?"

"Why Bob? What's up?" he asks eagerly.

"Jeff, it's nothing.... really. I was hoping to grab you for a coffee and talk about a few things, if you have some time."

"How about when I get out of the meeting?"

"That would be just fine. Drop by my office when you're finished."

Jeff's face lights up again. "Did you want to come to the meeting to hear Sarah's presentation?"

I smile unconvincingly. "No thanks, Jeff. It would be great to hear Sarah again, but I have some really important paperwork I need to get to." A little white lie.

"Maybe next time. I'll see you after the meeting," he says, and then he is off down the hallway.

I make my way into my office and see right away that the message light on my phone is flashing. As I walk in I trip over the case that holds my new laptop computer from the company. More useless technology, I think to myself. I pick it up and move it under the desk where it belongs. On the side of the desk is the other computer I barely use. Use it for what? They buy these expensive computers for us and all I end up using it for is email. How bad is that?

The top of my desk is littered with all of the things I have started and not finished. To look away from this stuff I take off my suit jacket and hang it up on the hook behind the door.

As I settle into my chair I look at all of the golf paraphernalia I have collected over the years. Some are great gifts, some are gag gifts, but all of them are treasures. On the walls are two pictures; both of which have inspirational sayings at the bottom that I can't read or remember. I look at my watch. I have got an hour and a half before Jeff is out of his meeting and I realize that if I don't start returning these calls I won't have any clients at all.

I push the message button and the messages start rolling off, one after another. I jot down notes and numbers to prepare to get back to these people. I hate voicemail as much as my clients do, so I make a conscious effort to answer my calls personally and return messages as soon as possible.

For the most part, my clients love me. Even with this good service, however, I am losing some good clients and, more recently, I haven't been able to replace them, let alone grow my client list. Then I decide on the first call and I pick up the phone. "Good morning," I try to sound cheerful, "is Nadia in?"

"Who's calling, please?"

"It's Bob Stephens. I'm returning Nadia's call."

"Just a moment, please." Within a minute I can hear Nadia on my speaker. "Good morning, Nadia Tremis speaking."

"Hi Nadia, it's Bob Stephens calling. How are you doing?"

"Good Bob, thanks for returning my call. Do you know when I can expect those papers we discussed?"

"Well Nadia, I put everything together myself and I handed it to the courier yesterday. You should have it on your desk this morning," I say with pride. "If for whatever reason you don't get it, give me a call back and I will drop it off to you personally."

"Don't worry about it, Bob. I am sure it will be here this morning."

"Remember, though; if it doesn't show up just give me a call. I know you are waiting for the information," I say, trying to emphasize my great service.

"OK, Bob, I will." She hangs up.

I guess it is clients like Nadia and her company that have kept me going. I really enjoy delivering great service, and they really seem to appreciate it. For the next hour or so I return call after call. There are some problems, but most of them are minor. I swear, some of my clients call just because they just want to visit with me.

I am right in the middle of a phone call when I hear the knock on my door: being so consumed with my calls I had totally forgotten about my meeting with Jeff. Jeff pops his head in and sees me talking on the phone. I motion for him to come in and he does and stands there silently, waiting for me to finish. I have a good client on the phone so I add a little extra happiness to the call, seeing as how Jeff is listening. After a few minutes I exchange closing pleasantries with my client and hang up.

"Sounds like a good client, Bob! Are you ready for coffee?"

"Sure, Jeff. I just need to drop off a couple of things for the staff on our way out." I quickly jot down some 'to do's' and gather up several forms from the top of my desk.

I haven't thought about what Jeff and I are going to talk about, but I am feeling better about my situation after talking to my clients. I pick up the pile of papers and start towards the door. Jeff has already swivelled and is walking off ahead of me.

I close the door to grab my jacket from behind it and I catch of glimpse of myself in the mirror on the back of the door. I see a man looking back at me whom I have become all too familiar with: the shadow of someone who at one time was a respected leader in this office. I take a deep breath, artificially raising my shoulders high, and rummage through my pockets to find a single piece of gum, which I pop into my mouth and chew feverously to get the maximum effect.

With a spot on my tie staring back at me, I button one, then two buttons of my jacket to cover the evidence. Again I look at myself in the mirror and I wonder what looks sillier; a stain on my tie or the appearance of a straitjacket? I opt for the straitjacket look and make my way out of the office.

Jeff has now stopped halfway down the hall and is waiting for me. By the time I catch up to him I have already disposed of the gum back in its wrapper and into my pocket. I've got to remember to get rid of this later or Sandy will kill me.

As we stop at the front office, Jeff chats with a couple of the staff as I make my rounds. I drop off the forms with different people and give them detailed instructions. Within minutes, I am ready to go. On the way out, Jeff asks, "Where do you want to go?"

"Doesn't matter to me," I say, although it does. I don't want to go to the regular coffee shop where I have wasted so much time with the 'Old Guard'. I know this is the time of day when Teddie and Sarah will most likely be there, and I don't want them to see me with Jeff... particularly Teddie!

"I know of a spot where they have good coffee, and it's quiet," Jeff says as he starts off ahead again. Within a few minutes we are sitting in a little coffee shop I have passed by a thousand times, but have never stopped at. It's funny how you get into habits.

We are the only people in the coffee shop, which makes this choice even better. We settle into a table near the back and within minutes the waitress is standing there, waiting to take our order. She asks Jeff, smiling when she speaks, "Do you want tea with no tea bag again?" Obviously the man has been here before, I think to myself.

"Sounds great," Jeff answers.

"And what can I get for you, sir?"

"Coffee would be just fine."

As she walks away I look at Jeff. "Tea with no tea bag?"

"Actually, I just like hot water but I don't want to come here and order that so I just ask for tea, with a bag on the side."

This guy really is a health nut. "I thought you said the place has great coffee. How would you know that?"

Jeff smiles and shrugs his shoulders. "That's what they tell me!"

In a flash, the waitress is back at the table with our order. I start feeling anxious, realizing I haven't taken the time to plan out what I was going to say.

"Bob, would you mind if we leave here by 11:00 so that I can make my next appointment?"

"Sure, Jeff. I think we can be done in fifteen minutes." I don't want to appear to have too many problems.

"What did you want to talk about?" he asks, ready to sip his hot water.

I need more time to think so I stall with, "So how's that squash game, Jeff?"

Jeff gives me a puzzled look. "It's great, Bob. Thanks."

I decide to cut to the chase and blurt it out. "Jeff, for the past few years I have had difficulty finding new clients. Both my sales and my income have dropped substantially as a result." Mid-sentence I think about my experience from the day before, and I switch directions. "Yesterday I was out with this golf pro named Russ Atkens. At one time he coached some of the greatest golfers on the tour, and now he is giving lessons over at Canyon Meadows." I can feel my face turning red as I realize how confused I must sound. I have a thousand thoughts in my head, but there is a traffic jam occurring in my mouth as I struggle to get the words out.

"I could sure use a lesson or two myself!" Jeff says, trying to lighten the moment.

"I'll be sure to get you his card, Jeff," I say as I try to re-group my thoughts. "Anyway, we talked about how even the greatest golfers need a coach or mentor of some kind. It occurred to me that the same thing might be true for salespeople. John Andrews used to be my coach, but since he left I haven't really had anyone to talk to. I don't know if you can help me, or if you are even interested, but I would like to find out."

Jeff has a surprised look on his face and he speaks clearly when he says, "You want me to be your... coach?"

"I don't know for sure, Jeff. But what I do know is that I need someone who can help me."

"I'm flattered," he says, and then pauses. "What exactly do you want me to do?"

"That's what you and I are going to figure out. I was also thinking about something else: How has it been going over the last six months here, Jeff... honestly?"

Jeff's expression turns serious and he pauses. "Not as well as I would like. The division is way behind on the numbers, and I have had a difficult time getting to know the people here. I'm not sure what the problem is."

"Well, Jeff, part of the problem is people like me." I have a hard time believing I am actually saying this.

"I appreciate that, Bob. But, unfortunately, the bigger problem is my lack of experience as a manager. The funny thing is that although I might be green as a manager, I do know this business. I started out in sales and achieved some impressive numbers, even if I do say so myself."

Curiosity gets the best of me. "Well, how well did you do as a salesman, exactly?"

"I was in the top ten in the eastern division, for three years."

Just like me, I think: Great start then downhill. That's probably why he ended up in management. "And then what?" I ask.

"I was #1 for the last two years," Jeff says, almost apologetically.

"So why did you go into management?" I ask, bewildered.

"I wanted to lead people, Bob." Jeff stares out the window. "But, well, it hasn't worked out quite like I planned." Jeff grabs his empty teacup and sips, as if to avoid saying more.

I find that I really feel for the guy, but I'm not sure why. Quite frankly, I should be envious. "Jeff," I tell him, "I don't know a lot about management but I do know a fair amount about being managed. Maybe you can help me and I can help you. What do you say?"

Jeff's spirits pick up. "That sounds great, Bob. I would be more than happy to work with you. In fact, I really appreciate you approaching me; I wish more experienced veterans would."

"So when should we meet again?" I say, hoping it will be sooner rather than later.

"How about next Tuesday morning at 8:00, before everyone gets in?"

As I am nodding in agreement, Jeff looks down at his watch. "I've got to get going."

I reach to pay for the bill, but Jeff shakes his head and throws some money on the table. As we get up he asks, "So how was the coffee, Bob?"

"It was great coffee!"

"I told you so!" Jeff says with a big smile.

Jeff and I part ways; him rushing off to his appointment and me making my way back to the office. Walking along, I feel a sense of renewed energy. It's like I have taken a huge step in solving my problems - the first step!

Chapter 4
The Situation Today

*O*n my way out the door, I pick up the phone to call Sandy. "I'm on my way," I tell her. "See you shortly!" I add, hoping to make a quick break.

"Bob," she asks, "why didn't you call me today?" She is speaking quickly, to avoid being hung up on. Sandy has come to expect to chat with me at least once or twice every day.

"Sorry about that, hon, but I had a great day! I met with Jeff this morning and it went well. It ends up, well, I'm not the only one having problems. Jeff himself has been having trouble over the last six months and I'm going to see if I can help him out. Anyway, we're meeting again next Tuesday at 8:00!" I am talking enthusiastically, almost spilling my words together.

"Bob, did you forget?" Sandy jumps in.

I search to think of what I could have forgotten, and then I give up. "What did I forget?"

"Remember you said you would drop the kids off at school on Tuesday? I told you I have a dentist appointment at 8:00. Bob, you never listen to me."

I slap myself on the forehead. I remember Sandy giving me all the details only a few days ago, but it has totally slipped my mind. I have been so involved thinking about my situation and my meeting with Jeff that this didn't even cross my mind. "I'm sorry honey, we're going to have to make other arrangements. I've got to make that meeting with Jeff - it's already set!" Hoping to ease the moment I say, "Remember, I said I want to increase my income... "

She cuts me off at the pass. "If I recall, Bob, you wanted to increase your income to pay for golf lessons."

I hate it when she thinks faster than me - which is most of the time. "Come on Sandy, work with me on this," I plead.

She gives in reluctantly. "OK Bob, I'll make some calls. When are you going to be home?"

"Thanks Sandy. I appreciate it. I'm leaving the office right now. See you in a bit... ." She casually hangs up the phone without saying "good-bye". She knows I hate that.

When I get home I find that Sandy has held off feeding the kids. After supper, Amanda promptly hands me a piece of paper and drags me off to her room. Scanning the paper, it becomes apparent that it is the lines for her upcoming play. "Why do we have to practice in your room, honey? There's no audience in here."

"I don't want anyone to hear me, Dad," she confesses.

"OK, but you're going to have to learn to get comfortable saying your lines in front of people. After all, it is a play, right?"

"OK, OK, Dad."

Mechanically, we read through the lines, switching back and forth. Within a few attempts Amanda goes from reading word by word to being able to periodically glance up at me, all while reciting her lines.

"Why is practicing your lines so important?" I ask. Amanda rolls her eyes before answering, as if I shouldn't have asked since the answer is so obvious.

"Mrs. Dias said that it's difficult to try to remember lines and act all at the same time. The better we know our lines, the better we will act," Amanda explains slowly, as if I don't understand. Then we look at each other. "Let's do it one more time," Amanda says. And we do.

By the end of the evening I sit back and admire the passion and conviction in my daughter: She really is my hero!

I am up before both the alarm and Sandy, so I roll out of bed so I don't wake her and I slip towards the bathroom. Then I am halfway through brushing my teeth when I hear the alarm go off beside the bed. Damn it! I forgot to turn it off!

I race back to the bed, trying to get to it before Sandy wakes up, but I know my effort is in vain. Sandy is a light sleeper and there is no way she is going to sleep through the alarm. Just as I get to the clock her hand flops out of bed to turn it off. "Good morning hon," I garble, with my toothbrush sticking out of my mouth.

She doesn't say anything and recoils under the covers, so I make my way back to the bathroom and continue to get ready for the day. By the time I am finished Sandy is already up, has made the bed, and has opened the curtains. Although I'm all for sunshine, I hate coming out of the bathroom in my underwear and I have to crawl to my closet to get dressed. I'm sure there are no neighbours outside our window waiting to get a glimpse of me walking around in my skivvies, but I'm not so proud of my body that I'm willing to take a chance.

I get over to the closet half-stooped, and quickly pick a suit and accessories. Within a couple of minutes I am dressed; I figure this unique ability to dress quickly is the only thing Superman and I have in common.

Just as I am about to make a mad dash for the car, Sandy interrupts. "Bob, it's still early and you have lots of time to get to the office by 8:00. Sit down and talk to me. Have a little breakfast before you go."

I realize that she is right: It is still early and after all, having breakfast is supposedly good for the mind and I want to be sharp today. "OK, Sandy," I say and move to the table.

She puts cereal in a bowl and then pours skim milk overtop of it. I wince at the sight; I hate skim milk, I think to myself! I should never have told her the doctor said my cholesterol is a little high. I get up and grab some sugar to sprinkle on top; this seems to be a fair trade-off for having to eat cereal with skim milk.

Sandy sits down beside me. "So honey, are you nervous about your meeting with Sparky today?"

"His name is Jeff," I say. It seems strange for me to be correcting Sandy on this point, considering I was the one who came up with the name in the first place.

"Whatever. So, are you?"

I purposely take a big spoonful of cereal and chew it slowly so that I will have a moment to think about my answer. "I'm not nervous... I just don't know what to expect."

"Just be yourself, Bob. Just sit down with him, tell him what you think, and hear what he has to say."

The more we talk about the upcoming meeting, the more nervous I am getting. I decide to switch gears to something more fun. "So Sandy, what are you getting done at the dentist this morning?" I ask with a smirk.

The smile on her face disappears as she contemplates the morning ahead. "You jerk!" she shoots back, "you know I hate going to the dentist!"

"Touché" would have been better, but "You jerk!" is good too. I lean over and give her a kiss good-bye. "I've got to get going; I don't

42

want to be late for the meeting. Thanks for breakfast." I put my coat on and I am out the door.

Since I am negotiating my way to work earlier these days, I come to the realization that I can actually avoid traffic by leaving early: that thought had never occurred to me even once over the last few years! When I get to work, Jeff's car is already in his stall.

In the office, I am surprised at how much activity there is this early in the morning. I drop by my office to hang up my coat and pick up a pen and pad.

Arriving at Jeff's door, I see him working away behind his desk. When he sees me his face lights ups with a smile and he gets up to shake my hand. "Good morning, Bob! It's nice to see you. Grab a seat," he says and points to one on the other side of his desk.

"Good morning, Jeff," I hesitate slightly before making my way to sit down.

"What's the problem, Bob?"

"Nothing. Don't worry about it," I say, and sit down. I can't tell Jeff, but sitting on the other side of a manager's desk makes me feel like a subordinate... not at all like we're players on the same team. But he is a new manager, so I allow him his power trip.

Jeff is busy organizing the papers on his desk when I spot the 'big, fat, file' with my name on it. That file might as well be titled *The Rise and Fall of Rocket-Man,* because that is exactly what it shows. The knot in my stomach grows, the more I stare at my file. Although I know I have some accomplishments in there, I also know my statistics lately don't look too good. I sure hope Jeff's not planning to spend an hour sifting through my dirty laundry, or this could be the longest meeting of my life.

At that moment the phone rings and Jeff picks it up. The conversation goes on for a few minutes, and from my perspective it doesn't seem to be particularly important. Sitting in that uncomfortable chair, on the other side of Jeff's desk while the man himself completely ignores my presence, I start to feel a little angry at my treatment. I signal to Jeff, "Do you want me to go?" in the hopes he will say "yes". There is nothing more awkward than sitting idly in front of someone while they chat away on the phone, as if you don't exist.

Jeff signals back with his fingers to indicate the call will just be another second or two. Unfortunately, the call goes on for several minutes before Jeff finally hangs up and apologizes for having to take that *important* call from head office.

"Bob," Jeff says, "I have been thinking lots about our conversation and I am really excited to work with you. I think there are some things I can help you with, and you can help me as well. I thought this morning -"

he cuts short as the phone rings again. "Just a minute, Bob; this will be quick."

I can feel the tension starting to rise and my face getting red as I listen to Jeff's side of yet another telephone conversation. Fortunately this call is shorter and Jeff apologizes profusely again when the call is over. "As I was saying, Bob, I thought this morning we could spend some time learning a little more about each other and trying to figure out exactly how we can work together."

I try to calm my nerves, decide to give him another chance, and focus on why I am here. "Jeff, I have been thinking a lot about our conversation as well. I really am interested in getting my sales back up again. You see, I have thought a lot about the success you have achieved in sales and I am interested in learning more about how you -"

At that point we both hear the 'toink' that computers make to indicate that a new piece of email has arrived. I continue talking but I can see Jeff slowly and inconspicuously rolling his chair back and reaching over to press a key to bring the screen to life. With the screen now alive, Jeff's eyes flip between the message and myself as he attempts to read it and appease me all at the same time. The whole time I am talking; trying to make Jeff understand how my whole career seems to be ending and how I don't know what to do to bring my sales back up... and if he hears anything it is between the lines of his email.

Now, I don't usually lose my temper - particularly with a manager - but at this point I am officially offended. I jump to my feet, scoop up my pen and pad, and start walking to the door. Looking straight ahead I shout, "Jeff, it appears you are far too busy to be spending time with me!" And then I am out of his office and down the hall.

Jeff tries to recover. Over my shoulder I can hear his voice fade away as I disappear. "Bob! I'm sorry. Karen is on the brink of selling the largest contract for our division so far this year... and there are some snags with head office... "

All the way to my office I wonder how I could have been so stupid as to think that Sparky could help me. I get into my office, close the door, and sit down to think about what I should do next. While I am extremely upset with my treatment, I am also concerned about my future: over the last twenty-four hours I have convinced myself that I can't turn this around on my own.

Within minutes of getting settled I hear a light knock at the door, and Jeff sticks his head in. Before I can say anything Jeff jumps in - both hands in the air - as if to surrender. "Bob, you have every right to be upset with me... I am extremely sorry for my behaviour."

I think to myself that at least Jeff has the courage to say sorry. I sit there, saying nothing, to allow the moment to sink in. After an extremely long pause I speak. "Jeff, I appreciate your apology. But if you're too busy I'm not sure we can work together."

"No excuses, Bob. I made a mistake and I'm sorry. I *am* interested in working with you. Let's go back to my office and try again."

At that moment I have an idea: Lesson #1 for the new manager. "Jeff, I am going to give you some advice. Do you mind?"

"Not at all, Bob. Go ahead."

"Let's go back to your office... " I say and we make our way down the hall.

Jeff returns to his comfortable chair behind the big desk with me standing across from him with my hands resting on the back of the chair.

"What did you want to say, Bob?" Jeff says, reclining in his chair.

I take a deep breath and focus, choosing my words carefully. "Jeff, it starts with this desk and these chairs. When I sit across from you it just doesn't feel right... it doesn't feel like we're on the same team, let alone on the same field. "

My attention turns to the round table. I walk slowly to the table and sit down at one of the chairs without saying a word. Slowly and deliberately I begin with, "Jeff, when I meet with you, I'd like to sit over here. It might be a small point, but I want to know we're working together. Don't you?"

"Good point Bob, I never really thought about it that way," he says, getting up from his chair and making his way around the desk.

Before he gets too far, I move on to the second point, "And Jeff, I realize you are busy, but it would make me feel a lot better, and a lot more important, if you would hold your calls and turn that damn computer off."

"I know, I know," Jeff says with an apologetic grin. "I promise that won't happen again, Bob," Jeff says and takes a chair beside me at the table.

"Enough said... I appreciate you letting me speak my mind." At that moment I spot the big fat file with my name on it. I have just got to say something, I prod myself. I put my hand on the big, fat, file. "There is one more thing, Jeff. It's this file. This file contains everything there is to know about me and where I have come over my fifteen years with the company. But what I did, or didn't do, in the past isn't going to give us the answers to the future. I would like to start with a clean slate; I don't want any baggage for you or me." Without saying another word, I grab the file, stand up, walk across the office, and drop it in the wastebasket with the loudest bang you can imagine.

I turn to see the shock on Jeff's face. As I walk back to the table I break the moment by asking, "Now, if you want to get the file out of the garbage, I understand." I say, walking back to retrieve it.

"Bob, I am impressed. When you talk about that file I can sense how you feel. I certainly don't need any of the information in your file to figure out what we are going to do from this point forward."

Jeff gets up, grabs his notepad, and writes down several notes from our discussion. I am not sure if he does this for his benefit or mine, but all the same I am impressed. It is nice to see a manager that is open to learning something - particularly from a weathered salesman like me.

Jeff switches gears and puts his manager's hat back on. "Bob, tell me about yourself; tell me about Bob Stephens."

I settle in to the real purpose of this meeting... me! I take a deep breath and try to relax and then I begin. "I started with the company just out of university. The first few years I did really well. Then, well, I am not sure exactly what happened... but slowly the sales numbers dropped off. For the last few years I have really struggled to build up my clientele." I go on and on; bragging about my successes, venting about my frustrations, and exposing my fears. Jeff does the best thing he could do: he listens.

"Bob, did you want to tell me anything about your personal situation?"

"Sure, I don't mind. I'm married to Sandy and we have two kids; David is nine and Amanda is twelve. When we decided to have kids we both thought it would be best if Sandy temporarily gave up her accounting career, but in the end Sandy decided not to go back; it's difficult to both have full-time careers when you have a young family. The problem is, though, now that my sales have dropped it is getting harder and harder to live on my income."

"So what does Sandy think about you getting your sales back up?"

"Both her and the kids are 100% behind me on this." As these words come out of my mouth I question whether they are behind me or not. Obviously Sandy would like to see me making more money, and the kids would certainly like the little extras that come with that, but are they prepared for the extra commitment this will take? I decide that I need a plan to get their 'buy-in'.

"That's great, Bob. Let me tell you a little about my background." Jeff goes on to talk about his history with the company; how he got started, his success in sales, his challenges, and even a little about his personal life.

"Yesterday morning you said you were looking for a coach along the lines of a 'Russ', if I'm not mistaken. Why do you think a coach is the answer?"

I sit there, slowly rubbing my chin as I look for the answer. "The problem is, I don't know what I need to do to get my sales back up. I am hoping a coach will help me figure out what is wrong. I also want someone who I can talk to from time to time; someone who will pat me on the back when I do a good job and who will give me hell when I don't. Most of all, I want someone who cares about me... and whether I succeed or fail."

After the words had come out, I wonder if I am just describing my relationship with John Andrews. In that instant I remember that John Andrews is gone forever, and perhaps asking Jeff to be his clone isn't likely to work.

Jeff hesitates. "Bob, I think I can help you. Let me tell you how I work with new salespeople. You can then tell me how that might work for you."

He continues. "My belief is that if a salesperson becomes brilliant at each basic step of the sales process, they can't fail. Perhaps my downfall is I don't understand when the new salespeople I hire can't do well. I work hard with them... damn hard. The sales process I train them on is the same one I learned when I was selling."

He sits back with an impish grin on his face. "Some of the new salespeople, like Karen, have been trained on different parts of the sales process two or three times since they started. The new salespeople hate it, but what I keep finding is that their skills keep slipping, so I keep on training them."

"Jeff, if you don't mind me saying... it all sounds a bit like a boot camp."

He laughs. "I guess it is in some ways, but I am convinced that they need to be brilliant at the basics to be successful!"

I shudder at the thought of being forced to follow a 'canned' sales presentation; losing my individuality for this manager and his ways. "Jeff, does every salesperson you train follow the sales process exactly the same way, with every client?"

"Not at all, Bob. The steps of the basic sales process are always the same, but everyone is different and they inject their own personality into their presentations. I want them to know the sales process so well that the client has no idea they are even following a process."

I feel some relief with Jeff's explanation. I am definitely not interested in becoming a Jeff Townes clone any more than he is interested in becoming John Andrews.

"Bob, let's take the remaining time to figure out how we can work together," Jeff says and checks his watch. "Where do you think we should start?"

"I'd like to figure out what's wrong with my current approach. I also would like to set some goals and put together a plan to achieve them."

"Do you follow a sales process of your own, Bob?"

"Not really. Over the years I have learned through experience to adapt on the fly with each client."

Jeff winces slightly. "Well, Bob... I think there is a standard process."

"Jeff, maybe the new people need a 'canned' sales presentation to get them through an interview, but I certainly don't."

"Are you sure you don't need to follow a process?" Jeff persists.

I sit there saying nothing, neither agreeing nor disagreeing, but I can feel my tension level rising. I did not come here to learn Jeff's canned sales presentation: My clients would fall over backwards laughing if I walked into their offices like a sales robot and delivered some mechanical presentation. No way; it's just not me.

"Jeff, I appreciate where you are coming from but I think you have been spending too much time with the new salespeople. I don't think following a canned sales process is the answer for me."

Jeff gives in. "OK Bob. I want you to keep an open mind on this. Would you be willing to sketch out the sales process you are following?"

"OK. I'll write it out but I'm not sure what it is going to tell us."

"Thanks, Bob. I appreciate your cooperation. When you are writing out your process I want you to think of which parts of the process you are most comfortable with, as well as those areas you find more difficult. Also, think about which parts you put the most effort into, and into which parts you put the least effort. Are you willing to do that?"

"OK, Jeff," I agree... reluctantly.

"Bob, you also said you wanted to set some goals. Would you mind putting together some of the goals you would like to achieve? Also, make a list of all the good prospects you have right now, agreed?"

I think about my schedule today. I have some follow up work with my existing clients and this afternoon I have another appointment with Selectrum; a great prospect I have been working with over the last few months. If I have to, I'll get it done tonight. It's probably a good idea to get Sandy and the kids involved in my goal-setting anyway. "I'll get it done, Jeff."

"Great, Bob. Do you want to meet again tomorrow morning at 8:00?" Jeff asks, checking his watch.

"I'll be here!"

"I have enjoyed spending time with you today, Bob. We got off to a rocky start but I appreciate you handling it the way you did; I will take the advice to heart." As he gets up, we walk to the door together. Jeff waits until we have eye contact and then he says, "By the way Bob, there's one more request I have of you. I know you came up with my nickname 'Sparky', and although it is really cute I would appreciate it if you didn't call me that."

I am lost for words. I laugh, but I can feel my face turning red. That Sarah has such a big mouth... she has pinned the whole 'Sparky' thing on me. "Jeff," I say, "let me explain... "

Before I can say anything, Jeff jumps in. "No need to explain. I'll tell you what; I won't call you Rocket-Man if you don't call me Sparky." He gives me a smile, and then a wink.

She not only told him about Sparky, she told him about "Rocket-Man"! I am so consumed with my thoughts of Sarah I have to force myself to reply.

"It's a deal," I say. Then, as I walk from Jeff's office, I have only one thing on my mind: how am I going to get even with Sarah?

As I head down the hall, the thoughts race through my head as I scheme about how I'm going to get back at Sarah. I could stomp into her office, accuse her of having a big mouth, and rant and rave about how it made me feel... but the problem is, the pain she would feel wouldn't last long enough, and it wouldn't be nearly as much fun as devising a more appropriate payback. Sarah forgets how much I really know about her and her sordid past.

I think of a few scenarios, and this calms me down; by the time I am back in my office, I have put Sarah behind me, and I start getting organized for the day. In fact, I find myself looking forward to my next appointment with Selectrum this afternoon. It's nice to have a good lead drop in your lap every so often. I remember getting the call from my client a few months ago telling me that Selectrum was in the market for our services and that I should give them a call. I hadn't been up to calling new clients... so, unfortunately, the lead gathered a little dust on my desk. All things have a way of working out, though, because about a month later, Peter Most from Selectrum actually called me! I can just sense that Selectrum is going to sign a contract! Over the last few months, I have invested so much time pulling this deal together; they've just got to buy!

I don't know how many times I have received leads from clients and then didn't call them - at least not right away, anyway. I open my desk drawer and grab a small stack of business cards along with a handful of torn pieces of paper covered with scribbles. I fan all this like a deck of cards, thinking of all the time I have spent collecting them. These leads are an indication of the great work I do for my clients; I look at them as my security. As long as I have got leads in my desk, there's still hope. Perhaps that's why I am reluctant to call them. After all, if I got on the phone and called them all, I'm sure I would get some appointments. But then, all my leads would be gone... and the thought of that scares me a little.

I know I have got some important things to get done, but I am not sure where to start. Whenever this happens, though, I have my trusty time managers. One is an in-basket full of email and the other, my voicemail.

I flip around to the keyboard and tap it to bring the monitor to life; I find reading my messages is a great way to ease into the day. As I bring up my in-basket, it 'toinks' with each new message. Each 'toink' represents a little something to keep me busy, at least for a while; some are office jokes while others actually require action. Throughout the day, I can be busy on one thing or another, but when I hear the 'toink', it's like this big magnet draws me to the monitor, and I have to check on my new arrival.

It's funny; when I look at the screen, I see programs, files, and company-provided tools that are supposed to help us... and all I do is send and receive email. At least, I think, I *can* send and receive email: some of my colleagues retired rather than learn even that! That said, I check through the new messages of the day.

I start with reading the message at the top of the list from Teddie. Scrolling through Teddie's message provides me with the clues to its origin. A while ago, I handled a simple task for one of Teddie's clients while he was away and then notified him by email. Today, he has replied simply: "Thanks!" Being the polite guy I am, I press the 'Reply' button and then I begin to hunt and peck: "You're welcome!" With the message complete, I manoeuvre the mouse ever so carefully to position the pointer directly over the 'Send' button and triumphantly slam the 'Enter' key. I smile as I think; email is such a great communication tool!

Just then the phone rings for the first time, and my day is off and running.

As it approaches noon, I search around for the bag Sandy packed me, and as soon as I open it I know what's in store: "Tuna salad on brown; hold the butter", and judging by the weight, there must be an apple down there, too.

Here it is noon, and I still haven't thought about the things I agreed to have ready for Jeff tomorrow morning. My appointment at Selectrum should only take about an hour, so I decide to put off the work on the stuff I promised Jeff until I get back.

I gobble down my lunch and begin preparing for my afternoon appointment. The more time that passes, the more anxious I become that I have left this too late. In a panic, I fumble through file folders looking for the right information. Slowly, the material for my presentation begins to take shape and my confidence re-builds. I check my watch one last time and hurriedly stuff everything into my portfolio. As I jump in my car and drive away, it's as if my car knows its way without me: Over the last few months I have been back and forth to visit Selectrum a dozen times or more. I smile, thinking of the time Peter Most asked me, "Don't you have any other clients to visit?" Naturally, I took it as a compliment; I wanted to show him the kind of service he could expect if - I mean when - he signs a contract with us!

On the way to the appointment, I re-play in my mind all the meetings I have had with Selectrum. The first meeting went great! I razzled and dazzled Peter with all of the great things we could do for them. The next few appointments were a breeze; I have found that my experience has made me very intuitive as to what my clients' needs are! When it came time to present the solutions, even though we had scheduled an appointment for one hour we ended up talking for over two! I must admit that the last month or so has been a bit of a challenge: It seems we have been spending a lot of time trying to mop up the final details... but I have a sense that today is the day!

As I pull up to Selectrum's office building, I take note of the structure itself; the foyer is expansive and modern. Selectrum is the best kind of prospect you can have - one with lots of money!

"Can I help you?" the young receptionist asks. The other continues responding to incoming calls.

I am actually surprised she doesn't remember me. "Yes. My name is Bob Stephens, and I have an appointment with Peter Most, your controller, for 2:00 pm."

"Peter is on the phone. I'll let him know you're here when he is available. Have a seat over there, please," and she points.

I make my way to the leather chairs along the window, pick one, and sit down. The seats are very low and not that comfortable, considering what they probably cost. While I wait, I pull out my portfolio and start organizing my material into some semblance of order. I am only halfway through when Peter Most - a heavy-set, middle-aged man - walks up.

I struggle to get up out of the chair in order to shake his hand. I gather up my papers, and we make our way to his office, with Peter leading the way and not saying a thing.

Even though I am a little disorganized, I still feel confident about my approach: I have been through this a thousand times. We walk into his office, which is large and opulent. Peter starts out, "Bob, over the last few months, we have talked a lot about Selectrum and our expansion. I am interested to see the answers to the questions I gave you last time we met. Why don't we go through your material and then we can talk about next steps when you're done?"

Now I am in my comfort zone; I start walking Peter step-by-step through the information. One question comes up, and on the fly I answer it easily. Then a second question, and a third. With each question, I try to come up with a logical, reflective answer.

Then it becomes my turn to ask some questions. "So Peter, you've had a chance to look at all the material and I've got the contract right with me. All I need is your signature and we'll be ready to go!" I reach into my portfolio, searching for a copy of the contract.

Peter leans back in his chair with his hands raised. "Bob, I'm going to need some time to go through the material you presented today. I need to pass it by the management team before I can give you a final answer. How about I give you a call?"

"That would be great! Peter, I know we can do a great job for Selectrum if you give us a chance," I say politely. Then I sort through my proposal and leave the most appropriate information, stuffing the leftovers in my portfolio.

"Thanks again for coming in, Bob. We are close to making a decision; I will get back to you soon." He shakes my hand. "Can you find your way out?"

"I can. I look forward to hearing from you," I say, and I start my way down the hall.

I wait to get in the car before giving myself a one-handed high five. What a great prospect... what a great call - I was brilliant! Sure he had some objections, but every time he threw one at me I was right there; ready with an answer!

Unfortunately, it's now 3:10 and now I'm really behind schedule. I can't wait to tell Jeff about Selectrum: he'll be impressed. Maybe I haven't lost it after all, I muse, maybe it was just a dry spell... more like a drought, I correct myself, laughing out loud. On my way back to the office, I mentally prepare for my morning meeting with Jeff. I am starting to feel anxious about not being ready for it, however.

When I walk into my office, the message light is blinking as usual, but this time, I ignore it. I go directly to the notes from my meeting with Jeff. The first point reads 'Existing Sales Process'.

I get out a clean page and start writing. I figure out that my sales process is really just the steps that take a prospect all the way through to becoming a new client. Once I have the general steps defined, I write down what I do at each step in more detail, and identify which parts I am strong at and then where I need help. Finally, I think about how much effort I am putting into each of the basic steps I have identified.

It is after five o'clock when I realize I've forgotten to call Sandy about when I'll be home. The phone rings only once, and then I hear Sandy say, "Hello."

"Hi Sandy, I'm just finishing up, and I'll be on my way," I say, expecting to get a little backlash for not calling.

"How did your meeting go with Jeff?" she says, and I can hear the smile in her voice.

"Great! You know, he really is a good guy. You should have seen, though - just as I was finishing up with him, he asked me not to call him Sparky any more. I could have died!"

"Have you been calling him Sparky?" Sandy asks, puzzled.

"No, no... at least not to his face. I think it was just his way of letting me know that he has a pulse on what goes on in the office. In the end, we agreed that I won't call him Sparky, and he won't call me Rocket-Man!" I say with a laugh.

"Rocket-Man... I always thought that was such a dumb name."

I think to myself that I didn't actually mind it when I was on top of my game.

She continues. "How did he know about Sparky and Rocket-Man?"

I hesitate. "Sarah told him."

There is silence on the other end of the phone. Then Sandy blasts, "What, is it any of her business anyway?"

I can feel I have struck a cord, so I say, "It's no big deal; she didn't mean any harm."

"That Sarah has such a big mouth. I guess I don't have to tell you though, do I?" she accuses me.

"Hey! Whoa, let's not go there, Sarah. I mean Sandy!" I caught myself too late. It's a minor faux pas, I think, but I know it won't be to Sandy. The phone goes 'click' in my ear, and she is gone. There is no point in rushing home now, I think to myself, so for most of the night I put together my list of prospects, sifting through file after file searching for information on my existing pool of potential prospects. A common thread that runs through these companies is that I have been working with most of them for several months, but I just haven't been able to land them. Perhaps my problem is closing, I think. I can only assume if Jeff led his division, he had to be a good closer. Maybe that's how he can help me.

By the time I am done, I have twenty-five companies listed that are 'that close' to buying. On top of my list is Selectrum.

Now that I have documented my sales process and I have my list of prospects, it's time to figure out my goals. What do I really want to achieve? I realize that whatever goal I set has to be measurable: a specific timeframe and I have to make it public. A goal that you keep to yourself has no consequences. Some of the only secrets I have kept to myself have been goals I set but never achieved. I figured it was a great way to protect myself from the embarrassment of not achieving something that I said I would do.

In my best year ever, I attracted fifty new contracts, and in my worst, ten. I'm not sure if I can hit fifty again, but forty would be nice. No, forty would be fantastic! I'll tell Jeff thirty-five... but I decide to shoot for forty!

Even with my list of twenty-five existing prospects, I still have an empty feeling about where I am going to find that many new clients. I don't get that many referrals given to me, and at my stage in the business, I'm not sure I want to start doing cold calls.

I pick up the phone and call Sandy back. I really shouldn't be calling her; she should be calling me... to apologize! The phone rings again and again, but no one answers. I go from being upset to immediately being worried. After four rings, David picks up the phone, and I try to hide the anxiety in my voice. "Hi, David, how's my little trooper doing?"

David, however, has only one thing on his mind. "Where are you, Dad? When are you going to be home?" he says in a whining voice.

"I'm on my way. What's your Mom doing?"

"She said she's waiting for you to get home."

"Tell her I'm on my way," I say with some relief. It appears another mini-crisis is behind us. I check my watch and see that it is already 8:00, and the office is vacant and dark as I make my way out. This has been quite a day! With my notes in hand, I am in the car and on my way.

When I get in the house, Amanda is the only one to greet me. As we hug, I ask, "Where's David?"

"He's already in bed."

I feel overridden with guilt; every day, I like to make sure I see the kids either before I leave or at least at the end of the day... and today I missed both.

I have a short chat with Amanda about her day, and she tells me about her experience with the upcoming play. "Dad, you know when I first said I was going to be in the play? Well, Kirsten and I decided to go in together; we thought it would be easier that way. I remember the first day we were both terrified as we walked up on stage to do our parts. When we finished, I was jumping up and down, excited about doing it again."

She continues. "I couldn't believe it when Kirsten walked off and described it as the scariest thing she's ever done. Anyway, she decided to quit, and now they have to find someone else to do her part!"

"Sweetie, I'm proud of you for sticking with it. I'm looking so forward to seeing you up on stage. So how's the practicing going?"

"I know all my lines off by heart, Dad! I've been practicing them at night *and* at school. I even practice them in the shower!" she says, adding a beautiful little laugh.

"In the shower! Boy, you must be good. That's funny, Amanda... I don't remember any shower scenes!" I give a huge laugh to support my own humour, and Amanda gives me a half-hearted smile to let me know she gets it.

"Well," I say, "I am going to give David a kiss good night. Why don't you run off to bed, and I'll tuck you in after I'm finished."

As I make my way to David's room, I look for signs of Sandy... and find nothing. Once in David's room, however, Sandy's whereabouts become clear. I kiss them both on the forehead without waking them, work my way back to Amanda's room, and we say good night. Then it occurs to me that I haven't had supper yet, and I head for the kitchen. As I am scavenging through the fridge, Sandy walks in. "It's in the microwave," she says, her voice toneless.

Even warmed up, the supper still is great and hits the spot. We talk about my day, her day, and even Sarah.

"Honey, don't worry about Sarah," I say to her, "I know that... incident still bothers you, but it was a long time ago. Sarah and I are just two people who work at the same place - nothing more."

"I know, Bob. And, well... I'm sorry for hanging up on you," she gives me hug and a kiss on the cheek, and suddenly everything is all right again.

So, with that behind us, I want to get her feedback on my goal. I lean back and say, "Sandy, Jeff asked me to put together a goal for the year. Well, I have decided to set my goal as thirty-five new contracts. I actually think I can sell forty, but I want to leave myself a safety margin. Do you think that sounds reasonable?"

Sandy is in touch with the number of new contracts I am selling: every time I get a new one, she is one of the first I share the news with. I feel it is my obligation to share the good news, seeing as how I always share the bad.

"How many did you sell last year, Bob?"

I look up at her from my plate. "Fourteen."

"You want to go from fourteen to thirty-five?" she says pointedly.

I hadn't thought about it in quite those terms. "How about thirty?" I say, and I am somewhat uncertain now.

"Bob, thirty sounds like an awful lot to sell!"

"Sandy, I need to get our income back up, and anything less than thirty isn't going to do it," I speak and realize that I am trying to convince myself now.

"Bob, I just don't want you to be disappointed again."

"Oh, great! You're so supportive! Thanks a lot, Sandy. You're a real confidence builder!" I can feel my stress level peaking, and nothing more is said. The rest of the night, we are both quiet. Sandy goes off to bed early, which gives me even more time to question myself about my goal.

Chapter 5
Theory of Scarcity... Theory of Plenty

$\mathcal{W}$hen I get into my office, I hang - or I should say hide - my golf clothes inconspicuously behind the door and drop my lunch and notes on my desk. I've got my golf game with the Butcher and the Baker later this afternoon - a little secret that nobody here needs to know about.

I still have ten minutes before my meeting with Jeff; the message light is an ongoing reminder of what I have put off since the night before, so I listen to message after message, scribbling notes as I go. The messages are a constant reminder of how important I am to my clients. When I hear the voice on the last message, I sit up with anticipation: I recognize the voice - it's Peter Most. What a great way to start the day! He is probably asking me to come back to sign a contract.

I listen carefully to every word. "Hi Bob, it's Peter Most from Selectrum. Thanks for coming in today. We've finalized our decision. We have decided to go with another company. Give me a call if you want more information."

Shock! Nothing! Impossible; my heart sinks. The thoughts race through my mind, pointing blame first on myself and then him. What went wrong with my presentation? What's wrong with me? What's wrong with him? Why wouldn't he choose us? Can't he see we are his best alternative?

I have invested so much time and energy over the last few months trying to close Selectrum, and now they are gone! I was counting on them to come through!

I have been through this situation so many times that I have given up counting. All of a sudden, nothing matters. Not my goals, not my plans, not my meeting with Jeff... nothing. My eyes start to well up with tears of frustration and fear, so I lean back in my chair, take a deep breath, and stare at the ceiling looking for an answer. I'm not sure how much time passed when I heard a knock on the door.

The door opens and Jeff sticks his head in, all smiles. "Ready to go!" After we make eye contact, Jeff's tone changes. "What's wrong, Bob?"

I shake my head back and forth, and then look back up at the ceiling. "I just lost another great prospect," I whine. "I was counting on Selectrum to come through."

"That's it?" he asks, relief evident in his voice. "I thought someone had died by the look on your face. Bob, grab your plans and come see me in my office," he says before disappearing down the hallway.

I immerse myself deeper in self-pity, thinking about how easy it is for him to react that way. Something has died all right - my career - one prospect at a time, the worst kind of death! Last night I started off thinking how forty new contracts was a great goal. What kind of fool am I? Sandy was right!

I have to shake myself to break my line of thinking. Then I take a deep breath and walk over to my door, looking in the mirror to get a better view of myself. My face looks pale and drawn, but at least I don't look as though I am on the verge of breakdown. It's funny... looks can be so deceiving.

By the time I get to his office, Jeff has his jacket off and is standing at the whiteboard. As if scripted, Jeff starts the routine. "Bob, can you close the door behind you? Grab a seat at the... round table." He then picks up the phone and tells Bruce he is having an important meeting with me and that he doesn't want us to be disturbed. Jeff then turns off the computer and makes his way to sit beside me at the round table. He then says, "Oh, just a second, I forgot something. What time is it, Bob?"

I look down and reply, "It's five to eight."

"Great. Today we will have a whole hour together. Thanks for making the effort to get here on time." A grin stretches across his face. "How was that, boss?" Jeff asks like an eager puppy.

Even in the pit of my despair, I can't help but smile.

"Thanks for those tips, Bob. I used them with every salesperson I met yesterday and what a difference!" His tone changes when he says, "Now, obviously you are pretty upset about losing Selectrum, is that right?"

"Right," I admit.

"One thing I learned when I was in sales is that your success is not built by selling one prospect, and losing one prospect won't ruin your career either." Jeff looks at me intensely and with the index finger of his left hand raised, says, "We operate under the Theory of Plenty!"

I don't understand what the Theory of Plenty is, but for some reason, his conviction about it is enough to make me feel a little better about my future and myself.

Jeff continues. "I don't want to dwell on Selectrum... but why are you so disappointed?"

I think to myself, isn't it obvious? I humour him and say, "Well, good prospects are hard to come by. I haven't had too much success getting new contracts lately, so the news from Selectrum really hurts."

Jeff gets up and makes his way to the whiteboard. "I have an idea. I want to show you something. Remember we talked about mapping out your sales process? What did you come up with?"

Slowly, I reach for my notes. "I guess it starts with prospecting. In other words, you need to gather names in order to have people to call, right?"

"Sounds reasonable," Jeff turns and writes down <u>Prospecting</u> on the board. "Bob, how would you describe the prospecting you do?"

"Prospecting, for me, is when one of my clients picks up the phone and calls me with a name, or when someone a client has referred calls me directly."

"Sounds good. So what do you do when you get a prospect, Bob?"

"That's simple: I call them to book an appointment."

"Then the next step in the sales process is <u>Getting Appointments</u>," and Jeff writes it down. "Do you have any scripts that you follow?" he asks.

"Are you kidding? I pick up the phone and call. The last time I looked at a script was when I was starting out... with John Andrews."

"Then what do you do once you have an appointment?" Jeff continues.

"I usually go to meet them to tell them about our company, myself, and our services; you know - the same old stuff."

"Let's call that the <u>Initial Interview</u>," Jeff says. He writes it at the bottom of the list.

"Is your Initial Interview with your prospects structured at all? For example: do you have a set time frame with clear objectives and so on?"

"At one time, I had a structured initial interview, but as I got more experienced, I learned to adapt to each new client. Sometimes the initial interview lasts ten minutes, and sometimes it takes up to two hours. The objective is always the same, though: I want to sell them on myself and our services so that I can get another interview."

"Then what?"

"Then I usually have another meeting where I ask all of the questions to see exactly what kind of needs or problems they have that I can solve."

Jeff writes <u>Discovering the Needs</u> on the board. "OK Bob, I understand. Keep going; what's next in the process?"

"Once I know what the need is, I put together the solutions and present them to the prospect."

As I am talking, Jeff writes down <u>Presenting the Solution</u>. He turns and smiles. "I think I know the answer, but I'll ask anyway. Do you use the presentations that have been created on the computer?"

"I like the human touch," I smile.

"After you have presented the solution, what do you do then?"

"I close them... or at least I try."

He writes at the bottom of the list <u>Asking for the Business</u>. Then Jeff makes his way back to the table, and we both look at the board.

Prospecting

Getting the Appointment

Initial Interview

Discovering the Needs

Presenting the Solution

Asking for the Business

"So, this is your sales process, Bob. You know, it really is the same for everyone. We all do it a little differently, but basically those are the steps. Wouldn't you agree?"

"Of course," I say, "we all find prospects and try to get an appointment, meet to introduce ourselves, find the need, develop and present the solution, and then ask them for the business."

"Exactly," Jeff agrees. "I think part of the problem is, my friend, that while you follow the general sales process, you don't follow any processes beyond that. Would you agree?"

"Jeff, we've been down this road before. Following a sales process is for new people, not for me. I don't believe in canned sales presentations."

"Hold on, Bob. Just because people follow a sales process doesn't mean it has to be canned. Although the process is the same, everyone is different; no two people are going to deliver it exactly the same way. They are going to inject their own personality and their own experience. Also Bob, once a person learns the sales process, it doesn't come across as mechanical at all! In fact, it becomes the natural way they do business; they do it unconsciously." He pauses, staring at me, wondering if I am getting the message. Jeff knows we are at a critical point: either I am going to buy in, or I am not, and Jeff waits for me to decide which. I sit in silence... and then all of a sudden, it makes sense.

"Jeff," I start, "the other day, you'll remember I told you I went for a golf lesson with Russ Atkens." Jeff gives me a disoriented look; he is no doubt wondering what I am talking about. He nods his head without saying anything.

"The problem with my sales game is the same problem I have with my golf game," I continue, "I have lost touch with the basic process." Jeff sits down to listen more carefully.

"Russ talked about how the basic golf swing is made up of fundamentals. You see, throughout the history of the game, the fundamentals of the basic golf swing have been proven time and time again; the greatest golfers do not create a golf swing from scratch. No way! They learn the fundamentals by practicing and playing, taking golf lessons, reading books, watching others, and so on. Even though the fundamentals of the basic golf swing are exactly the same for everyone, no two golfers swing the club exactly the same way. They personalize the fundamentals based on their body and mind. And, mind you, although they personalize the fundamentals, they never compromise them.

"When these pros are playing in the tournaments, the fundamentals may always be there in the back of their minds, but the mechanics of the swing are unconscious. In other words, when they are in the game, they are not focusing on the swing; they are focusing on the shot they are about to make."

I get up, walk over to the board, and point at the sales process Jeff has written. "It's no different in sales. The sales process is made up of Prospecting, Getting Appointments, the Initial Interview, and so on. The sales process for our company is as tried and true as the basic golf swing."

For a full minute, I take in the words on the board; it has been a long time since I have seen them written out like that.

"Over the years though, I have moved away from the basic sales process. Geez... it happened so slowly I didn't even realize it was changing. John Andrews taught me all of the basics you are teaching your people today. The problem is, over time, with experience and results, I tried to streamline the process - a cut here, a nip here, a tuck there. I think... I think the sales process I am following today has evolved to the point where it looks totally different than the one I was originally taught." I turn to look at Jeff. "The reality is," I tell him, "is that I am not following any sales process at all anymore."

Jeff gets up, shaking his head and smiling but not saying a word. After a moment, he says, "You know Bob, this makes so much sense not only for you, but also for me and the rest of the people here. Whenever I start talking to salespeople about following a sales process, their eyes glaze over just like yours did. They think because it is structured that it only applies to new people. The reality is, great salespeople are really no different than great golfers - both have to be brilliant at the basics!"

"Jeff, I'd like to take credit for this discovery, but it was really Russ who said it to me. I didn't see the relevance of his comments until you started talking about the sales process in our company. Right now I am not sure if I am ready to go back to boot camp with the new salespeople, but I am open-minded about hearing more about the sales process you are teaching them."

"That's all I ask, Bob: an open mind. Let's go on; I have some more things I think you might be interested in." I sit down while Jeff points at the steps in the sales process written on the board. "I want you to think of where you currently are, focusing on the biggest effort. Is it at the top of the sales process: <u>Prospecting,</u> or is it at the bottom: <u>Asking for the Business?</u>"

"That's easy - it isn't prospecting, at least not these days; most of my prospects are referred to me from satisfied clients. I like to think it's one of the rewards of being 'long in the tooth.' Based on my list of prospects - and where they are at in the sales process - it is pretty clear I spend a lot more effort closing the sale."

Jeff draws a triangle over the six steps of the sales process.

Prospecting

Getting the Appointment

Initial Interview

Discovering the Needs

Presenting the Solution

Asking for the Business

"After my first couple of years in the business," Jeff says, "I too had a period of time where my results slipped. Fortunately, I had a manager who recognized the symptoms and got me turned around quickly; he introduced me to this triangle, which measures effort for each step in the sales process. What I learned is that my efforts were focused on the wrong part of the sales process - the part I couldn't control. That realization is what helped me turn my sales around quickly and come back to lead the division. Are you interested in learning more?" Jeff asks as if he knows the answer.

"Are you kidding?" I say, smiling.

"Let's walk through your sales process again to make sure I understand your situation fully." Jeff points to <u>Prospecting</u>. "As you were saying, you don't put a lot of effort into prospecting, so when a prospect does land in your lap, you treat them like gold. Am I wrong or right?"

"I guess you're right."

Jeff points at <u>Getting Appointments</u>. "You're not that comfortable with making phone calls, so sometimes you put off calling the prospects, or perhaps you don't call them at all. Right?"

"I hate to admit it but yes, it's true."

Jeff moves his finger to the <u>Initial interview</u>. "When you are into the initial interview, you start to get more comfortable. You work to sell them on yourself and your services so they will move to the next stage in the process. Maybe you hold off asking too many tough questions for fear of turning them off. Am I on track?"

I think back to my first meeting with Selectrum; that's exactly what happened. "Go on, Jeff. So far so good."

He moves his finger down to <u>Discovering the Needs</u>. "Your comfort level is continuing to rise. You ask some of the questions to uncover the need, but with your experience, you know what their needs are and you've got a pretty good idea of what the solution is going to look like, too. Right?"

"Right." I smile, wondering exactly where this is leading.

Jeff moves to <u>Presenting the Solution</u>. "Now you are on home turf. You know our services inside out, and you show the client. Most salespeople are most comfortable talking about the product. Would you agree?"

"I don't know about most salespeople, but I definitely am."

Before I can say any more, Jeff moves to <u>Asking for the Business</u>. "When you start asking the client to make a decision on signing the contract, they apply the brakes, and you start dealing with all different types of objections. Asking for the business can take a lot of energy. Isn't that what you said, Bob?"

Selectrum jumps to the front of my mind. I think about how many times I had to go back to get the deal closed. I think to myself that I knew closing was the problem right from the start! When I started writing out my prospect list last night, it became clear how much time I have spent trying to get these prospects to sign the order.

"That's exactly what I said, Jeff. I put a huge effort into closing the deal but I can't seem to get them to buy my solutions. Did your manager give the secret to closing all of those prospects to you as well?" I ask with a grin.

Jeff turns around and looks at me. "Bob, my manager helped me to see that closing wasn't the problem. My problem is that I was operating under the Theory of Scarcity."

Now I am confused. "What is the Theory of Scarcity?"

Jeff points at the triangle on the board. "This represents the Theory of Scarcity," he says, "and salespeople who operate under the Theory of Scarcity believe there are very, very few prospects out there who are either qualified or have needs for our services. Over my first couple of years, my prospecting efforts went down and down and I invested more time uncovering needs and presenting solutions. The truth was I was operating with fewer and fewer prospects, and so I had to work harder at the bottom parts of the sales process, trying to turn whatever prospects I got into clients. I held on to every prospect I got like gold, hoping they would be worth something someday. I figured out, while some of them were gold, a lot of them were fool's gold. Bob, the problem is if you don't get rid of your fool's gold early in the sales process, you end up with a bunch of prospects who will likely never buy from you but who consume your time and energy. The thing about this is... "

My attention has faded from Jeff's presentation; Jeff's mention of time and energy reminds me of something that John Andrews taught me and that, over time, had completely slipped my mind. I slip back in time to a conversation with John Andrews.

John Andrews came into my office asking to look at my list of prospects. After studying it a few moments he said, "Ah-ha, just what I thought." Then he dropped the list, which floated gently down and landed right in front of me.

I grabbed it, looking for clues. "What are you talking about, John?"

"Bob, I was looking at some of your old prospect lists from a few weeks ago and I noticed that the same names keep re-appearing."

I studied the list more closely. "John, I keep those prospects on there because there is still a chance I can do business with them; it's not like they're taking up a bunch of time. Every couple of weeks or so, I pick up the phone and give them a call to see if they're any closer to making a decision... no big deal!"

John leaned over with one hand on my desk, his finger pointing to the top of my head. "Bob, it's not the time they are taking... it's the mental real estate they occupy!"

"Mental real estate? What's that?" I asked, confused.

At that moment, Jeff stops talking momentarily, which brings me back to reality. "What's the matter, Bob? Doesn't this make sense?"

"I'm sorry, Jeff. When you were talking about all the time and energy those fool's gold prospects take, it reminded me of when John Andrews told me about mental real estate... when I was new in the business."

"What is mental real estate?" Jeff asks, smiling.

I point at my head just as John Andrews had done. "Mental real estate represents the total mind space we have available. Those fool's gold prospects you talked about can consume a lot of mental real estate. The problem is, as long as you are thinking about them you can't be thinking about those prospects who really deserve your time and attention. I believe we need to learn to manage our mental real estate like we do our time!"

Jeff looks at me with a smirk, "How much mental real estate did Selectrum take up?"

I shake my head, "I am afraid it was a lot. Over the last few months, I thought about them day and night. And as long as I was thinking about them, I wasn't thinking about anything else."

"That is a great concept!" Jeff says. "I like that - mental real estate."

Jeff's comments about the Theory of Plenty pop back in my head. I blurt out, "It makes sense - I get it."

"You get what?" Jeff asks, confused.

"The Theory of Plenty! When you were trying to calm me down about Selectrum, you said we operate under the Theory of Plenty. Obviously that means we are operating under the assumption that there are lots of good prospects, so losing one doesn't matter. Is that right?"

"You're bang on, Bob." Jeff gets up and draws a new triangle over the old one.

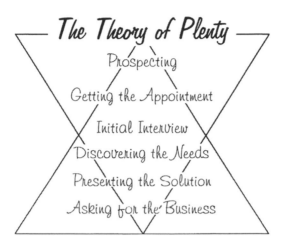

The Theory of Plenty

Prospecting

Getting the Appointment

Initial Interview

Discovering the Needs

Presenting the Solution

Asking for the Business

"With the Theory of Plenty," Jeff instructs me, "the bulk of your effort goes into the top half of the effort triangle: things like Prospecting, Getting Appointments, and the Initial Interview."

"Jeff, this is good in theory, but are there really lots of good-quality prospects out there?"

"Bob, you are good - both you and I know it. You do a great job for your clients; you understand their needs and you know your products and services better than anyone. There are plenty of high-quality prospects who are interested in dealing with you."

I think to myself; damn, I'm good! My clients love me. Jeff is a genius - even if I do say so myself! For a second I think that ol' Jeff and I should start our own 'mutual admiration' society! And then I smile at the thought.

Jeff continues. "The best thing about the Theory of Plenty is that it puts you in control of your sales funnel. You control how many prospects you add in the top, and you decide which ones you are going to deal with. The Theory of Plenty gives you the power to say "No" to those prospects who do not meet certain criteria *early* in the sales process. After your prospects have been filtered out in the initial interview, only the high probability prospects will be left. Those are the ones where you are going to invest your time, effort, and mental real estate."

Jeff steps beside me, puts his hand on my shoulder, and looks me straight in the eye. "Bob, operating under the Theory of Plenty means that companies like Selectrum don't matter as much because there's lots of great prospects right behind them that are ready and willing to deal with you."

Before I can say anything, Jeff quickly switches gears. "Based on the Theory of Plenty, Bob, where should you be investing the bulk of your energy?"

"The top of the sales process," I answer. "Prospecting, Getting Appointments, and the Initial Interview," I speak confidently.

"That's right, Bob - that's where we need to start. We need to show you how to find those great quality prospects that are out there, and how to get appointments with them. The other thing we have to figure out is how to 'filter' all those prospects so that only the 'high-probability' prospects are left. Those are the ones where you are going to invest your time, energy, and mental real estate. Agreed?"

"Sounds good to me Jeff"

"OK Bob, the last thing we were going to talk about was your goal. What did you come up with?"

I find myself confused at this point and don't know what to tell him. "Well," I start, hesitating, "my first thought was that my goal should be forty new contracts; then I dropped it to thirty-five... and then thirty. Right now, I don't know what to do."

"Bob, this is your decision - it's your goal. I don't want to impose a number that is either too high or too low. The only thing I will say is that you know more about this business than almost anyone in this office. You have got great people skills, some great clients, and I think you are determined to improve your results. I think any goal you set your mind to achieving, you will achieve."

"Thanks for the confidence builder, Jeff. I appreciate it." I think to myself that the only thing he was missing was 'atta boy!'

"I'll talk to Sandy again and get back to you," I say, and then I gather up my notes from the meeting, and we both get up from the table. "Jeff, in one hour with you, I learned more about myself than I have in the last three years looking in the mirror trying to figure out what was going wrong. I appreciate your time."

"Bob, you don't know how much I learned as well. Tying the sales process back to golfing is a great idea. Thank you." Jeff and I shake hands and we part ways.

In the hall I see Karen and two other new people I recognize, but I don't know their names. They are kibitzing back and forth but I can't really make out what they are saying. Normally, I would pass them by without saying so much as a word... but this morning is different. "Good morning, Karen," I announce.

This abruptly breaks up the momentum of their dialogue. Karen smiles at me and says, "Good morning, Bob." The other two people - both young, both male - look at me but don't say anything.

"Hi, I'm Bob Stephens." I reach out to shake hands and they reciprocate. "I'm Rudy," one says, and the other follows along with, "Nice to meet you, Bob. I'm Al - Al Boucher."

We make small chat, although we are all a little out of our comfort zones. "So what's the sales meeting on this morning?" I ask as sincerely as I can.

Karen pipes up and says, "Discovering the Needs." Her eyes light up and she asks, "Why don't you come to the meeting and tell us what it really takes to be successful!" I can tell she is just making conversation, but it is flattering nonetheless.

"I'm sure Jeff wouldn't want you to be learning all my bad habits," I say as we part ways. I think to myself that maybe I should talk to them sometime - I couldn't do any worse than Sarah.

Then, on the way to my office I think about Jeff's challenges with the new salespeople. Maybe all it takes is just making an effort to get to know them and trying to keep the spirit up. That would be a switch for me - one of the founding members of the 'Old Guard'.

I spin into my office and hang up my coat behind the door; the golf attire hanging there is a friendly reminder of my golf game late this afternoon. I think about my lesson with Russ and of all the minor adjustments he suggested for my swing, but I cringe as I remember his words about practicing. I make a commitment to myself to get out at least one hour before the golf game, in order to practice my swing.

The flashing message light on my phone brings me back to my real priority; turning my business around. The meeting with Jeff was great and I feel that the points on the Theory of Scarcity and the Theory of Plenty really hit home. Then I consider how the conceptual world is so much simpler than the real world here in my office, where I have a list full of old prospects consuming my time, a cluttered desk, and messages and emails begging to be dealt with. I know the moment I start on the mini-tasks my day will slip away, as will any opportunity to move to the Theory of Plenty.

As I am sitting there Teddie marches into my office and drops the day's newspaper, in a loose pile, on my desk. "Hey Bob, you want to read the paper?" he asks and turns to leave, not really caring what my answer is.

He is already out of the door by the time I have a chance to reply, "Thanks, Teddie... "

Teddie and I have pretty much made this a daily ritual for the last few years. He sneaks the paper from the reception area and reads it front to back, so by the time I get it the paper looks like it is ready for the kitty litter box. Whenever I finish reading it, I carefully fold it back into its original shape and return it to its rightful spot.

So I pick up the paper and I become drawn in, article by article. I glance over every page, scanning some articles and studying others. As I finish each section I carefully fold it, attempting to remove as many of the creases as possible.

Within ten minutes I have made it all the way to the sports section - my favorite. I sit back in my chair and put my feet up on the desk. However, instead of reading the sports page I drift back in time to a conversation with John Andrews, from when I was first starting out. Come to think about it, we didn't actually talk... although John spoke volumes.

I was sitting in my office celebrating my success by reading the paper. As I recall, I was sitting in the same position I am right now. John walked by my office and stopped for a moment to see what I was doing. Without saying a word, he turned and kept on going down the hall. Being young and cocky, I never gave it much thought and dipped back into the sports page. Within a few minutes he walked into my office in silence: he was holding a giant sheet he had ripped off the easel in the meeting room. Although I was relatively new, I was smart enough to know this had something to do with reading a newspaper at my desk during the day. I attempted to fold it and slide it off the desk, but it was very awkward and suddenly quite pointless.

John held the paper to the wall directly in front of me with one hand while he taped it with the other. John wasn't a big man, but he was positioned so that I still couldn't see what was written on the paper. Without us exchanging a word, he walked out of my office and disappeared down the hall. The writing was somewhat illegible, but after studying it a moment I made out the message:

Throughout your day you are taking small steps; some towards the success you are striving for, some towards your eventual failure.

He didn't have to explain it; the message was clear. I left that paper up for a week or so. John never said anything about that day until a few months later: I was overwhelmed with the administration, my sales were starting to slip, and I was in John's office looking for answers.

"Bob, you need to hire some help!" John coaxed me after patiently listening to my problems.

I was expecting this advice, and I was prepared. My income had dropped down slightly as my sales dipped, and I didn't want to forego any compensation for administrative help. "I can't afford it, John," I tried to convince him. He and I both knew that wasn't true, but he didn't debate it.

"It sounds like you may be thinking this is going to cost you money. Is this true?"

Being somewhat naïve at the time I replied, "Well, doesn't it?"

"Depends. An assistant costs roughly twenty dollars per hour. If your 'selling time' is worth less than twenty dollars per hour, it costs you. If it is worth more, then it is an investment. So? Which is it?"

I was good, so I knew I was making a lot more than that when I was doing my job. "OK John, I get your point. But what is an assistant going to do for me?"

"Do you remember the message I taped to your wall about the steps towards your success or failure?"

I nodded, thinking; how could I forget?

"Well Bob, there are certain tasks that come with the job. Some of those tasks contribute directly to your success, some contribute indirectly to your success, and others take you away from the success you are trying to achieve. The tasks that contribute directly to your success, like prospecting for example, are the ones you need to focus on - they are *your* responsibility. The tasks that do not contribute directly to your success but still have to be done are the ones that usually can be delegated. The tasks that are contributing to your failure are the ones that you need to get rid of. For the next week I want you to keep track of everything you do in a day. At the end of the week I want you to check off which things contribute directly to your success and which tasks can be delegated. Got it?"

Once I had a list of tasks that could be delegated, that became the job description for my new assistant. After following John's advice I found precious time I never knew I had, and I continued to rise on the charts.

Over the years, though, as I started avoiding the prospecting tasks, my income dropped off. In an effort to maintain my take-home pay I cut back my assistant's time and assumed more of the administration myself. I convinced myself that if I didn't handle each and every administrative task for my clients, it either wouldn't be done right or maybe wouldn't be done at all. I also felt that doing my own administration was in the name of good service: my clients need me at their beck and call, I told myself. In fact, I actually became pretty good at handling all of the administration and I was able to justify my actions with one bad reason or another.

When I look back now I wonder if maybe my love of administration didn't come from my dislike for prospecting and making appointments.

After reflecting over this time from my past I realize something: If I do not re-think the handling of all my own administration I am going to be stuck living in the land of the Theory of Scarcity. The sad thing is that the company provides me with basic administrative assistance, and I haven't even taken advantage of that.

The past gives me a clue to the future: I pick up the phone and dial a three-digit extension. "Hi Tina, can I see you for a minute?"

As I am reflecting on my past I hear this tap at the door. "Can I help you, Bob?" Tina asks in a timid voice.

"Hi Tina. Come in and sit down." She makes her way to the chair across from me. Tina is in her mid 20's and she is rather attractive. She sits there with her steno pad and pen poised.

"Tina, I need your help. The problem is... I don't really know how you can help me."

She sits there, saying nothing and waiting for me to continue. After a few moments of silence she asks, "What would you like me to do?" with a confused expression on her face.

"I was hoping you could tell me, Tina. You see, I have an in-basket full of emails, voicemails coming out of my ears, and some things I promised I would get done for some clients."

Her confidence appears to build as the request takes on more definition. "Mr. Stephens, if you give me access I could review your emails and voicemails and handle anything that you don't need to be involved in. Do you have any confidential situations I should be aware of?"

"Besides my girlfriend in the Bahamas?" I say to display my wit.

She gives me a fake smile to show she doesn't appreciate my humour. I was going to tell her to call me "Bob", but with my bad joke fresh off my lips, that doesn't seem as appropriate now. "No, Tina, thank you. There aren't any confidential situations."

"Mr. Stephens, I will need you to give me shared access to your inboxes. Anything I do for your clients I will copy for you. Is there anything else?"

"I am glad you asked," I say, remembering my list from the voicemails that came in before my meeting with Jeff, "because there is one more thing. Can you handle these requests for me?" I find the notes and hand them over; Tina takes them, looking for the additional information she needs to get the work done. It seems the more I am willing to let go of the ownership of these tasks, the more initiative Tina shows.

"Is that all, Mr. Stephens?"

"Yes. No! Wait: every time a new piece of email arrives this computer, uh... 'toinks'. How do you turn that off?"

"Easy!" Tina moves around to my computer and a few keystrokes later lifts her head and smiles. "Done!"

"That was easy! By the way, Tina, will you call me Bob? You're making me feel as old as I really am."

"OK, Bob. I'll get back to you if I have any questions," she says. And then she is gone.

That felt good, I think, really good! It makes me realize that I need to look for other ways to free up more time for finding new clients, and I pat myself on the back for taking another small step towards the success I am striving for. But, I know, I need to find more ways to free up my time so I grab the pad I used in my meeting with Jeff and search for a clean page. As I flip though the pages I am drawn into the notes.

Although the two triangles make perfect sense, there is a missing piece. These days my time is consumed between keeping my clients happy and trying to turn some of those prospects on my list into new clients. My attention is drawn to my list of twenty-five prospects; over the last six months I have sunk a huge amount of time trying to turn these prospects into clients. I look through the list and it is easy to spot several prospects that have been stuck at one point in the sales process or another.

While the names of these prospects are different, the story is always the same. I meet with them to do a presentation and leave them some material to review. Then a week or so later I call them to find out what they have done with the information I have left with them, at which point they tell me they haven't looked at it yet. Then I coax them to take the time to go through the material, and they promise they will. Two weeks later I call them back and the cycle continues. The problem is, they are good prospects - or so it seems - and I don't have the courage to cut them loose. This, I realize, is a classic case of the Theory of Scarcity.

As I look at the two triangles illustrating the Theory of Scarcity and the Theory of Plenty, the answer comes into clear focus. The two small triangles at the bottom represent all those prospects that ended up on my prospect list because I didn't have a filter. What a revelation! That's where I need to start, I realize; I need to clean my funnel out first.

.   I need to find a way to filter this list of prospects; I need to either move them forward in the sales process or else eliminate them as prospects - at least for now. The time and effort saved could then be reinvested back into the top of the sales funnel, where it belongs.

71

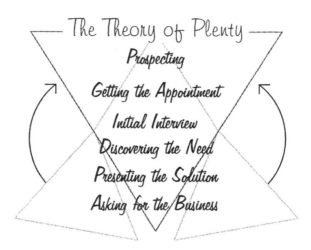

I start by taking my list and mapping out where each of the prospects is in the sales process. Then I convince myself that getting these prospects to say "No" is as valuable as getting them to say "Yes". Every "No" represents future time and effort saved (not to mention mental real estate) that can be re-invested back into finding new clients who really do need my help.

I am lost in this, deep in concentration, when Teddie raps on the door. "Coffee time," he announces. I say nothing and stare at him and realize that the amount of time Teddie, Sarah, and I have spent having coffee over the past few years is overwhelming. A couple of times a day, either myself, Teddie, or Sarah leads the troop down to our favorite coffee shop. By the time we get back, sometimes half an hour has passed! There is a bigger problem though - and that's what we talk about when we are at coffee. I don't need to go down that road today so as casually as I can I announce, "I am going to have to pass, Teddie. Sorry."

"Your loss, Bob," he says and turns to leave.

Quite frankly, I never thought that saying "No" would be quite that easy. Now I pull out my list of twenty-five prospects and I phone them... one by one. Some I talk to directly; others I leave voice messages for. In the past, I usually didn't leave voice messages, for fear they wouldn't call me back. I realize now that if they don't call me back the message is clear anyway.

On one number I listen to the phone ring and it is answered with, "Good morning. Stan Wise speaking."

"Hi Stan, it's Bob Stephens calling."

"Good morning, Bob. How are you?"

"Great, Stan. Last month I dropped off a proposal on my services. Have you made any decision on that yet?"

"Actually Bob, we haven't. We have been so busy with other things we haven't had a chance to get to it," Stan explains apologetically.

"I understand. Do you feel you have all the information you need to make a decision?" I ask.

"Bob, when you walked me through the package it looked very good. I think we've got everything we need for now."

"Stan, would it be all right if I left this with you? If you decide you want to take advantage of my services you know how to get a hold of me, right?"

"I do, Bob. Thanks for calling." As I hang up the phone I stroke Stan's company off my list. I realize the chances of them moving forward in the *short run* are slim, and I do not want to dedicate more time, effort, and mental real estate to them at this point. I have to be confident that I have done a good job of presenting our solutions, and that when the time is right Stan will contact me.

With each prospect, I do everything in my power to move them to the next step in the sales process. Some say "Yes", some say "No", and some are like Stan and defer. If they are not prepared to make a decision, I make the decision for them. Then, from these reflections, I see that part of my problem was that I stopped asking the direct questions at each step in the sales process that would draw out either a "Yes, I want to move forward" or a "No, I am not interested", for fear the answer would be the latter.

I now know that not asking direct questions that will either move a prospect forward or out of the sales process is comparable to disconnecting your gas gauge because you don't want to see that your tank may be empty; if it is empty you might as well know so that you can do something about it.

The phone interrupts my thoughts and I pick it up. "Hi Bob, it's Allan from Standard Enterprise. You were trying to get hold of me?"

I fall into my regular spiel. "Thanks for calling me back, Allan. I would like to move to the next step with Standard. Can I catch you for forty-five minutes one day next week to arrange a meeting to discuss that?"

"That sounds good, Bob. We've been waiting for your call."

We agree on a time and say our good-byes. I resist the temptation of getting excited about my chances with Standard. At this point it is just another appointment, I tell myself; dwelling on 'what could be' is only a waste of enthusiasm.

For a few moments my office is quiet. I realize how I have been guilty of rewarding and punishing myself for things that were out of my control; things like getting the client to sign the contract. The client is the one who holds the pen and writes the check for the order - I cannot control what they do. I decide that I need to reward myself for things I *can* control, like picking up the phone and asking for an appointment regardless of whether they say "Yes" or "No".

Throughout my day I move from call to call; some are good, some not so good, but regardless I feel great about what I am achieving. One dramatic difference in my day is that instead of having my time controlled by the 'toink' of my email and the ring of my telephone, I am in control. Tina pops back in my office periodically, looking for more information and direction on the tasks she has taken responsibility for. Very soon I am thinking that this is really going to work out well.

I check my watch and see that it's almost 3:30: I can't believe what a great day I have had! Besides handling the regular customer requests, I have talked to sixteen of the twenty-five prospects on my list; I booked follow-up appointments with seven and eliminated the rest. When I look at all the downfalls of the Theory of Scarcity, one of the biggest drawbacks is how desperate it can make you feel. Clients can sense this desperation: most are turned off by it because nobody likes to buy from someone who is desperate. As your prospecting slides the need increases to sell to a higher percentage of the prospects you are meeting, which increases your desperation. The Theory of Scarcity really is a slippery slope.

I straighten up a few things on my desk before heading out the door for my golf game with the Butcher and the Baker. Even though I am leaving early, I pat myself on the back for a job well done today. As I look at my telephone I notice how the message light isn't blinking. That's a first.

I walk over to the door, close it, and retrieve my golf clothes hidden behind. With the door shut I catch a shot of my face in the mirror and see a new Bob Stephens looking back at me... and it was only this morning when I was standing here devastated by the news from Selectrum. I shake my head, thinking about how many different Bob Stephens that mirror has seen over the years.

Chapter 6
Small Steps Towards Success

*I*t has been so long since I've gone home after a productive day: I feel like I have earned my golf as I settle into my car and plot out the fastest way to Eddie (the Butcher)'s club. It would be great if one of us was a member at some posh private club, but unfortunately we have all experienced varying levels of mediocrity in our careers. Eddie is so funny - he says, "Let's golf at *my* club this time" like he owns it or something. The truth of the matter is, he has a twenty-game pass and it just kills him to finish the year with a game or two left.

While driving along I spot the laminated card Russ gave me poking out from under the seat. It occurs to me again that I had promised Russ I would practice before playing my next game, so I check my watch and figure that I might just have enough time to hit a bucket of balls before teeing off.

After making it to Eddie's club I run up to the main building, drop my clubs carelessly in the rack, and immediately slow to a stroll as I walk into the pro shop. "Small bucket of balls, please," I announce before the young man behind the counter can speak. "Oh yes," I add, "I'm golfing nine holes with Eddie".

The clerk hands me the bucket of balls and asks, "Eddie who?" with a confused look on his face. Obviously, this is Eddie's club in Eddie's mind only.

"Never mind, just charge me for nine holes and a small bucket of balls." I give him a large portion of my pocket money and he gives me some change to jingle in exchange. I make my way to the change room and ask, over my shoulder, where the driving range is.

Standing on the range matt, I warm up using my 'w-*one*-der' wood. I know you're supposed to start with the higher loft clubs, but I thought I might as well work the kinks out quick. I hit a couple of balls - both slices, and decide it is time to look at Russ's checklist. I study each point on the card, trying to remember the adjustments Russ had suggested. I practice the swing slowly and methodically, trying to commit the adjustments to memory. Then it's time to put the new swing to work.

I put a ball on the tee and pull the club back while incorporating every new change I can remember, and then follow through. I miss the ball all together. The only two good things are that I don't have to reload... and even better, no one saw me.

Just a bit of bad luck, I tell myself. I review the card, take a couple more practice swings, and then go for it again. This time I make contact with the ball; but unfortunately I ground out on the matt three inches behind the tee. I can still feel the ache in my hands as panic starts to set in. I look at my watch and realize that I only have another fifteen minutes before I tee off.

After a quick attempt to relax, I tee up ball after ball and hit some good, but mostly bad. By the time the basket is empty I am hitting only about fifty percent of the shots in a decent way. Feeling less confident than I was, I pack up my clubs and head to the first tee, trying to convince myself that I have gotten rid of all my bad shots for the day at the driving range.

Both Eddie and Brian are ready and waiting when I arrive. I hardly have my driver out of the bag when they both start chattering about the number of strokes they are going to give me *this* time. I swear they must have both signed up for the same psychological warfare option offered in their respective universities.

Between the two of them they have already decided that I am first up. I take Russ's advice; put away the card, and then I confidently walk up and place a ball on the tee. During my practice swings I try to forget about the tips Russ has given me, but they keep coming to the forefront of my mind. At this point I step up to the ball; and to my surprise I hit a fantastic drive! It is one of those drives that starts low and seems to arc up while drawing gently right to left. Then it lands, hops several times, and rolls to a stop in the center of the fairway. It kind of looks like one of those golf ball commercials... even if I do say so myself.

Unfortunately, that shot is the height of my game; slowly and steadily my game declines from that point forward. About halfway through the round I pull out Russ's card in a desperate attempt to save my game, but the embarrassment only continues to mount. The only thing that saves me is that the 'gimme's' get longer the farther I fall behind.

My friends and I also have this bad habit of improving each others' lie, so that helped my score a little as well. Eddie has this saying; "If you don't cheat at golf, you're only cheating yourself!" and we all laugh as we make favourable adjustments to our score.

By the time we are done, painful as it is, the strokes that Eddie and Brian have given me are still not enough for me to save either my pride or my money. Even with the generous 'gimme's' and the foot wedges, I still end up with a forty-eight. Could have been worse, I muse; it could have been over fifty - now that would hurt!

Fortunately with golf, even when I play bad I still always enjoy spending time on the golf course with Eddie and Brian. As we settle up the accounts of the day, we make our way to the clubhouse for a little refreshment.

"How's it going at work, Bob?" Eddie inquires.

"Actually, I'm looking to turn my business around: I've almost totally stopped prospecting for new clients over the last few years and my business has really suffered. I've got some great clients who like me, but I haven't been able to translate that into new clients. Anyway, I might be taking some sales training from the new manager in the hopes that it will help me get my business back to where it used to be."

Brian pipes up. "Well Bob, when you find out what the secret is, let me know. It seems that in my business we work hard to get clients and once we have them, we spend all our time keeping them happy. Finding new clients isn't something we particularly enjoy, so it's an activity that gets dropped to the bottom of the priority list. When we do get a referral, we tend to wine and dine them to get them to use our services - but that doesn't seem to work either."

Eddie starts laughing. "Bob," he says, "I can just imagine the sales training you are going to take!" He does his best imitation of someone other than himself (a real stretch for Eddie); "OK class, the first thing you need to understand about being successful in sales is that you need to be sincere. So, this morning we are going to teach you how to *fake* sincerity!"

Brian and Eddie burst into laughter. After an awkward moment, I join in as well, although I have never been great at making fun of my career and myself. Over the years Eddie and Brian have poked fun at me being a salesman - perhaps it's because I am an easy victim. I take a long sip of my drink to avoid giving them any more ammunition for the attack, and I wait for the joke to run its course. It's no surprise how Eddie is the one who laughs the hardest, as well as the longest.

"Sorry about that, Bob... I just had to say it," Eddie explains, still trying to gain control. With his dig in, he continues with, "Seriously; we need help finding new prospects, too. It's not quite so bad for the people in our firm who already have an established clientele. But I tell you, new associates coming into the firm really do find it difficult getting new clients. In law school they teach lots about being lawyers, but very little on how to find good-quality clients. A good lawyer who has the ability to constantly find new clients is worth their weight in billings."

For the next hour or so we talk about ideas for getting new clients. By the time we part ways, both Brian and Eddie have each given me a token lead - pity is such a powerful tool!

By the time I get home supper is done... and I feel like I am, too. However, this is not a time to show weakness. Sandy doesn't appreciate it when I drop on the sofa like a dead fish, saying how tired I am after I have been golfing.

"Bob," she tells me when I walk in, "there are some leftovers in the microwave for you. The kids and I have already eaten."

"Thanks, Sandy. How was your day?"

Sandy goes on to tell me about the regular things that keep her busy, and that keep our life as a family in order. "You had better make sure you're home in time for Amanda's play," Sandy tells me, "she has really worked hard at it."

"I wouldn't miss it for the world," I assure her. "When is it?"

"Tomorrow night at 7:00. By the way, she wants to practice her lines with you so hurry up and eat your supper."

With food still in my mouth, Amanda drags me off to the family room. At the same time she is summoning David and her mother to participate as the audience. "Guess you got over your stage jitters, Amanda," I joke. She ignores my comment and hands me my lines.

For the next twenty minutes Amanda recites all of her lines without any reference to the script. More notably, she lives the part... even though I am doing a poor job of being the supporting actor.

"I'm really looking forward to seeing you in the play, dear. You did great!" I give her a hug on the assumption that my part is over.

"Dad," Amanda demands, "I want to do it again!" So, for the next hour we practice the lines again and again, with Amanda's confidence building each time. By the time she is satisfied, our audience of two has parted ways and I am physically exhausted; I fall into bed and sleep sounder than I have in months.

In the morning I am ready to face a new day. I know that Jeff has a meeting but it would be nice to catch him for a few minutes before he gets into it. On my way to the office I pass the turnoff to Canyon

Meadows. With the embarrassment of my golf game still fresh in my mind, I decide that I will make the time to practice.

I pull into the parking lot and see that Jeff has already arrived. I jump out of the car and head straight for Jeff's office; he is behind his desk - busy with one thing or another - when I walk in. Jeff looks up at me with his usual wide-smiling face. "So, what do I owe this pleasure to so early in the morning?"

"Well Jeff, I wanted to thank you for yesterday: I had a great day. After I left you I figured out that the next steps are that I need to get organized and that I need to clean out my sales funnel. I have to get rid of all of those prospects that aren't qualified buyers, or that don't see the need for my services. Those prospects have slipped into my sales funnel because I was afraid to ask the tough questions for fear of losing them - a classic case of the Theory of Scarcity."

"That's excellent, Bob!" The phone rings and both Jeff and I look at it. I know exactly what he is thinking.

"Go ahead, Jeff," I tell him, "I really don't mind."

Jeff reaches to pick it up. As he listens he checks his watch. "I'll be right there," he says and hangs up the phone and then looks at me apologetically. "Bob, I lost track of time. My meeting started at 9:00 and it is already five after. I really have to run, but maybe we can pick up on this conversation later."

"Great, Jeff. Don't worry about it; I was the one who popped in on you. I'll talk to you later today."

Jeff gathers up some notes, heads to the door, and then stops. "Say, Bob, at this meeting I am talking about the Initial Interview. Why not come and join us?"

I stand there in silence for a moment, thinking. I am not sure I'm ready for Jeff's boot camp, but I don't want to go through another disappointment like Selectrum. So, to both Jeff's surprise and mine, I agree.

When we walk into the training room the people are ready and waiting. I recognize all of them, but only know the names of Karen, Rudy, and Al, so I grab a seat at the end of the table next to Rudy.

Jeff starts the meeting by introducing me. "It's my pleasure to introduce you to Bob Stephens. Bob started with the company fifteen years ago and had some of the most impressive sales numbers this division has seen when he was first starting out. I asked Bob if he would be willing to sit in and listen to the training on the initial interview."

After these introductions Jeff rolls up his sleeves and goes to work. He starts by talking about the objectives of the Initial Interview, why salespeople need be brilliant at it, and more important, how to do one properly.

About forty-five minutes into the meeting Jeff says a word that makes my face go hot and my palms go cool: role-play! How he actually said it was, "OK, I want everyone to role-play the initial interview with the person sitting next to them."

I quickly count heads and see that there are exactly six (not including Jeff or myself), which means I am the odd man out. As a sense of relief flows over me, Jeff sits down beside Karen. "Karen, do you want to start or should I?"

This can't be happening. If Karen partners with Jeff, there will be one person left over, and any money says the extra person is going to want me as their partner. I can feel the panic taking hold: There is something about role-playing that terrifies me, especially in front of a new salesperson. After all, I am supposed to be the experienced one: I can just see it now - this person is going to do a great job of role-playing and then when it is my turn I am going to freeze. They are going to snicker, point, and laugh, and I will be the butt of all their jokes for years to come. I can feel my heart starting to race. Rudy looks at me calmly and asks, "Are you ready?"

Ready? I think to myself. Ready? Oh yes, I'm ready... ready to throw up! I reply as casually as I can with, "Actually, I just came to watch. Thanks."

"Would you mind being the client, then?" he asks innocently.

Reluctantly I give in. "Well.... I guess I could do that."

Rudy walks through the initial interview flawlessly. He actually sounds pretty convincing. Being the nice guy I am, I don't subject him to the usual objections that clients have. Before Rudy can finish, I jump in. "Nice job, Rudy. You are very convincing!"

"Thanks, Bob. OK, now why don't you give me some objections?"

Poor Rudy doesn't know how many objections I have heard over the years. I throw out a couple of my best objections, and to my surprise he handles them calmly and professionally. Just as I am getting warmed up, Rudy hands me a card and tells me to call *him* if my situation changes. This is not what I was expecting. If this were a real client I would have jumped into a 'song and dance routine', and kept pushing for the next appointment. My motto is: Never say die! "Rudy," I ask, still holding the card, "is that how you would really handle a client?"

"Of course, Bob. If I am confident I have described my services accurately and I have asked all the right questions, then if he or she still doesn't see a need for my services I am probably wasting my time if I go further. After all, I operate under the Theory of Plenty! There are lots of companies that are interested in what I have to offer."

I stare at him. "Interesting, Rudy."

We sit there quietly as the rest of the group finishes up their role-plays. Rudy leans over and asks, "Do you want to give it a try?"

"That is very kind of you, but I'm afraid I've got a sore throat." And then I proceed to give my best fake cough.

For the balance of the meeting Rudy role-plays and I basically watch. Each time I listen to Rudy, though, I become impressed with how well he has learned the training material.

After the meeting I make my way back to my office to get the day rolling. I no sooner get behind my desk when Jeff appears in the doorway. "So what did you think, Bob?" Jeff asks, as if he is the one who needs an 'atta boy'.

"Good... very good. That Rudy is a sharp young guy."

"Thanks, Bob. I know he'll appreciate hearing that. What did you think about the role-playing?"

"Well Jeff, let me explain it this way. You know when you have to leave a message on voicemail? Well, I get stage fright every time I hear that little beep. And, you remember those little Dictaphones people used for dictating letters? I couldn't use mine because I would clam up every time I pushed the record button. Also, have you ever noticed that I always close my door when I am making calls? Well, the reason isn't so much that I want privacy - I don't want anyone to hear me talking besides the person on the other end of the phone. That pretty much sums up how I feel about role-playing."

"Sounds like some pretty deep-rooted problems, Bob," Jeff says in mock intensity. "Seriously, you really should try role-playing. It is one of the most powerful tools you have for learning new approaches."

I brush him off. "Sure Jeff, maybe another time."

"Keep an open mind on it, Bob - it really can make a big difference." He then turns and makes his way down the hall.

I get on the phone and call the remaining clients on my prospect list. My successes are getting further apart, but that's OK. After all, I keep reminding myself, I operate under the Theory of Plenty.

Mid-afternoon there is a familiar double rap on the door. "Ready for coffee, Bob?"

I look up to see Teddie giving me a wink.

"Sorry, Teddie. I think I'm going to pass."

"Come on, Bob. You need a break! I noticed your car was here when I got in, so you *must* be tired by now. It will just be a quick one - I promise."

Although I hate losing the time, the bigger problem is what Teddie and I talk about when we go for coffee. One of us usually starts griping about one thing or another, which the others feel obligated to support.

The truth is, talking about 'what's wrong' has become the only thing we have in common anymore, and it has also become a bad habit!

Also, we always talk about the problems... never solutions. Worse yet, most of the problems we talk about are beyond our control, so even if we do want to solve them, we can't. Some people feel that talking about your beefs is an excellent opportunity to vent, but the truth is I typically come back from these coffee sessions feeling drained. Maybe not drained of my energy, but always somewhat drained of my enthusiasm and optimism.

I might as well figure out a way to deal with Teddie, so I concede reluctantly and say, "OK, Teddie - but just a quick one. I've got a lot of work to get done."

Teddie and I make our way to the regular coffee shop in silence. On the way, I reflect back on Teddie's history with the company. Teddie started shortly after me, but the only difference between him and me is that he never really had a period where he did well - except for the odd burst here and there. He has always plodded along at his own pace... just doing enough to keep his job.

We grab our coffee and take our usual seat. "So why were you here so early this morning, Bobbie?" he says as he takes a loud slurp of coffee. Teddie thinks every name should end with either "ie" or "y".

"I met this morning with Jeff," I say, and leave it at that.

Teddie asks with a smirk, "So how is Sparky anyway?"

It seems funny, but calling Jeff "Sparky" doesn't fit and it doesn't feel good. "Oh, he's fine," I answer.

On the other hand, it is a little awkward defending Jeff, considering I was the one who came up with the name in the first place. Teddie and I sit there in silence, sipping our coffee and checking out the other patrons in the shop. I decide to change the direction of the conversation. "So Teddie, have you sold any new contracts lately? Last time I talked to you, you had a couple of clients holding the pen ready to sign."

"Don't get me started... " he says, sitting up straight with his body coming alive.

I know this means exactly the opposite. It might be more appropriate if Teddie said, "Thanks for getting me started. I didn't know what else to talk about anyway."

He continues with, ".... I can't believe the company - they screw everything up. I hand them this great client all signed, sealed, delivered, and they mess up the whole thing! First, it started with the admin staff, and then home office screwed it up too. When I found out about it, I marched into Sparky's office and unloaded the whole mess on him. Didn't you say the same thing happened to you just a few months ago?"

By this time, I can see clearly see the pattern forming: He wants to drag me into the 'doom and gloom' world, where we often live. Unfortunately, Teddie is right about me complaining; I did sit there in that same seat and I complained exactly the same way Teddie is now. But, I decide, today is a new day and it is time to break the chain.

"You're right, Teddie; I did gripe about those problems. But you know what? My biggest problem is the person looking back at me when I look in the mirror," I say, "it's me. Not the admin staff, not head office, and not Jeff. In fact, that is why I was meeting with Jeff this morning: I am looking to turn my business around and get my sales up where they should be. This starts with taking ownership for my success or failure... it starts with looking for solutions instead of problems."

Teddie looks at me with a shocked expression on his face. Before he says anything I continue. I put my hand on his shoulder and say, "Teddie, you and I have got to stop meeting like this," I say, smiling. "You and I need a 'check-up from the neck-up.' I enjoy your company, really. But, I do not want to come down here and then waste our time beefing about what's wrong. I want to talk about what's right, and what you and I can do to get better. I want to talk to you about my ideas, and hear your ideas too!"

Teddie sits there in silence. He grabs his coffee and takes the last drink. After a few moments he responds quietly with, "You're right, Bob. We do have to stop meeting like this." And he proceeds to get up and leave without saying another word.

I sit there, watching Teddie disappear from the coffee shop. That was not the reaction I was hoping for, but the reality is that old habits die hard. I pay the bill and go back to my office; maybe Teddie will get over this and maybe he won't. The bottom line is, I can't afford to take what precious optimism and enthusiasm I have and waste it complaining about things that I can't change. I need to surround myself with people who see the cup half-full: people who recharge my energy and brighten my outlook. Hopefully, Teddie will soon be one of those people.

Then, back at my desk and still consumed with thoughts of my conversation with Teddie, Tina brings me back to reality when she pops by to give me an update on her progress. With every task she completes, my confidence in her ability grows.

"Do you have extra time available that I could purchase, Tina?"

"I'm not sure... but I think there must be at least an hour or two a day if I was able to unload some of the general office administration."

"Why don't you check that out?"

"I will, and I'll get right back to you. Here is everything else you wanted done. By the way, Denise from Savoy called back and asked if you could see her tomorrow morning. She said you had called asking for an appointment."

"I did call her; I have been trying to book an initial interview with her for some time and finally decided to just leave a message."

As Tina walks out the door I think to myself; this is perfect! With training on the Initial Interview fresh in my mind I'll be ready for Savoy in the morning. Maybe I should have role-played with Rudy after all, I tell myself. The shiver up my spine confirms I made the right choice.

By the time I am ready to leave I am happy with the progress I am making. I have now contacted all twenty-five prospects and have eliminated all but ten. I know now that I need to start rebuilding my prospect list with good-quality names. Tonight is the big play, though, and I don't want to miss a minute of it.

When I arrive home the house is a buzz. It is apparent how Amanda has pre-stage jitters, judging by the way she is mocking David's every move. Actresses can be so high strung.

After a rushed supper we all head to the school early to give Amanda enough time to get into costume and character - and to secure some choice seats at the front, of course.

Little by little the place fills up with parents, and eventually the lights dim as the anxiety level of the parents rises. I am almost sure that all of the parents are far more nervous than the kids, but I can only speak for myself. Soon enough, the first child stomps onstage to announce the name of the play as *The Life and Times of Danny Digby*. That's funny... in all the time I practiced with Amanda, I never bothered to ask her what the play was called.

The story is set in the early 1900's, and is about a boy named Danny who is being raised in a family of seven. Danny's challenge is that he happens to be disabled, in a time when there is very little medical support and equipment to help him cope. Danny is being played by one of the schoolchildren who is actually disabled.

Some of the kids start off with almost a whisper, but as their confidence grows so does their volume. Some know their lines well, and others require coaxing to remember. The ones who know their lines are alive in their characters and their parts, while the others focus all their energy on trying to remember what to say next.

About half an hour into the play, Amanda walks onstage. She is playing a nurse who is helping Danny deal with his challenges, and I can feel my pride swelling as Amanda recites the lines she has worked on over the last several weeks. It feels funny, seeing my little girl up on stage speaking with such confidence and passion. The whole time she is up there I sit on the edge of my seat, anticipating her every word. Whenever she hesitates before saying a line, I want to jump up and blurt it out.

Fortunately, and with impeccable timing, the words always come out. It is as if Amanda is playing the audience intentionally.

Towards the end, Amanda's part grows. Her character pushes and challenges Danny to reach physical and mental heights no one thought possible. In the final scene, Danny and Amanda's characters say their goodbyes as Danny goes off to chase his dream: to go to university in a far away place. Amanda's character stays behind to continue her dream: helping people. The tears well in my eyes as Amanda walks back onstage to take a bow with the rest of the kids. Amanda really is the hero: My hero!

I glance over at Sandy, who is also dabbing her eyes by this point. We both smile at each other, our pride overflowing. It's not so much the play or the story line, but more to see all of Amanda's effort come to fruition. It also has to do with seeing a little girl turning into a little lady.

It takes Amanda and David over an hour to settle down for bed. After the kids are finally asleep, Sandy and I take the time to re-live some of the moments from the night. I start with the obvious. "Amanda is a natural; we need to get her into some acting classes!"

"She's just a little girl in a little play, dear. She's not a star."

"Are you kidding? Didn't you see how she handled herself on stage? She's definitely a natural."

Sandy tries to help me keep things in perspective. "I was very proud of her too, Bob. She did a beautiful job but she's not a natural. Do you realize how many hours she put into practicing her part? That's why she did so well!"

I recall all of the times I saw Amanda in her room practicing, not to mention all the times she pulled me in to help. "You're right, she did work hard... but she is still a natural!"

Sandy switches directions in the conversation. "How is it going at work, dear?"

I realize that with both of us being so busy, I haven't taken the time to bring Sandy up to speed on my new focus. So, for the next half an hour I tell her all about my meetings with Jeff, as well as my own revelations. I describe the situation that morning, in Jeff's meeting, when I was almost sick with anxiety when the role-plays started. Sandy and I both laugh until tears roll down our cheeks, and after we regain our composure she asks, "Why does Jeff make those poor people role-play, anyway?"

I answer her question and the message becomes clear for both of us: "Sandy, it is no different than with Amanda. When she gets up on stage she can't be focusing on trying to remember her lines - she needs to focus on the part she is playing. The same is true for salespeople! If they learn each part of the sales process so that they can deliver it unconsciously, they will be able to focus all of their attention on what is most important: the client."

Sandy looks at me with a confused expression. "Well, if that is true then why don't you role-play?"

"Because it terrifies me, that's why!"

"That's crazy! If you know it will help you then just do it! After all, if Amanda can role-play why can't you?"

Oh sure, throw that back in my face, I think. "Easy for you to say: I'd like to see *you* role-play," I come back. I can see by the look in her eyes that I have just put up a challenge that she is not going to let go of. Definitely a mistake.

"OK Bob," Sandy says with a 'gotcha' tone, "let's role-play."

This is exactly what I was afraid of - Sandy has outwitted me again. "All right," I answer, "I'll play Amanda's part and you can be Danny." I say this knowing that Sandy doesn't know the lines.

"Don't be ridiculous - let's role-play something more meaningful. What were they role-playing at the meeting today?"

"The initial interview, but ... "

"Great, you take the role of the salesperson and I'll be the customer."

I can see that she is not going to let go of this, so I reluctantly agree. I set the stage with, "OK, you have agreed to see me for thirty minutes and you were referred by one of my clients. Oh, there's something important you need to know, Sandy: you're a nice prospect - not a jerky prospect. All right?"

"I'll be nice," she promises.

We go through the initial interview again and again. At first, all of my attention is focused on the fact that I am role-playing, which makes me feel even more uncomfortable. But then, slowly but surely through repetition, I forget all about the role-play and start concentrating on what I am saying. Sometimes Sandy critiques me, and sometimes I critique myself.

Eventually I figure out that the key to using role-play as a tool starts with finding a person you truly trust. The next step is to just do it, and keep doing it, until your attention switches from the act of role-playing itself to the skill you are trying to improve.

Time goes by so quickly we can hardly believe how late it is. But then, even at 12:30, I can see the strides I have made and more importantly, Sandy can see them too.

"We have got to get to bed, Bob," Sandy grins, "you're going to be exhausted tomorrow."

"I know, I know," I hesitate for a moment. "I want to thank you for pushing me to role-play, Sandy. I honestly thought I could never do it, but you made the difference. Thank you."

Glowing with a warm smile, Sandy reaches across and grabs my hand. "Bob, I didn't mean to hurt your feelings when you were talking about your goal: you know I support you one hundred percent in your career, and I love doing stuff like this with you. It's nice to know more about what you're doing and to be involved in some way."

"I know you meant well, Sandy." I sit up straight, grab hold of her hand, and look directly into her eyes. "After talking with Jeff, I am convinced I can reach that goal of forty new clients that I originally set. It's going to take commitment on my part, and I am going to need both you and the kids' help."

"How?" she asks cautiously. "You're not going to be working day and night, are you?"

"The days might be a little longer, but you always know that you and the kids are my #1 priority. All I need from you and the kids is to help me remain focused on my goal. Also, everyone needs to remember that when it's work, it's work. I can't be running personal errands when I should be working."

"That's fair, Bob... but what about when you get home? Are you going to leave your work at work?"

"You're right, Sandy. When I get home I'll focus my time on the family."

Sandy's eyes light up. "Bob, you know the kids really do support you. Why don't you let them know what your goal is, and then we can have a little family reward if you reach it. They'd love it! But what could we do... "

We both sit there in silence, looking for an answer. "Disneyland!" I blurt out.

"Bob, we can't afford to go to Disneyland!"

With a smug look on my face I respond with, "We can if I sell forty new contracts!"

"It would be great if we could take the kids there; they'd just love it. It's been so many years since we have taken a good holiday."

Sandy's right. Over the last few years it always seemed that there wasn't enough time or money to take a nice family holiday. The problem was that I was taking 'mini' vacations every week: Get into work late one day, leave early the next, an afternoon off here or there. It didn't seem like a lot of time off, but when I added it up over a year it became significant. I was cheating myself, and more importantly I was cheating my family.

"Sandy, this sounds great. Why don't we both tell the kids about it over supper tomorrow night?"

She leans across and kisses me on the cheek. "Bob, things are going to be just fine. Now get to bed!" she insists.

By 1:00 am Sandy is sleeping soundly while I lay beside her with my mind racing: I know I have to be ready for my appointment tomorrow morning with Savoy Metals, and that makes it even more difficult to fall asleep. I feel as though I have overcome a tremendous hurdle tonight: It is not so much that I have perfected the initial interview, but more that I have opened myself up to a new way of honing my skills. My next hurdle is to be able to role-play with someone in the office, although that thought still scares me a little.

In an effort to slow my thoughts I turn to golf. With my eyes fixed on the darkness of the ceiling I think about my lesson with Russ, and his words of advice concerning practice. When it comes right down to it, I realize, perfecting your golf swing is no different than perfecting your sales presentation. I remember Russ talking about how the greatest golfers have perfected the art of practicing, and how Russ stressed the importance of practicing everything I was learning.

In sales, role-play and joint calls are to the salesperson what the driving range and practice greens are to the golfer. Role-play allows you to learn new approaches - or to hone the old ones - with no risk. Perhaps becoming a 'great' salesperson is no different than becoming a great golfer – to become brilliant at the basics, you need to become 'brilliant at practice!

Morning comes sooner than it ever has, and I roll over in bed, batting at the alarm to make it stop. I'm not sure what time it was when I finally fell asleep; there comes a point when looking at the clock is only a depressing reminder of how tired I am going to be in the morning.

As my mind clears, I remember that my appointment with Savoy Metals is this morning at 9:00, which helps me gain sufficient strength to force myself out of bed. I want to make a favourable impression so I put a little extra effort into looking good. On my way to the appointment, I run my mind through the role-plays that I did the night before with Sandy. On the radio, two DJ's banter back and forth trying to outdo one another's verbal antics, and I click this off to allow me to concentrate.

Then I try something I have never done before; I start role-playing with myself. At first I start off slow, just saying a line or two under my breath. But within five or ten minutes, I am talking loudly, using my free hand to emphasize my points. At one red light, I am speaking rather emphatically when I notice that the lady in the car on my right has a big smile on her face, as if to say, "I caught you!" I break eye contact with her only to notice the young man in his car on my left. He is in his early 20's and is craning his neck to see if there is anyone else in my car. I smile politely and then stare straight ahead, waiting for the light to turn green.

I arrive at Savoy Metals ten minutes before my appointment. With my car parked, I do my best to visualize each step in the initial interview while I wait for the time to pass. Just before 9:00, I walk in and introduce myself to the receptionist.

"Denise is on the phone; she will be with you shortly," the receptionist informs me.

I make myself comfortable in the reception area, trying to clear my mind and focus my attention on the person I am about to meet. A couple of minutes later, a middle-aged woman walks up to me, and I jump to my feet with my hand extended. "Hi Denise, my name is Bob Stephens."

She shakes my hand firmly. "Actually, I'm not Denise. My name is Judy, Denise's secretary. Would you like to come with me?"

I follow her down the hallway to an office around the corner. As we walk in, Judy announces our arrival. "Denise, Bob Stephens is here." Denise, who has her back to us, swivels her chair around and stands up. When our eyes meet, it becomes painfully clear she was the lady in the next car, the lady who was smiling at me at the red light. A shiver runs through me: do I try to explain myself, or do I say nothing in the slim hope that she doesn't recognize me? Denise makes the decision for me.

"Didn't I just see you in your car on my way in to work?" she asks, with the same smile I had seen earlier.

"Yes, that was me, I was just... "

She interrupts with. "Don't worry about it; I love to sing in the car, too. Although I usually stop singing when I get to the red lights."

"I'll have to remember that for next time," I say with a smirk on my face.

That was smooth, I think, and after our short introductions, I move into the initial interview I had practiced. Although I am able to stick to the plan for the most part, from time to time, I switch between my old presentation and the new. The amazing thing to me, though, is that Denise plays her part almost exactly how I had imagined she would.

As the interview approaches the end I ask, "Well Denise, based on what you have told me I believe it would be worth both our whiles to move to the next step. Would you agree?"

"Bob, I can't promise you anything but there seems to be a good fit. What is the next step?"

"I need to come back and spend some time with you to figure out exactly where your company is at today so that we can assess what your needs might be for the future. I will give you an outline of the information you will need to have ready, so that you can be prepared in advance."

"That sounds good, Bob. Why don't you talk to Judy to set a time?" We both get up to shake hands and Denise walks me to the door. "By the way Bob, what song were you singing anyway?"

Now it is my turn to smile. "Rocket-Man," I say. "You know - that old song."

"Oh, I love that song! I haven't heard it in years."

With my next meeting arranged, I make my way to my car shaking my head. I can't believe I said "Rocket-Man", although I have never been too good at thinking on my feet when I'm on the spot.

All the way to the office, I replay the meeting in my mind again and again. It was a little uncomfortable at first, but yet it was probably the most focused initial interview I have had in years. Although I did a pretty good job, doing the initial interview *live* tells me I am going to need a lot more practice before I can deliver it unconsciously. Perhaps practicing your approach does work, I tell myself; just look at how well that meeting went! Maybe you can teach an old dog some new tricks!

Once I am back in the office, I make some quick notes from the meeting with Denise while it is still fresh in my mind. Presently I hear a small tap at the door and look up to see Tina standing there holding a stack of papers and her steno pad in hand. "Bob, I checked with the office, and I can free up another hour a day for you if you are interested. If you need more time than that, they are going to have to re-arrange some of my workload."

"I'll take that extra time, Tina. I think an hour is a good start."

She looks at my scrawl on the page on my desk. "Is that something you need to have typed?"

"No, it's just the notes from my meeting with Savoy for my files."

"Why don't you give them to me, and I'll put together a short letter thanking them for the initial meeting. I've got some copies of similar letters we use in the office that I can modify."

"Good idea, Tina! I also promised her a list of the information we will need for the next meeting. Can you include that as well?"

"I'll type it out, but you should double check it before I send it off." She looks down at the notes on her steno pad. "Oh yes, Bob, I went through your entire in-basket and I have either handled, filed, or deleted most of the messages. There are some important emails left there that I think you should read."

"Why don't you print them off, and I'll read them later today."

She shakes her head slowly, saying, "There is no sense wasting paper and cluttering up your office. Would you mind just reading them on-line and then deleting them when you are finished?"

All of a sudden, Tina doesn't seem nearly so timid. "OK, OK. I'll read them on-line." I know she is right, but I have got in the habit of printing off almost everything that comes to me. There is something about having that piece of paper.

"Bob, there's something I wanted to say about your email etiquette," she says hesitantly.

"What's that Tina?"

"I noticed all those emails you have sent to people to say "Thanks"... I even saw one you sent to someone to say "You're welcome" after they sent you a 'thank you' email!"

"Tina, what can I say... I'm a polite guy!"

She shakes her head once again.

"What?" I ask sheepishly.

"Bob, a lot of people are inundated with too much email already. Most of these people you are sending 'thank you' messages to, already know you appreciate what they have done for you. Do them a real favour and minimize the number of emails you send them... and if there is something that is significant that really deserves a heartfelt thank you, mention it the next time you see them or talk to them on the phone."

"Point taken Tina."

On that note she turns to step out the door.

"Oh Tina... "

She stops and looks back.

"By the way... *thanks.*" As her smile develops, I shrug my shoulders and wink. "Just a habit I guess!"

With Tina on her way, I sit at my desk realizing I have more free time than I am used to, the more work she takes on. On top of that, I am now finished calling the prospects on my list, and I am not sure who I will call after that. All of a sudden I feel a familiar sense of anxiety building, but the answer comes to me before the anxiety takes control. I slide my top drawer open and pull out the stack of leads I have accumulated... but never called.

The edges of the cards and papers are tattered from playing 'Prospect Solitaire'. Prospect Solitaire is a game that has been played by generations of struggling salespeople - myself included. The game starts by fanning out the leads on your desk. You then organize them into piles from oldest to newest, or from the best lead to the worst lead, or maybe even geographically. The goal of the game is to arrange them in the perfect order to call. Usually at about that time, either Teddie or Sarah walks by and asks me to go for coffee, which signals the end of the game. At that point, I scoop all the names back into a random pile and place them in my desk, ready for the next game.

It's funny - I still remember the lectures I would get from John Andrews whenever he saw a lead on my desk. He'd say, "Bob, if you are like most salespeople, you probably hold on to the leads you get like you would pennies in a piggy bank. You don't mind taking money out as long as there are always a few jingling in the bottom. No one wants an empty piggy bank, right?"

I would say, "Right," knowing exactly what he was going to say next.

"Bob, leads are like milk; they have an expiry date. If you don't use them, they go bad. I want you to call all the leads you have saved up right now."

Then when I did call them, he would wander back in my office and say, "I notice you don't have any leads anymore, Bob. You better get out there and find some."

With John, it was such a catch-22. He either wanted you panicking because you did have leads and they needed to be called, or he wanted you to panic because you didn't have any.

I fan the leads in the pile, and out of habit, start to spread them out on my desk. I catch myself, knowing it doesn't really matter which order I call them in if I have to call them all anyway.

Throughout the day, between client calls, I phone one after the other in whatever order they come up. I guess I could have put off calling them even longer by convincing myself I need to send a nice letter out first, since some argue that sending a letter in advance allows you to introduce yourself ahead of time, which will increase the likelihood of making an appointment on the phone. On the other side, the doomsayers say sending a letter only gives the prospect a chance to figure out why they don't want to see you.

I guess I believe that sending the letter adds administration and lost time, and only delays the inevitable. In most cases, if they are interested, they will say "Yes" and if they are not, they will say "No", and the letter will likely have little bearing on the outcome one way or the other.

Early in the afternoon, Teddie pops by my office again, although this time he's here to talk. "So Bob, do you still think I am the root of all your problems?" he speaks with a hurt look on his face.

"I'm really sorry about that, Teddie; I didn't mean to come across that way. I have just come to a realization that I have got to either turn my business around or else I'm in big trouble. You know how I've fought to get new clients over the last few years."

"Fair enough, Bob. But I don't think I am the cause of your problems."

"Hold on! I never said you were, buddy. All I said is that I don't have the time or energy to talk about what's wrong with the company, or our services, or whatever, anymore. It really drags me down."

I can see his face getting red. "You're as big a whiner as I am, not to mention Sarah!"

"You are quite right, Teddie, and maybe that is part of the reason my business has dropped so much over the years. I think what I have figured out is that being negative is just like a bad habit, similar to smoking. You and I and Sarah are not negative people, but when the three of us get together as a group, the conversation gravitates to 'what's wrong with everything' because that's what we always talk about. I want to spend time with you, but I also want us to make a pact that when we get together, we will use the time productively. In fact... I have an idea."

"What's that, Rocket-Man?" Teddie asks in a mocking tone.

I ignore his jab. "Relax Teddie, have a seat." I think to myself that maybe I can help Teddie and he can help me. I muster up my courage and spit out the words, "Teddie, would you be willing to role-play with me?"

He breaks out with a roaring laugh, and then slaps his knee in an over-exaggerated motion.

"You really have lost it, Bob," he laughs.

I wait for his laughing to subside. "Seriously," I say, "I went to one of Jeff's training sessions on the initial interview; he had these young guys role-playing their hearts out. I didn't want to do it with them, but last night, I spent about an hour role-playing with Sandy. Hell, I even was doing it in the car on the way to my appointment this morning." I am speaking with a smile and shaking my head in disbelief.

Teddie turns the corner on the issue. "So, what would I have to do?"

"All you have to do is be the client - the 'nice' client. At the end, tell me what you think." Another idea comes to my head. "I'll tell you what - how about I take you out and buy you a coffee, and we'll role-play there."

"Hey, if you're buying the coffee, I'll play your silly game."

On the way to the restaurant, I give Teddie a quick overview of the initial interview Jeff was teaching the new people. I also give him some idea on the type of client that I want him to play. As we sit down with our coffee in hand, I go straight into the role-play. The first few times we try, either Teddie or I break into laughter, and we have to start over again. Although Teddie and I have our differences, he really has become a good friend over the years, and that makes this whole exercise tolerable. Within fifteen minutes or so, we are able to piece together a few parts.

"So, what do you think?" I ask, in an anticipation of an 'atta boy'.

"I think you are a better salesman than you are an actor."

I stare at him without saying a word, waiting for him to give me the feedback I am looking for.

"It's good, Bob. You did a good job of it. I'm not sure it would work for me, but you seem to be pretty convincing."

I push him for more feedback, but he avoids getting into detail. I can tell by the look in his eyes he wants to say something, but I can't figure out what it is. "Come on, Teddie, tell it like it is... "

"Bobbie, you bonehead, your presentation is fine," Teddie hesitates for a second before continuing. "Did you hear the scuttlebutt on Sarah? Or are we allowed to talk about that?"

I think back to our pact, convincing myself this really isn't negative or a problem... and if it involves Sarah, it's got to be good. More important, I still haven't had a chance to get Sarah back for opening her big mouth and telling Jeff about Sparky and Rocket-Man.

"Of course we can, Teddie," I say, like the cat about to eat the canary.

"Sarah's got a new love of her life - and nobody knows except moi! You'll never guess who it is," he adds, to tease me.

Oh this is good, I think to myself; I better probe further. "We better get the facts straight, Teddie. How do you know?"

He says proudly, "I'm just really, really, smart - that's how!"

"We both know that's not true, Teddie. Seriously, how do you know?"

"Flattery will get you nowhere," Teddie leans across the table, his voice a whisper. "The other night I went to a new restaurant downtown. In the dark back corner, I saw none other then our good buddy, Sarah, holding hands and making kissy faces across the table while giggling like a schoolgirl."

"So, what did she do when she saw you?" I say, trying unsuccessfully to conceal my excitement.

"Saw me - are you kidding? She had a love trance on this guy like you can't imagine. The last thing she cared about was me sitting across the restaurant staring at her from behind my menu."

"Oh, you're so sly... " we instinctively reach up and give each other a high-five over the table. My curiosity is peaking. "Who is it? Come on tell me!"

In a single word, he almost blows me off my chair: Out of his lips, Teddie whispers, "Bruce!"

We both explode with laughter. We have to contain ourselves when we notice everyone in the coffee shop staring at us. "Bruce? He's half her age!" I say in disbelief.

On our way back to the office, we send one-liners back and forth like two amateurs playing tennis: When I drop one line, Teddie picks it up, adds a little spice to top it off, and sends it back to me. Then we both laugh again, amazed at our wit.

We both glance into Sarah's office to see her sitting behind the desk and do the standard 'nudge, nudge, wink, wink' routine while concealing our hilarity.

As I step into my office and move behind the desk, Teddie sticks his head in the door and in a sincere tone, he says, "Thanks for coffee, ol' buddy."

"Thank *you*, Teddie. And I appreciate your role-playing with me. You really are one of the few people here I could do that with."

"Anytime, Bob," and with a little salute, he is off.

It feels nice to be on good terms with Teddie again. It feels even better to have the bait for Sarah... all I need now is the trap!

With Teddie on his way, I reflect on how far I have come in such a short while. It's the small steps toward success that really matter!

Chapter 7
Prospecting -It's a matter of Leverage!

*O*n the way home the turnoff to Canyon Meadows is a friendly reminder of the fact that I still haven't made a commitment to practicing my swing. My lesson with Russ is coming up and I haven't been out hitting the ball, except for my disastrous experience with the Butcher and the Baker.

Later that night, with supper behind us, I call the family to attention. I give Sandy a wink, looking for her approval, and then begin. "Your mom and I want to talk to you about something important," I say.

A concerned expression comes across Amanda's face. "You're not getting a divorce, are you?"

Sandy and I break into laughter. "Why would you think that?" I ask.

"You know Jody Templeton... this is exactly how her mom and dad told her."

Sandy pipes up. "No dear, we're not getting a divorce. Your father and I are very happily married."

David comes to life. "What's the news then, Dad?"

"Well, I've decided that I need to start doing better at work, and so I've set a goal that I want to hit."

While David's expression turns to disappointment, Amanda crunches up her eyebrows and looks at me as though I am crazy.

"Kids, there's a couple of reasons I am telling you this. First and foremost, because I need your help. Your encouragement and support means the world to me, and I need you to push me to reach this goal. I also need you to understand that when I am at work, it's work. My days might be a little longer than you are used to."

David jumps in. "What's in it for us, Dad?"

It's just like David to cut to the chase. "Good question, David. Two things: First, I will make a commitment that when I come home I will leave my work at work."

"What's the other thing?" Amanda asks.

"Well, if I reach my goal - and it's not going to be easy - your mom and I are going to take the family to... You tell them, Sandy."

Immediately both David and Amanda focus their attention on their mother.

A smile comes across Sandy's face. "IF your dad reaches his goal, we are going to take the family to Disneyland, but..."

Both kids launch off their seats, as if this is a 'done deal'.

"Settle down for a minute, kids; this isn't for sure. Your dad has a lot of work to do and there is a chance that he might not reach his goal."

Amanda calms down long enough to put her thoughts together. "Dad, what do you have to do to reach your goal?"

The more excited they get about Disneyland, the more concerned I get about missing my goal and disappointing them. "Good question, Amanda: I have to sell forty new contracts before the end of the year. Last year I only sold fourteen, so it's not going to be easy..."

Amanda cuts me off. "No problem, Dad! You're the greatest!"

In unison, both kids throw their hands up in the air, running out of the room in celebration while calling out, "We're going to Disneyland!"

A fear drifts over me. I stare at Sandy, who is staring back at me. "Are you thinking what I am thinking?" I ask, and all of a sudden I feel a huge responsibility: I can hear the kids still cheering down the hall.

"It will be all right, Bob. When they calm down - in a day or two - we'll explain to them exactly what you have to do to reach your goal. As long as we keep them involved in how you are doing with your goal - I mean *our* goal - they'll be fine. I believe in you, and I think that if we pull together as a family, Bob, we can do it." As I look in her eyes and listen to her words, calm and confidence flows over me.

Sandy gets up, walks over, and sits next to me at the table. She puts her hand on my back and rubs my shoulders, softly. "I really enjoyed doing that role-playing with you, honey. It's so nice to actually see what you're doing at work."

"If you hadn't pushed me to try that with you, I'd still be muddling in my fears," I tell her, putting my arm around her and kissing her affectionately.

Our kiss ends all too soon. "I want to get back to sharing in the excitement of your career," she tells me. "Remember the days when we would celebrate every time you had a success?"

I remember, and give Sandy a wink. "I don't remember the days so much as I remember the celebrations!"

"You know what I mean, Bob," she says with a frown. "By the way, how did your appointment go today?"

"Very well! I made it through the initial interview and actually booked a second meeting." I speak like I have just been pronounced 'king of the castle'.

"See, Bob? That's what I want to hear about. I want to know when things are going well... and even when they aren't. I also want to practice with you... so that I can learn more about what you do."

The word 'practice' cues me to my commitment to improving my golf game. "Sandy, I know we just talked about hitting this goal, which means me having to spend a little more time at work, but like they say: All work and no play makes *Bob* a dull boy!"

"What are you talking about, Bob?" Her eyes sparkle like a light has come on inside her head. "This is about golf, isn't it?" she asks with a small frown.

"Well, this probably isn't the best time to bring this up, but I really do need to find some time to get out and hit some balls. I've taken one golf lesson and I've got another one booked, and I promised Russ I would put in some practice before we got together again. When do you think would be a good time?"

"How about after the kids and I are in bed?" she asks, nudging me with her elbow.

"Seriously, Sandy; when is a good time? I don't want to disrupt our family life any more than you do."

"Let's see... David has baseball Tuesday nights and Saturdays. And don't forget you need to help him get out and sell chocolates. If you don't we are going to have a year's supply of candy sitting in the back closet!"

"I'll help him sell the chocolates," I assure her. "Maybe I'll take them to work and pawn them off there. Heaven knows how much I have spent on everyone else's kids over the years."

"I think David should sell the chocolates himself. It doesn't hurt for him to pay part of his way," Sandy insists.

"Fine, no problem. I'll take him out to sell his chocolates. That still doesn't help figure out when I should practice my golf swing, though."

"Why not do it on the way to work? You're gone before the kids are up anyway."

I kiss her to seal the deal. "Good idea: I'll start in the morning."

Accordingly, the next morning I bounce out of bed an hour earlier than normal: There is something about getting up for golf that makes the morning so much more enjoyable. I arrive at the driving range at the same time as the attendant opening for the day. From him I grab a large bucket of balls and make my way down the pathway. I have always loved the sound and feel of clicking metal spikes beneath my feet on the pavement.

In the clear morning air I decide that one day, I am going to make a tape of all the great sounds of golf. It will have sounds like the tap of an expensive putter stroking the ball, the plop of a ball dropping into the cup, and of course, the clink of a solid drive with an overpriced metal wood. Oh yes, and I will include the sound of metal spikes on pavement. Golfers all over the world will play this tape in their homes and cars as a sort of relaxation tape. I'll be rich, I declare!

I set my clubs down, and with my laminated card in hand I review each of the basic steps over and over again. After hitting several balls, I finally look up to take note of how beautiful and serene the morning really is. Dew glitters on the grass in the early morning sun for as far as my eye can see, and I stare for maybe too long of a time.

Then, for the next half-hour I hit ball after ball, trying to commit Russ's adjustments to memory. By the end of my bucket I am starting to see the results of my efforts. I check my watch, pack up my clubs, and make my way to the car: I have a couple of stops to make on the way to work and I don't want to be late for my meeting with Jeff.

Unfortunately, when I walk into Jeff's office I can see that he is not in the same bubbly mood that I have become accustomed to. "You wanted to see me?" he asks, speaking in a matter-of-fact manner.

"If you're busy I can see you another time," I assure.

"No, Bob, I'm sorry. I'm just a little distracted."

"Is it something I can help with?"

"Not unless you have a bunch of new contracts signed," Jeff sighs, and holds up a company memo. "I'm getting heavy pressure from home office for results in our division, particularly from the new salespeople. They want me to push harder; yesterday I had to terminate one who was falling behind."

I try to lift his spirits. "I'm sorry to hear that, Jeff - I know you work very hard with them. What about Karen?"

"Oh, she's doing great... but some of the other ones are not. The funny thing is, I have sat down with each of them and told them the results they need to bring in. I give them the training and even tell them how many calls to make, but some of them always seem to fall short. It is very frustrating for all of us."

When I hear Jeff talking it reminds me of so many of the conversations I have had with managers. They ask you how many new contracts you are going to bring in this week... this month... this year. When the results aren't there they tell you to go do this or go do that, but they don't realize how difficult it really is. It's so easy to sit by the sidelines shouting for results. I am tempted to say something, but then realize that I have enough of my own problems to solve before I start tackling Jeff's. "Sorry to hear this, Jeff," I say, and leave it at that. I have learned from experience that people who talk about their problems aren't always looking for solutions - sometimes they just need someone to listen.

"Well Bob, you didn't come in this morning to hear about my woes," Jeff says as he gets up from behind his desk. "Let's sit over at the round table; I want to hear about how you are doing."

We make our way to our regular chairs at the table. "I have some good news and some bad news," I say with a smile on my face, looking to change the tone of the conversation.

"I really don't think I can take more bad news - give me the good news first."

"The good news is that I have cleaned out my existing pool of prospects. I have eliminated a lot of the ones who weren't serious about moving forward, and I have booked new appointments with the ones that are. Also, I had a stack of leads in my desk that I had been ignoring. Yesterday I got on the phone and called all of them; I booked a few more initial interviews."

"That is great news, Bob! So what's the bad news?" he asks, cringing; his fingers ready to plug his ears.

"The bad news is that I don't have any prospects left; that is why I wanted to see you. I want to hear about how you found so many great prospects to sign contracts."

"That's the bad news? I can take more bad news like that!" Jeff cries, throwing his hands in the air.

"Well, Jeff? How did you get all those great clients?"

Jeff crosses his arms and says smugly, "Leveraging."

I'll play your cat and mouse game, I think to myself. "What is Leveraging?"

Jeff leans forward and locks his eyes on mine. "How hard do you work at keeping your clients happy, Bob?"

I think to myself of how many happy clients I have. "I work damn hard. In fact, for the last number of years it has been one of the few things I have done right."

"You have done a good job, Bob; I hear it all the time from your clients. But... how much effort have you put into turning your successful relationships into many more new relationships, with high-quality prospects?"

I think of all the times that I have received calls from clients pointing me to new prospects. "I've got my fair share of leads over the years."

"I bet you have. Did you proactively go out and ask for those names, or were they dropped in your lap?"

"I have tried to get names of prospects from my clients over the years, but it never felt right: I always felt like I was begging, and that asking for the leads was a sign that I wasn't successful. Even when I did ask, most times I didn't get any names anyway... so eventually I just stopped doing it."

Jeff raises his hand; his pointer finger directed at the heavens. "Bob, have I got something for you! I want you to put together a list of ten accounts where you feel you have a good relationship. Those accounts should be the ones where you have gone 'above and beyond the call of duty' delivering great service. Do you think you can do that?"

As Jeff is talking, the names of clients start jumping to the front of my mind. "No problem!"

"You get that done and I'll meet you in the training room. How about I give you half an hour?" Jeff checks his watch.

As I am heading out the door, I stop and turn back. "Why do you call it Leveraging, Jeff?"

"I'll tell you that when you get your list!"

I head back to my office and start going through my files. Most of the names come easily, but as the list grows time stretches out between names. By the end I am flipping through my client lists alphabetically, looking for another possibility. As I am jotting down the last names I hear a double rap at the door.

"Here's the paper, Bob. Do you want to go for quick coffee? I've got some interesting news!" Teddie throws the paper on the empty chair.

I glide past the bait. "Teddie, I can't. I'm just going into the training room with Jeff. Maybe later."

"Boy oh boy, aren't you the perfect student! Are you bringing an apple for the teacher too?" he taunts.

I ignore his simple humour so that I can keep our conversation short. "Jeff is talking to me this morning about how to get some more prospects. I'm curious as to how he did so well when he was in sales," I say, and then think of the perfect way to end our conversation. "Why don't you join us, Teddie? I could ask Jeff to talk slower, so that you can understand."

The joke is either missed or ignored. "Sounds good," Teddie says, "I'll go get some paper." And he turns and walks out the door. I am dumbfounded! I can't believe he said he wants to come to the meeting - I am not sure if Jeff even wants him there!

I get up from my desk and jog down the hall to Teddie's office, cursing under my breath along the way. I slow to a casual stroll as I enter his office, waving my list of names in the air like a bullfighter with a cape. "Teddie, you need to come up with ten names of happy clients. I know that is going to be a bit of a stretch for you."

"What's wrong, Bob? Don't you want me to come?" he snaps.

Realizing this strategy is not going to work either, I give in. "Teddie, if you want to come to the meeting I am sure Jeff won't mind, but I am supposed to be in the training room right now. Why don't you quickly jot down the names of some of your happy clients and I'll let Jeff know you are joining us. Now, hurry up!"

By the time I get into the training room Jeff is standing at the front in anticipation. "Let's get started!" he announces.

"Jeff, Teddie wants to join us. Do you mind?" I ask apologetically.

"Of course not! The more the merrier."

Within a couple of minutes Teddie fumbles into the room, bumping into every chair as he makes his way to the front. He chooses the chair directly across from me and I can see that on his paper he has five names instead of ten... but I guess that's better than nothing.

"Hi, Teddie. Glad you could join us. Let's get started!" Jeff says, accompanied with a loud clap.

The meeting starts with us discussing different sources of prospects, and the pro's and con's of each. First, cold calls. We all agree that for those salespeople who can pick up the phone and make cold prospects endlessly, there is a significant advantage.

Teddie winks to get my attention. "Remember that one guy who did nothing but cold calling? He would set a goal for the number of appointments he wanted per week, and he would keep calling until he hit his goal. Sometimes he would be on his phone all day long - it was almost as if he enjoyed it," Teddie laughs.

I begin the banter with, "Why wouldn't he, Teddie? He was selling more than most of us here!"

In a sarcastic tone Teddie says, "Oh sure, Bob; he was a great salesman. By the time he left he had sold his car, his boat, and everything else that had any value! Don't you remember?"

The words reach my mouth before they register in my brain. "No, Teddie; don't *you* remember? He escaped from sales just in time to become a manager!" Teddie holds one hand up to the side of his face to block his expression from Jeff, while struggling to hold in his laughter as if it were a sneeze. I do my best to look composed on the outside while driving my embarrassment inward, hoping my comments will go unnoticed.

Jeff either chooses to ignore or possibly doesn't catch on to my unintentional dig, and continues. "Cold calls, without a doubt, are not for everyone. My hat goes off to the people who can build their business strictly from cold calls. The problem is, most salespeople burn out if all they have is a steady diet of cold calling."

"I agree," Teddie says, shaking his head. "Cold calls are the worst."

"Not necessarily, Teddie. There's usually an unlimited supply of cold leads, so you don't have to worry about running out of prospects. Also, with cold calls there is almost no risk," Jeff explains.

"No risk. Are you kidding?" I shout, remembering how I felt after hearing "No" again and again from the few cold calls I made, once.

"I'm not saying cold calls are the best source, Bob, but the great thing about a cold call is that if the prospect says "No" you haven't really lost anything. Cold calls can be a great 'no-risk' way of learning how to ask for an appointment and how to handle objections. Let's move on - what's another source of leads?"

"Existing clients!" Teddie lights up, as if he is on home turf.

"And what are the advantages of calling existing clients?" Jeff prods.

Teddie answers. "First of all, they are a lot friendlier to talk to and usually there is more business if you do a good job."

"I agree," Jeff says, "continuing to call your clients is all in the name of providing good service. If you're not calling them it won't be long before our competition is wining, dining, and signing them away from us." He stops for a moment and then asks, "Can you call them too often?"

I know from experience over the last few years that this can be a problem. "Of course you can," I say. "It is almost like going back to the well too many times. If existing clients are your only source of new business, it won't be long before the opportunities dry up."

"Good points, Bob. What's another source of leads?" Jeff asks.

"What about 'walk-in's'?" Teddie suggests.

"How would you describe 'walk-in's', Teddie?" Jeff asks.

"'Walk-in's' are those leads that fall into your lap either from advertising the company does or maybe they just walk through the door begging to be sold," Teddie explains, rubbing his hands together.

"'Walk-in's' are great," I remind Teddie, "but we all know from watching salespeople come and go over the years that you won't last long if 'walk-in's' are your only source of new business."

"So far, all I have learned is that no prospecting source is good," Teddie comes back.

The 'idea light' goes on over my head. "Actually, Teddie; it is exactly the opposite. All the lead sources we discussed have advantages, but when you rely on any one of them as your only source of new business you can run into problems."

Jeff backs me up. "Exactly right, Bob. You should have balanced prospecting, where you take advantage of all the different sources of prospects you have available - you should never rely on any one source exclusively for new business. A 'balanced' approach is a 'healthy' approach!"

Teddie lights up again. "What about referrals?" he asks.

"Good point, Teddie. Now we are going to talk about how you can improve your skills for getting referrals. You need to remember, though, that even if you become an expert at this source you should still make the cold calls to keep your skills sharp and you still need to call on existing clients to make sure you are addressing all of their needs... "

Teddie cuts in, ".... and we still need to take care of those poor lost souls who walk-in looking for our help!"

Jeff smiles politely to acknowledge Teddie's persistent attempts at humour. "How do you feel about getting a referral from a good client?"

"Are you kidding?" I jump in, "I love getting referrals. They're the best lead of all!"

Jeff walks over and sits on the table in front of us. "OK guys, if a referral is the best kind of lead then why don't you ask for them all the time? What stops you from becoming brilliant at getting referrals?"

For the next twenty minutes Jeff makes notes on the whiteboard of all the excuses - I mean reasons - Teddie and I have for not asking for referrals.

1. **Pride**. Many times we don't ask for names because we are too proud to suggest to our good clients that we need their help growing our business.

2. **Oops, I forgot!** Sometimes we do have good intentions to ask for referrals, but with everything else we are doing with our clients, we simply forget.

3. **I don't want to screw up my relationship with my client.** Teddie and I discuss how hard we work to make our clients happy, and we are concerned that if we push for referrals this might somehow jeopardize both the relationship and the existing business.

4. **I ask my clients for referrals but they can never think of anyone.**
    Both Teddie and I talk about how we have tried to ask our clients to
    identify others who they know of that need our services, but it seems
    the clients can never think of anyone, anyway.

    Jeff looks back and forth at both of us and then asks point blank,
    "Do you give referrals to salespeople who have done a good job for you?"
    We tiptoe around the question, but the reality is that we can both
    recall far more situations where we have been asked for names and said
    "No" than when we have been asked and said "Yes". Jeff writes the last
    point on the board.

5. **They don't give referrals themselves!** Jeff proceeds to talk about
    the difficulty of asking for names when you don't personally endorse
    the concept. He says that if you think the salesperson has provided a
    valuable service or product, and has delivered it in a professional
    manner, then why wouldn't you refer them to others if they ask?

    Jeff stands by the list we have accumulated on the board. "Before you
can open your mind to the opportunities of asking for referrals you need
to let go of each of these excuses for not doing it, and you need to do it
right now." Using his hand as an eraser, Jeff wipes the five points off the
board, as if to cleanse our prospecting souls. He walks towards us,
brushing his hands together to remove the residue. "Now let's talk about
Leveraging your way to success!"
    There is that word again. "Jeff," I ask, "exactly what is Leveraging?"
    Jeff sits on the edge of the table. "Leveraging is when you take all of
your happy, satisfied clients and multiply them into many more. For
example, you might take one client and with their help identify five more
potential clients. Perhaps two of those referrals become great clients.
Then you take those two and with their help identify ten more potential
clients, and so on. The more satisfied your clients are, the greater your
ability to get referrals. Does that make sense?"
    "Perfect sense!" Teddie says as he pounds his fist on the table.
    "Great! I want to make a list of all of the advantages of Leveraging."
    For the next thirty minutes Jeff, Teddie, and I come up with point
after point about why Leveraging is so important to our success.

1. **Referrals are warm, pre-qualified prospects:** Leveraging allows you to transfer the trust and credibility you have established with an existing, satisfied client to a new prospect that you don't know. With Leveraging you can turn what would normally be a cold prospect into a warm, pre-qualified lead. What could be better?

2. **There is an endless supply of referrals:** As long as you continue to have happy, satisfied clients and you Leverage those relationships, you should never run out of good prospects to call on to promote your services.

3. **Getting referrals is an endorsement of your services:** When a client gives you a referral, that gesture represents the best feedback you can get; it really tells you how the client feels about you, and the quality of your service.

4. **Referrals are a source of compensation for your time and effort:** Referrals are an excellent source of compensation for doing a great job for your client or prospect *regardless of whether they purchase your service or not*. Understanding this form of compensation allows you to invest time with high quality prospects who do not have an immediate need for your services that day.

5. **Giving referrals allows your clients to help people they know:** The reality is, many businesses need your services. Your client can help other potential clients that they know of by referring them to you.

6. **Best use of your time:** Every successful business needs to be continually finding new clients. Leveraging allows you to spend more time servicing your clients as opposed to spending endless amounts of hours sifting through unqualified prospects looking for new business.

Jeff stands back, admiring the list. "There really are a lot of great reasons to become an expert at Leveraging. Wouldn't you agree?"

Teddie and I nod simultaneously, like parrots in a cage. "OK Jeff, you've sold us on Leveraging. What's the first step?"

Jeff smiles. "Bob, the first step to being successful at Leveraging is that you need to re-define the goal you are striving for with your high-quality clients. When some salespeople meet with their clients and prospects, they ask themselves 'What will I have to do to impress this individual enough so that they will purchase my product or service?' Tell me, guys; what's the problem with striving for this level of service?"

Teddie and I sit quietly, each waiting for the other to answer. "Jeff, that seems like a pretty good goal to be shooting for. I don't really see any problem with it at all," I confess.

"Bob, would you agree that it is possible to do a good enough job for a prospect to get them to become a client, but a client who is not confident enough with you to give you referrals?"

"Sure Jeff, it happens all the time," Teddie jumps in.

"That is exactly the trap that many salespeople fall into; they focus on doing a good enough job to make the sale, and then stop there. To be successful at Leveraging you need to set your sights higher: Here's the goal you need to shooting for with each high-quality client you meet."

Jeff turns and begins writing on the board. He then stands back for us to read:

My goal is to impress my high-quality clients to the point where they are confident enough with me that they are comfortable introducing me to other high-quality people that they know.

Jeff continues. "When you reach this goal with your client they become leverageable. What kind of things do you think you need to do to make a high-quality client leverageable?"

I start the list off first. "Well, it's bunch of things... " Between the three of us, we come up with several points that Jeff writes on the flipchart.

- **Underpromise and overdeliver** – We agreed that some salespeople have a tendency to make commitments based on what they think their clients want to hear (overpromise) and then sometimes they fall short on delivering those commitments (underdeliver). Overpromising and underdelivering can really damage a salesperson's credibility. These salespeople can dramatically improve their client's impression of their service by simply adjusting the expectations of the client. In other words, salespeople need to *underpromise* - make commitments that they are confident they can deliver on (which sometimes means leaving a safety margin), and *overdeliver* - make sure they either deliver on or possibly even exceed the commitments they have made.

- **Put your high-quality client's needs first** – We all agreed that whenever we have put our client's needs ahead of our own, the long-term paybacks have been significant. Sometimes, putting your client's needs first means walking away from a sales opportunity; not an easy thing for a salesperson to do.

- **Be honest and up front with your clients** – Honesty and integrity go a long way when building strong relationships with clients. We all know, though, that there can be times when being honest and up front means having the courage to tell our clients something they may not want to hear.

Jeff then asks us to pull out our list of happy, satisfied clients. "I am assuming your list represents clients that are leverageable: where you have concentrated on providing excellent service instead of just focusing on selling them. Is that right?"

"I'd like to think so," I say proudly, scanning my list.

"That's great, Bob: That's the key to being successful at Leveraging. What about you, Teddie?"

Teddie picks up his piece of paper, leans back, and glances over the names. "These clients are happy, but I can't say all of my clients feel the same way."

"That represents a great opportunity. Your goal should be to make every client leverageable." Jeff walks behind Teddie to see the list he is concealing. "I notice you have five clients listed; you should find at least another five leverageable clients. If your other clients are not leverageable at this point, then you need to figure out what you will have to do to make them happy enough to be on this list."

"So Jeff, you want me to call these people up and ask them for names, right?" I ask.

Jeff shakes his head. "Not exactly, Bob; being an expert at Leveraging is no different than being an expert at selling your services. Many salespeople don't have success getting referrals because of their approach. Usually for them, asking for referrals is an afterthought - they are walking out of their client's office when they suddenly remember what they have forgotten to do. They pop their head back in the door and start their request for referrals by asking, "By the way, do you know of anyone... " and then it proceeds to go downhill from there. To really be successful at Leveraging you need to learn each of the steps of the process for asking for referrals, and then you have to practice them until they become second nature. Are you willing to do that?"

"I've already got my role-playing partner all lined up!" I say, with a wink to Teddie.

Jeff walks over and leans on the table with both hands. He locks his eyes on me, then on Teddie, then back on me again. "How would you guys like to get fifty high-quality leads on your desk in just one day?"

This peaks my attention. I look across to see Teddie sit up, and then simultaneously we ask, as if rehearsed, "How?"

"First things first. Would you like to have fifty qualified names?" Jeff pushes.

Teddie takes the lead. "I haven't had fifty names on my desk cumulatively in the last six months." Then his eyes look up to the ceiling for an answer, and he bursts into a laugh. "Hell, I haven't had fifty names in the last year; that would be great!"

I speak up, looking to be included. "The last time I had fifty prospects was when they called me... " I stop before the words can escape my lips. Teddie and Jeff's attention focuses on me, waiting for me to finish my sentence. I can feel my face turn red as I try to think of what to say next.

Teddie spots the weakness and comes to my rescue. "I am sure Jeff doesn't want to hear about our ol' war stories."

Jeff shakes his head, confused at our conversation. Then he continues. "If I could show you how to get fifty names in one day, would you agree you would never be short of good-quality prospects to call again?"

"That would make sense. But, I am still curious as to how you are going to do that," I say as I gather my composure.

"The two of you are going to have a 'Leveraging Blitz'! I want you both to check your calendars for a date when you can dedicate the full day to Leveraging appointments. Here are the rules:"

Jeff stands there, raising a separate finger as he announces each rule. "First, you are not allowed to do anything else that day, from morning until night, except for Leveraging meetings - no sales or service appointments, no returning phone calls, no golf! Second, you must be away from the office all day conducting your Leveraging meetings. Third, all of your Leveraging appointments must be arranged in advance of that day. Fourth, you must participate in the Leveraging training, and practice your approach ahead of time. Fifth, and most important, you have to be available at the end of the day so that we can have supper to celebrate your successes."

On that note, Jeff gives both of us a quick high-five to confirm the deal.

"One more thing, guys; you must set aside time the next morning to review your skills for turning those referrals into appointments."

Teddie laughs. "If I do all those things, they will be calling me a Leveraging Legend!"

Jeff pushes forward. "First things first, though. We need to agree on the day, and then you need to learn how to ask for a Leveraging appointment. After you have that mastered, it is your responsibility to make the calls and book the appointments. Are you prepared to do that?"

"I am!" I say, without really thinking about what lies ahead. Teddie follows suit. We scan our memories and reach an agreement on the date. I know I don't have a lot of scheduled appointments set for the upcoming weeks, and I am fairly sure Teddie has even less.

"OK, now that we have the date set, let's go over the script for requesting a Leveraging appointment. Turn to the second page of the Leveraging handout; I want you to read it out loud. Don't worry about how it sounds - just read it word for word."

I break the ice by starting first, and then Teddie follows; each time we try it the delivery slowly transforms from a mechanical to a more natural tone. From time to time Jeff takes the script and demonstrates, which then becomes the benchmark for Teddie and I to shoot for.

"Thanks for your big effort today guys," Jeff beams, "you really did great. Once you have those appointments booked I would be happy to walk you through the rest of the training on Leveraging. When do you want to have the next session?" Jeff asks as he checks his watch.

Between the three of us we agree on a time and date, then Jeff shakes our hands and makes his way out of the room. Teddie watches Jeff turn down the hall - I can tell by the glint in his eye he is up to something. I take his cue and sit silently in anticipation, waiting for him to speak.

He leans across and says in a musical whisper, "Bobbie, someone's love is in bloom!"

"Oh, is that so? Who might that be? Hmm, it wouldn't be Sarah, would it?"

"None other. This morning when I came in I noticed that on Sarah's desk there was a single rose in a vase, with a note clipped to the stem."

I tilt my head toward him, as if to suggest he might whisper the answer in my ear. "So, Teddie... what did it say?"

Teddie slams his hand on the table. "What do you think, that I am some kind of snoop or something? Even Sarah is entitled to some privacy!"

I can tell from his lack of sincerity that I need to push harder. "Come on Teddie, we both know you're not a snoop... you just have a natural, boyish, curiosity; that's all." I reach up my hand for the high-five, knowing that this is the final step to getting an answer.

Teddie concedes with the stinging slap of his hand on mine. "You're right, Bobbie. I'm just curious." Teddie checks the door to make sure the coast is clear and then whispers, "The note said, 'G is for how GREAT looking you are!'"

In harmony we both fall back in our chairs, bursting out in laughter. As I draw a breath, Teddie leans across and breathes, "That Bruce ain't much of a poet, but he sure is romantic!"

Chapter 8
The Leveraging Process

I can still hear Teddie giggling his way down the hall when I get to my office. Sitting at my desk - I'm still smiling myself - I peruse my list of happy clients, feeling proud.

I take out the telephone approach Jeff gave us and read it to myself again and again; something just doesn't feel right so I take a clean piece of paper and adapt the approach with my own words. After several versions - and multiple pieces of paper - I come up with something that feels comfortable; the message is still the same but now I feel like it is mine instead of something that comes out of a book.

I put the page down, thinking of how this type of practice is merely improving my reading skills and little else: I need to try this on a live person. I check my list of prospects, select one, pick up the phone, dial, and listen to the ringing. Once... twice... Before the third ring my hand slams the phone down, as if I had no physical control over my actions. I wipe my palms across my thighs to remove the dampness, and force myself to pick the phone up again. This time I dial a more familiar number and while there still is a temptation to hang up, I hold on. On the other end of the line I hear a familiar "Hello?"

"Hello! It's Bob Stephens calling."

"What are you doing, Bob?" Sandy asks, like she is questioning my sanity.

I start laughing at the situation and at myself. "Listen Sandy, I just got out of a meeting with Jeff and we were practicing a new approach. I wrote out a new script and I was, well... wondering if you wanted to hear it."

"I'd love to, Bob. Phone me back," Sandy orders. Then she hangs up.

Not what I was expecting, I think. I redial the number and on the second ring Sandy answers with, "Good morning. Stephens Manufacturing."

A smile stretches across my face when I hear Sandy's enthusiasm. "Good morning. Is Sandy Stephens in?"

"One minute, please... Good morning. Sandy Stephens."

I pick up my new script and work my way through it. As I listen to myself on the phone, it is amazing how different I sound compared to how I imagined I would when I was writing it out.

"Are you reading off a page or something?" Sandy cuts me off at one point.

I thought I sounded reasonably good, but Sandy's question tells me I need more work. "Actually Sandy, I am. This is the first time I have said it out loud and I don't have it committed to memory yet. Does it really sound that bad?"

"The message you are saying sounds good, but your delivery reminds me of those telephone solicitors - it's so obvious they are reading some sort of prepared script. Do you want to try it again?"

This isn't the warm and fuzzy feedback I was hoping for, but it is a point well taken. "I will, Sandy... but not right now. I'll practice it a few more times before I call you back."

Sandy's tone changes, "I didn't hurt your feelings, did I Bob?"

"Not at all, Sandy. I'm just glad I called you instead of one of the clients on my list. I'll give you a call back a little later."

For the next half hour or so I practice my approach again and again, checking back with Sandy from time to time. Finally the moment arrives: Even with the preparation I can feel my anxiety level on the rise as I dial the number of the first client on my list. As the phone rings, I glance around my desk searching for the script that had been committed to memory up until this very moment, but I quickly learn that I shouldn't have worried. As the client answers my instincts kick in, my anxiety evaporates, and I move effortlessly through each line I have worked so hard to perfect. My delivery is flawless, and fortunately... so is the result. If this were a football game I'd be the guy doing a little dance in the end zone after the winning touchdown.

With my first success under my belt, one by one I work through my list calling each of the individuals I identified for Jeff, and soon I am surprised at how easy this really is. Some people have minor questions, but everyone agrees to meet with me. Within an hour or so I have been able to talk to all but three of the people on my list. In my appointment book seven spots are already filled, and with my success rate so far I am confident I will exceed my target.

It's early afternoon before I realize I have missed lunch, but that's OK because I filled all my available time slots... including an early breakfast and a pre-dinner appointment. After a quick mental breather I grab my coat and work my way through the halls while I consider my options for food. Inconspicuously, I glance into Sarah's office and see her on the phone talking and laughing... with her 'trophy' rose positioned front and center.

Before seeking food I decide to make my way back to Jeff's office to pass on my good news. As I drift by Bruce's desk, I notice how much of his attention is concentrated on the screen in front of him; seems to me he's a little too focused for a man supposedly in love.

Jeff and Karen are talking beside the infamous round table when I walk up to Jeff's door. At this point, even though an 'atta boy' would be nice... it doesn't seem appropriate to interrupt. Jeff looks up and sees me before I can turn and make a silent exit.

"Come on in, Bob. Karen and I were just finishing up."

"Actually Jeff, I just wanted to let you know that I have booked nine meetings so far. Thanks for your help this morning." Jeff gives me two thumbs up while Karen looks over her shoulder and smiles. I go on and say, "I'm going to go through that training material you gave me and I'll be all ready for the next meeting." I'm still absorbing the attention... and loving it!

"I'm going to invite the new salespeople too. It wouldn't hurt for them to go through the Leveraging training again," Jeff announces.

Karen's smile disappears. "Jeff, you want us to go through that training... *again?*"

Jeff says, "Well Karen, that's why you're so good!" And he winks.

I leave them both and return to my quest for food, but I'm more eager to get back to work.

All of the re-learning starts eating up hours, and then days start going by; sometimes I feel like I've been re-born, I am learning so much. I find myself learning and adopting new approaches; something I wouldn't have thought possible just a couple of months ago. Life is good!

What amazes me, though, is that even with getting into work early and Tina's help with administration, there is hardly an idle moment throughout the day. And you know what? It feels great! I find that the peaks of my successes and the valleys of my disappointments are levelling out the busier I get; work is no longer an unpredictable series of extreme highs and lows.

Teddie is trying to turn over a new leaf as well. I have noticed he is arriving at work a little earlier, and his competitive spirit is kicking in again. When I quiz him on how many appointments he has booked for the Leveraging Blitz, he acts like I am asking him to kiss and tell... but that's Teddie; he wouldn't want to give me the satisfaction of beating him.

And then there is Sarah... who is bouncing around the office like she is walking on air. Between Teddie and Sarah it's not too hard to tell when a new rose has arrived for her. In fact, I am convinced that Teddie gets more excited than she does.

One morning, as I lie in bed waiting for the alarm to go off, I think about the Leveraging meeting we are having this morning. Although I don't want to be late for that, I am more concerned about something else... getting out to hit some balls ahead of time!

As I walk in the door of the shack at the driving range, the attendant has my bucket of balls ready and waiting on the counter. The rewarding part of practicing every morning is seeing the improvement. I line up ten balls, pick my target, and track my success while always focusing on the points on Russ's card. When I first started out the successes were scattered, but I can slowly see results starting to come. When I do hit all ten balls on target, I always take a moment to bask in the pride of a job well done. I only hope, I think, that I can maintain this composure and consistency at my upcoming lesson with Russ.

When I arrive at the meeting Teddie is already there, with Karen on one side and Rudy on the other; Jeff is standing at the front of the room, making some notes on the board.

He checks his watch. "I'm impressed - everyone is early. So let's get started! OK everyone... what is the key to being successful at Leveraging?"

In unison Karen and Rudy say, in monotone voices, "Providing 'above and beyond' advice and service," as if the answer is painfully obvious.

Jeff smiles. "That's right! The amount of leverage you have for getting referrals is directly related to the level of service you provide - it's that simple. Now, there are two ways you are compensated for doing a *great* job for your client. The first form of compensation comes as a result of your client purchasing your services; the second way is by getting referrals. Understanding both forms of compensation and communicating that message to the client up front is important to becoming successful at Leveraging, and is essential if you want to get beyond the feeling of 'begging' for referrals."

I can tell by the look on Teddie's face that something is short-circuiting in his belief system. "Jeff, you mean you want me to basically tell my client how I get paid?" Teddie crosses his arms and starts shaking his head. "I am not sure I feel comfortable with that."

Jeff turns his attention to Karen. "What do you think?"

She looks straight at Jeff and replies, "Jeff, whenever I am dealing with a new client the conversation always comes around to money. That's my cue to tell them about both forms of compensation - it's a natural."

Jeff's smile tells me he knew exactly what she was going to say. He continues probing, however. "So what do you say when they ask?"

With no sign of hesitation Karen says, "Do you want me to role-play it?"

"Sounds good - I'll start." Jeff pulls up a chair and sits across from Karen. "So Karen, all of your services sound impressive, but I am rather concerned about how much this is going to cost."

Karen looks calmly at Jeff while the rest of us watch from the sidelines. "I'm glad you asked, Jeff: cost is an important issue. I have brought along a sample proposal for you to look at. Once we have an agreement on exactly what services you require, we will provide you with a total price. I am confident that you will find our rates competitive with other companies providing a similar caliber of service. Jeff, there is another way we are rewarded for providing excellent service that doesn't cost you anything."

"What's that, Karen?"

Karen smiles confidently, looks Jeff directly in the eyes, and says, "Like most successful businesses, our goal is to grow our client base. There are different ways to do that, yes, but we find that the best way is to leverage the successful relationships we are building with high-quality clients like yourself. After you have had a chance to properly evaluate our services, if you were impressed I would ask that you help me identify others that you know of who might benefit from the work I do as well. Does that sound fair?"

No wonder she is doing as well as she is, I think. If she is this good in the training room I can just imagine how effective she is in front of a client.

Jeff crosses his arms and leans back in his chair. "Well Karen, I don't feel comfortable referring you to others."

A slight smile forms on Karen's face and she responds with, "I understand, Jeff. Have you had a bad experience giving referrals in the past?"

"Actually Karen, I had one salesperson referred to me who was a real pain. After dealing with him I decided I wouldn't want to do that to anyone I know."

"I appreciate your honesty, Jeff. And I respect your opinion. However, I truly believe you will be impressed with my professionalism and our quality of work. Would it be all right if I asked you to keep an open mind on the issue?"

"That sounds fair, Karen. I will."

I jump in with, "So why didn't you deal directly with the objection, Karen?"

Karen turns and looks at me. "Because it doesn't matter. Regardless of whether Jeff says he will help me or not, I have achieved my objective: setting the stage to ask for referrals later. If Jeff says "Yes", both of us now know that if I do a good job there is an opportunity to get referrals. If he has objections to providing referrals I now know what the objections are, which allows me to be better prepared if and when I decide to ask down the road."

"You've got me convinced," I say. "That's very good, Karen." I look at Teddie, and he seems to be riding the same wave I am.

When we move into the area of actually asking for a Leveraging meeting I sit up to attention. After all, I have booked appointments with almost everyone I called and I am not going to let the opportunity to share my successes pass by.

Jeff looks at all of us. "Who would like to role-play their telephone approach for requesting a Leverage meeting?"

Although I am anxious to brag a little, I am not sure role-playing is exactly how I want to go about doing it. To my shock, Teddie puts up his hand.

Teddie leans forward, with me watching his every move. He picks up the imaginary phone in front of him and begins. I watch as Teddie and Jeff alternate parts perfectly.

"Great work, Teddie!" Jeff says when they are done. Jeff sounds as if he is a little surprised.

That couldn't be my good buddy Teddie speaking, I think. "What have you been doing, Teddie? Practicing in your sleep?" I accuse him.

Teddie looks at me. "Nope. I've been practicing on the phone."

Now everyone focuses on Teddie. "You mean you practiced your approach with your clients?"

"I never said that; I said I practiced on the phone." Teddie sucks up the attention as everyone waits for him to explain. "I used my voicemail - I called myself and delivered my phone approach. It gave me a chance to actually practice on the phone, but I also got to play it back so that I could listen to how it sounded from the client's perspective. I don't remember ever getting so much voicemail in one day!" Teddy laughs and follows this with a slam of his hand on the table.

I laugh along, thinking to myself, that Teddie, he sure is dumb... dumb like a fox!

"OK, so now you have a Leveraging appointment and you have arrived at the meeting with the client. What then?"

Teddie cuts back in. "You ask for leads!"

Jeff grins. "Not quite yet, Teddie. First you need to confirm your position with your client. It is difficult, if not impossible, to get referrals from a client who is unhappy with you, your company, or your service."

"Hold on," I say, "I already know when my clients are happy with me. Why would I need to ask?"

"You should never make assumptions about your client's satisfaction with your service, Bob. If you don't confirm your position you could be left in an embarrassing position when you ask for referrals. Confirming your position just means asking some simple questions to allow your client to give you their honest impression of the job you are doing for them."

Karen leans forward. "Also Bob, with my new clients we agree up front that if they are happy with my services then they will refer me to others that they know of who might benefit from the work I do. You see, I need to know if they are satisfied before I can move to the next step."

Jeff seizes this opportunity to move on. "And what is the next step, Karen?"

She rolls her eyes and says, "The next step in the process is to describe your ideal prospect to the client. You want to paint a picture of the person or business that you can do your best work for. The more vivid and clear the picture is, the more likely your client will think of someone who fits."

Teddie leans across to me and whispers, "My ideal client is one who needs my services desperately, and who has a chequebook and pen handy."

Jeff puts his hand on Teddie's shoulder and says, "I'm glad you raised that issue, Ted. One of the biggest reasons salespeople have trouble getting referrals is because they expect their clients to understand the needs of the people they are referring. Your description of your ideal prospect should be based more on the quality or caliber of client you are looking for, and less on their needs for your service at this point in time. Over time needs change, but a good-quality client will likely always be good quality."

Jeff directs his attention to Rudy. "How do you get your clients to start giving you names of referrals, Rudy?"

"I just let them know it is a brainstorming exercise at that point. I hand them a piece of paper and ask them to jot down any names that come to mind as I describe the type of client that I do my best work for.

I let them know that after we are finished getting some names on the paper we will work together to decide which ones I should call. This really helps to get the names flowing."

"And what if they don't come up with any?"

"I prime the pump," Rudy explains.

After a moment of silence I ask, "You do what?"

Rudy grins. "This isn't my terminology... blame Jeff. He told us that with most pumps you have to prime them before they will pump, and Leveraging with some clients is no different. If they are having trouble coming up with names, I usually have some names of potential prospects that they already know; I have picked these up in conversations and various dealings with them over time. I might say, 'You mentioned Smith & Company... tell me what you know about them.' If I give them some names of prospects that they already know, sometimes that helps to get them thinking of others."

"What do we do then?" Jeff pushes.

Rudy continues with, "Once I have reached my goal for names I start asking all the qualifying questions. I collect background information on the referral, especially the strength of the relationship between the client and the person they are referring. I want to know what influence my client has with this referral. Then I sometimes ask my client to rank the prospects on the list starting with the best. I might even ask them to put themselves in my shoes, and identify which prospects they would call first and why."

"Excellent, Rudy," Jeff announces. "A qualified name puts you a step closer to getting an appointment. The next step at this point is to leverage the good relationship you have with your client. The most obvious thing your client can do to help you get an appointment is to allow you to use their name when you are contacting the referral. If the referral has a good relationship with your client, mentioning your client's name can make a tremendous difference when getting an appointment. What else can you do to leverage your relationship with your existing client to get that appointment?"

"I like to have the client contact the referral, to introduce me before I call," I say proudly.

"Great strategy, Bob... as long as you understand the risks. The first risk is that they won't call... the second risk is that they will! When you make an agreement with your client to call the referral prior to you calling, if they procrastinate they can either slow down or even stall the process. So, if you are going to have the client call the referral make sure you don't make your call contingent on them calling first. That way, you always have the option of calling the referral regardless of whether they introduce you or not."

"You said the second risk was that they *would* call, Jeff. What did you mean by that?"

"Bob, your client is not in the business of promoting your services - you are. If they contact their referral and try to sell 'you' it could be uncomfortable for both your client and the individual they are calling. The solution is to suggest that your client only call the referral to let them know that you will be calling, and then leave it at that. It's easy for your client... and easy for you!"

"What about the card?" Karen asks.

"Good point, Karen," Jeff nods, "tell them about the card you send out to referrals."

Karen pulls out a professional, postcard-sized brochure with her picture on the front and slides it across the table. "This is one of my secret weapons. When the referral gets this brochure in the mail they see a picture of me, a message about what I have to offer, and my client's business card along with a note from them endorsing my services. Each of these represents important 'trust-building' links that can dramatically increase my chances of getting an appointment!"

"Impressive, Karen!" Teddie says, inspecting the card.

"What's the last step of Leveraging?" Jeff asks Teddie.

Karen waits for Teddie to answer and when he does not she says, "The last step is to thank them for trusting in you! Every person cherishes the relationships they build with the people they know. Allowing you to contact people in their circle represents a risk to those relationships if you do not handle yourself professionally. Jeff has drilled into us how we have to make sure that once we have called the referrals we get back to our clients quickly, to let them know what the outcome was."

As I sit back, absorbing the information flowing back and forth between the people in the room, I realize how little I knew about getting referrals. I also understand now that my success in this area was as limited as my knowledge and experience. While I did get some referrals from some clients, it had far more to do with luck than good management.

Over the years, my idea of asking for referrals was usually on my way out the door from a sale or a successful appointment. It always seemed to start with: "By the way, do you know of anyone who might be interested in my services?" The client would typically smile politely and say, "No, but if I think of someone I'll have them give you a call." I would then hand out a wad of cards and ask if they would be kind enough to pass them on. I never understood why no one ever called, but I sure do now.

Jeff checks his watch and looks over the group. With an unusually serious look and tone he says, "There is one last thing I want to talk to all of you about: your success with Leveraging requires a new understanding. To achieve your true potential you need to always strive to go 'above and beyond' providing great service to your clients; your goal should be to make every client a source for referrals. You also need to understand that getting high-quality referrals is equally as valuable as selling your services to your client. If you set the expectation for getting referrals up front, you will dramatically increase your chances of being successful at Leveraging. Finally, you have to set goals. Each week you need to have a goal for the number of Leveraging appointments you want to conduct, and then you must pursue that goal as you would any other."

For a moment Jeff scans the room in silence. "I believe each one of you has the potential to be the best; to reach heights you have only imagined. The question is... do you believe you can be the best? Thank you for your time." He looks down to gather up his notes from the meeting.

It was one of those moments where you want to stand and clap, but your self-consciousness restrains you and you don't. I look across at Teddie, who is still fixated on Jeff. Awkwardly, he breaks the silence with a light clapping of his hands under the table, as if he is slightly embarrassed as well. That is all the convincing I need to join in! As I clap, Teddie looks across with a smile, raising his hands above the table to clap louder. Without saying a word Jeff raises his head to flash a smile of pride, looking first at Teddie and then back at me.

Karen and Rudy look at the two of us, confused by our excitement. Perhaps they have not yet experienced the empty feeling that comes from having no new prospects to call while your sales and your income slip away.

Hopefully, they never will.

Morning arrives with the sound of the alarm ringing in my ears. I thrash about, knocking the alarm to floor, and I hope the crash represents its dying breath. Although it was annoying listening to it when it was beside my head, it is even more annoying watching it vibrate helplessly across the floor, refusing to quit. I roll out of bed, falling directly to my hands and knees, determined to make the alarm stop. Not exactly a Kodak moment, I think as I picture myself.

I peer up onto the bed and see that Sandy has already started her day. At that moment she charges in from around the corner, looking at me first with a concerned and then a puzzled expression.

"I hate that alarm!" I blurt out before she can speak.

"Bob, you've complained about that alarm ever since the day we bought it. Why don't you go buy another one?" she asks, trying to conceal her grin.

I refuse to answer a question when there is no logical answer... especially this early.

"What are you doing on the floor, anyway? I thought one of the kids had fallen out of bed," she says as I rise to my feet. There's another question I don't feel like answering right now.

"Hey, honey... isn't today the day you have all those appointments?" she asks. Judging by her tone, I can't help but think that Sandy is as excited as I am. She has spent so much time with me preparing my Leveraging presentations I swear she knows them better than I do!

With my thoughts channelled on the day ahead, I feel my mind and body perking to life. As I walk out of the bathroom, freshly showered, Sandy is there to greet me; her hand extended to mine.

"I've got something for you, Bob!" she announces, her face beaming. "Close your eyes and come with me." Sandy grabs my hand and leads me down the hall into the bedroom. "Open your eyes!"

Lying on the bed is an assortment of new shirts, ties, and socks, along with two of my suits still wrapped in plastic from the cleaners. "Bob, I know we can't afford to go out and buy you new suits right now, but there's no reason why we can't freshen up the old ones. I took these two in and had them cleaned and pressed, and then I bought some new accessories to liven them up."

From under the bed, Sandy pulls out a pair of black dress shoes; brightly polished. "You know how David has been asking how he can help you reach your goal? Well, I came up with an idea: We've agreed that David is going to be responsible for keeping all of your shoes cleaned and polished."

I stand there for a moment, lost for words. "Sandy, this is the nicest thing you and David could have done for me!"

"Oh yes! I almost forgot: Amanda is working on a poster to help you reach your goal as well. She's not quite done yet, so she doesn't want you to see it." Sandy glances towards the clock and orders, "Now get dressed; you don't want to be late!"

Standing fully dressed in front of the mirror, I scan myself from head to toe. There is an aura that comes with looking your best... an aura that I haven't seen in years.

As I pull out of the driveway, I think to myself that normally I would be off to hit balls... but today is different. There is only one focus I have today, and that's Leveraging. It feels very strange to commit an entire day to building up my prospect lists; I have decided that if I am going to fail today, it won't be because I didn't give it my best effort.

It also feels unusual to be working away from the office all day, I muse. I remember back to when I first got started: I was expecting that

John Andrews would want to see me every moment of every day so that he could make sure I was working. In fact, it was quite the opposite.

Early in my career I was sitting in my office, flipping though some files, when John walked in. When he asked me what I was doing, I told him I was trying to find some new clients. John backed up to right outside my door and looked left down one hallway and right down the other. Then he stepped back into my office and whispered, "You know what, Bob? I have been in this office for years and not once have I seen a prospect walk up and down these halls looking for someone to write a contract. And you know what else? Today it looks like that's still the case." Before I could respond he continued. "I'll give you another tip: if you're looking for pumpkins you better get in the pumpkin patch." John then turned and walked away down the hall.

I realized then and there that my success was not going to be measured by the number of hours I was in the office. While most bosses were looking over your shoulder to see if you were working, John looked at both your activities and your results. He didn't care if he only saw you once a week as long as you could show you were out in the 'pumpkin patch' doing your job. Over the years, with the pressures of a building clientele, I broke the habit of getting out of the office to meet new clients. I convinced myself I could be far more effective working in my office than I could be driving around visiting clients. Obviously, it didn't quite work out that way.

But now I'm on a Leveraging blitz: My first appointment starts over breakfast with a client I have known for years. I realize I am under time pressures today, so I need to be diligent. After the usual "How are you doing lately?" conversation, I cut to the chase. I look at my watch and start with, "How is your time this morning?" and then I am off. I follow the process to a "T": First I confirm my position, then I talk about my leveraging strategy, next I describe my ideal client, and so on. The only part of the Leveraging process that didn't work out was the objections that I was expecting: they never came.

Afterwards, as I am sitting in my car, I flip through the list of names and related information, slowly savoring every detail. I can't believe I got eight names! This guy has never given me a referral in all the years I have known him: I always assumed he either didn't know anybody or he wasn't happy with my services. Now I know the real reason he didn't give me any names: I never asked.

Throughout the day I move briskly from one appointment to the next, and I have to do everything in my power to stay on schedule. With every call I wait for the hammer to drop, but it never does. There are some minor objections... but overall my clients really seem to appreciate the work I do for them.

I check my watch again as I am walking out of my last appointment. I can see I am going to be a little late for the meeting with Jeff and Teddie, but I am sure they will understand.

On my way to the restaurant I decide there is one more important phone call I need to make. I pull over to the side, grab my cell phone out of the glove compartment, dial, and listen to the ring.

"Hello," I hear on the other end.

"Sandy, I had a great day!"

"How many names, Bob?"

"Guess!"

"Well... I assume you must have at least fifty or you wouldn't be calling... "

Before she can guess I jump in. "Fifty-six! Fifty-six names! Can you believe it? I'm going to be busy for months trying to handle all these!"

"Good for you, Bob! You've really worked hard on this."

"The reason I called is because I want to thank you and the kids; your support made all the difference. I know I still have a long way to go, honey, but I finally feel like I'm heading in the right direction."

"My support? What about my role-playing skills?" she laughs.

"You're right, Sandy; Amanda comes by her acting talents through practice. Anyway, I should get going: I'm supposed to be meeting Jeff and Teddie and I'm already late. I'll try to get home as early as I can."

"You go have fun, Bob: you deserve it. The kids and I have a few activities planned already. I'll see you later."

"Bye, Sandy. I love you."

"I love you too," she says with a smack, and hangs up.

I pull back on the road and make my way to the restaurant. When I drive into the parking lot I spot Jeff's car right away, but Teddie's car is nowhere in sight. I conclude that he must have caught a ride with Jeff. Whenever Teddie bums a ride he calls it 'environmentally friendly'. The fact that he always leaves *his* car behind tells me he means 'economically friendly' instead.

I walk into the entrance of the restaurant, admiring the décor; I don't come to places like this very often. The odd time Sandy and I do go out she always wants to go to fancy restaurants where we can rub shoulders with the best. For these dates I usually figure out how much the evening is going to cost by looking at the number of utensils set on the table. If that doesn't give it away, I listen for the accent of the waiter. The harder they are to understand and the more dramatic their presentation, the bigger the price tag.

This restaurant is different; it's a guy's restaurant. All the walls and even the ceiling are littered with paraphernalia collected from the past.

Some of the items are hard to make out because it's a little dark - after all you need to be able to see the big-screen TV!

I spot Jeff sitting in a booth, by himself with his back to me. Upon my approaching the table it becomes apparent that Teddie still hasn't arrived. I check my watch, thinking that he either has had a very good day, or worse, a very bad one.

"Hi Jeff," I say as I slide into the booth.

Jeff's face lights up. "Hi, Bob. Glad to see you. How was your day?"

The waitress stands there, smiling. "Can I get you anything to drink, sir?"

I look across at Jeff for his lead. "I'll have a glass of your dark beer." The waitress begins to rattle off four or five names of familiar as well as foreign-sounding beers. Jeff picks one and I pick another.

First things first, I decide. "Where's Teddie?"

"Teddie called to say he is going to be a little late. He had one more appointment with a good client and he wasn't sure how long it was going to take."

My curiosity and my competitiveness take control. "Boy! It sounds like Teddie had a good day too. Did he say how many names he got today?"

Jeff begins to laugh. "Actually, he did say... but he asked me not to tell you."

I laugh along, although I can feel my face turning red from the embarrassment of being outsmarted by Teddie; he knows me too well!

Jeff saves me from the moment. "Tell me about your day, Bob."

"I had a fantastic day!" I say, and go on to tell him blow by blow of the events of the day, wrapping up with my total number of referrals as a grand finale.

Jeff slaps his hand on the table and then reaches across to shake my hand. "Bob, you must be proud of what you have achieved." I don't answer, but I sense the expression on my face tells it all.

The waitress gracefully strolls up with a tray; holding two brimming glasses balanced above her head with one hand. She hardly has them placed in front of us before we pick them up and clink them gently together, to celebrate the day.

Within minutes I spot Teddie walking toward us, holding a portfolio in his hand. Although the booths are roomy, I am hoping he will choose to sit on Jeff's side - a guy thing. I try to hold my position on the outside edge of the booth, but Teddie ignores my gesture and slides in on top of me, forcing me to scramble to get to my corner.

No time is wasted, and Jeff prods Teddie for a recount of his day. I attempt to look uninterested, but Teddie's grin tells me he knows I am dying to hear the bottom line. He flips open his portfolio to reveal a scribbled list of names and phone numbers. Inconspicuously, I try to mentally estimate the number: it looks to me to be twenty to thirty names, maximum. As I sip my beer triumphantly, Teddie flips to a second page that is equally full of names and numbers. Now he has my attention.

"How many, Teddie?"

"Geez Bobbie, I never bothered to add them up," he says, closing his portfolio. "How many did you get?"

A little less cocky than I once was, I answer, "I got fifty-six names."

"You did not!" Teddie accuses me.

"I did so," I say, ready to defend my honour. Jeff is smiling and watching us banter back and forth. Teddie opens his portfolio, carefully concealing the list from my view. He studies each page closely, tabulating in silence. When he looks up he is beaming at both Jeff and I, and he announces proudly, "I got forty-five names!"

My competitive spirit instantly disappears when I see the innocent grin on Teddie's face. Jeff and I simultaneously slap our hands on the table and alternately shake Teddie's hand.

For the next half hour we exchange our successes from the day. We talk about those clients that surprised us with their generosity, as well as those who put up some resistance. In the end, the great thing is that we not only got a lot of referrals, we also found out how our clients really feel about the job we are doing for them. Both Teddie and I agree the reasons for our success today are, first; we practiced before we played, and second; we prepared for the day by booking lots of appointments in advance. Finally, we were totally focused on Leveraging... no phone calls, no messages, and especially no office.

"You both did well, but more important, you proved something to yourselves beyond a doubt: If you can get that many names of qualified referrals in just one day you should never be short of good prospects to call again." On that note, up go our glasses one more time... to toast our discovery.

With Teddie and I still caught up in the day's events, I notice that although Jeff is now silent his expression tells me he wants to say something. Jeff finally speaks up. "I'd like to change the topic; I'd like get your opinions on what makes a good manager. I know you have both been around the company for years, and have been managed by some pretty good people."

"What's the problem, Jeff?" Teddie asks.

"I'm not sure, guys; it's hard to put my finger on it. When I first arrived I believed I could make every new salesperson successful so I trained them endlessly, attempting to perfect their skills. I role-played with them and I went out on appointments... heck, I even made sales for them! I told them exactly how many calls they needed to make and I watched them like a hawk to make sure they were at it."

I shudder at the thought; if I had been managed that way when I was first starting out I would have been finished in this business long ago. "So... what have you learned?" I ask, hoping he has found a better way.

"I guess I've learned that that doesn't work," Jeff says with half a laugh. "I'd like to know more about how John Andrews worked with you."

I think back to my John Andrews days. "John believed there are some things you can train people and some things you can't. For example, how do you train someone to be independent, confident, motivated, or to have good people skills if they aren't that type of person?"

"Makes sense," Jeff acknowledges. "So once John found the right salesperson, how did he manage them?"

"John spent a lot of time with his new people, but he never told us what to do... at least directly. He asked us to set goals and then to make plans to achieve them accordingly. The goals - and the plans - were ours so we put our heart and soul into them."

"Did he get upset if you didn't achieve your goals?" Jeff asks.

Teddie leans forward. "No way! All that John expected was that we would keep the commitments we had made to ourselves. We all knew that there were 'controllable' activities that we needed to do each week if we were going to successful– things like making phone calls for appointments, doing Leveraging interviews, and initial interviews... that sort of thing. John had us make commitments based on those controllable activities and expected us to live up to them."

"Jeff, early in my career, John introduced me to the 'best' boss you could ever have... yourself! He helped me to understand that we truly are our own bosses."

I stop for a moment as I reflect on my words. Being your own boss takes a conscious effort. It means making commitments to yourself around those activities that lead to your success –activities that you have direct control over -and then rewarding yourself for following through on the commitment. The great thing is, the 'best' boss notices all the little things you do -even when nobody else does -and gives you that well-deserved pat on the back to keep you going.

Over the years, my 'best' boss faded away, and I let the new managers in the division take control of my future and become my 'boss'. Instead of doing the things to keep that 'best' boss happy and succeeding, I was only doing enough to keep my manager happy.

Jeff rubs his chin as he takes all the information in. "This one manager I had was only concerned with the bottom line, with the money and the numbers. It was like he just didn't know or care about any other part of the sales process. He just hounded me on the one thing I had no control over... getting the client to sign a contract. There was so much pressure from him I almost gave up the sales game... but look at me now: I'm the manager!"

The topic of what it takes to be a good manager goes on for another hour or so; Teddie and I have lots to talk about. We talk about how managers have to truly care more about the people they hire, and how managers have to maintain a positive attitude even when they are feeling down: Good managers need to have a 'bounce in their step, and a smile on their face!'... even when they don't feel like it.

We all have a good laugh when Jeff describes how he cranks up the music on his way to work, to get himself pumped up. As we talk, I think to myself that if this guy was any more pumped up, he'd explode! But, after I picture him singing his lungs out in the car... I then picture myself doing the same thing back in the days of Rocket-Man. Maybe that wasn't as goofy as I thought.

Finally, much later, the waitress walks up to the table and places the bill in front of Teddie and he awkwardly fumbles for his wallet, glancing up periodically to see whether Jeff or I will win the debate to pay.

"I invited the two of you," Jeff insists, pulling the bill his way.

Teddie immediately halts the search for his wallet when he sees Jeff holding the bill; I've been out with Teddie before and he always goes through this ritual. Next he will say,

"Jeff, I insist. Let me pay. You bought last time," Teddie says, mustering up his sincerity.

Jeff looks at me and then back at Teddie. Jeff calmly says, "OK Teddie, you can buy."

I swallow the last gulp of coffee that is still in my mouth to avoid having it come out through my nose; I look at Teddie's face as it turns ash white. I guess Jeff knows Teddie just about as well as I do.

"Boy Teddie, that was sure kind of you," I say, after composing myself. Teddie slowly pulls his wallet from his jacket pocket and unfolds it. It's funny; in all the years I have known Teddie I've never seen the color of his wallet. Teddie pulls a credit card from a buttoned pocket on the inside and I think to myself; who keeps their credit card in a buttoned pocket? Who other than Teddie, of course.

Jeff looks at me with a grin on his face and slides the bill away, saving Teddie from the moment. "I'll get the bill this time, guys. You can get the next one," he gets up and makes his way toward the cashier.

"Thanks very much, Jeff. It was a great evening," I say, raising my hand to wave good-bye.

"Yes. Thanks, Jeff. I'll buy next time!" Teddie hides his card back in the buttoned pocket, and his wallet back in his jacket.

Jeff turns and makes his way back to say, "Don't forget about our training meeting in the morning. Now that you have all those leads, I want to walk you through the training on Getting Appointments. I've got a special guest helping out: Sarah! See you later, drive safely."

Teddie and I look at each other and both say in perfect harmony, "Sarah?"

"What is Sarah going to tell us about getting appointments?" Teddie asks with a bewildered expression.

"I'll guess we'll see tomorrow, won't we?" I answer, rubbing my chin. It's late... and I want to get home to my family.

Chapter 9
Getting Appointments

Something I've just noticed is that very few people come to work this early. As I walk through the office, Tina's casual smile and "good morning" tells me there is nothing urgent facing me after being away from the office yesterday. Teddie, on the other hand, seems to have his hands full to the point where he doesn't even look up from his desk to see me strolling by. I really do have to talk to him about getting some help.

In my office I find a small, manageable stack of miscellaneous papers piled on the corner of my desk. The most rewarding sight, however, is to see that the message light is silent. I declare, Tina is the most valuable person I know and before the day is out I will tell her so.

After sitting down I open my portfolio once again to review my list of referrals. I'm not sure what makes me feel better, the endorsement from satisfied clients or the actual referrals. Given the fact that I want to increase my business, the answer is obvious. In fact, the list also represents the reason why I am here this morning: I have worked too hard getting these names to not spend some time honing my skills so as to improve my chances of getting appointments.

I head for the meeting room with a pen and pad in hand. Sitting there, alone, I imagine the training session ahead. Even though I have grown more comfortable with role-playing, I still have to prepare myself for the inevitable. I also suspect Jeff will either give us approaches or expect us to write our own. As important as they are, it still feels foreign to write out what I am going to say but I tell myself I can deal with that.

Down the hall I can hear Jeff and Sarah approach by the laughter and talk they make on their way. I'm not sure why, but I feel out of place as they make their way into the training room.

"Good morning, Bob," Jeff says, patting me on the back as he walks by.

"Hi, Bob. I see you brought your pen and paper, you mean you didn't bring me an apple?" Sarah asks, a nervous laugh exposing her true emotions.

Now I know where my discomfort is coming from. It appears that Sarah is as uncomfortable in her role as I am in mine. I push my feelings aside, determined to make the most of the morning. "Bring an apple... you told me apples bother your dentures!" I am pleased at my own wit.

"Jerk!" she scowls a half-smile.

Jeff looks at both of us, wondering exactly what part he should take in this. In an attempt to change the topic he asks, "Where's Teddie?"

Through the door Teddie comes as if he was waiting to make a proper entrance. He also bumps every chair on his way to the front of the room, definitely Teddie's signature. As I watch Teddie get settled, a certain sweet smell catches my attention and I turn and take note of Sarah, who is looking down at her papers. This thing between her and Bruce certainly hasn't hurt her appearance: New clothes, new haircut, but even more noticeable...she has a glow about her. Good for her!

"Let's get started," Jeff announces. "About a month or two ago Sarah came to one of our meetings to get some ideas on making appointments. It ended up that I learned more from her than she did from me. Since then, Sarah has lead all of the sessions on Getting Appointments, and she has done a great job. I had to twist her arm to get her to talk to the two of you this morning, and she reluctantly agreed. If you find the session valuable then all I ask is that you offer to lead one meeting on a topic of your choice sometime in the future. Fair enough?"

Before we have a chance to agree, disagree, or possibly even debate the condition, Jeff makes his way out of the room and calls over his shoulder, "Sarah doesn't need me here, so if you don't mind I am going to walk up and down the halls practicing *the bounce in my step,*" and he closes the door behind him. The three of us sit there, not exactly sure what to do next. This feels radically different from the last time the three of us got together.

Sarah stands up, grabs her notes, and moves to the front of the table. "OK, boys, I don't know exactly what you have been up to, or what you are expecting, but I have to admit that this is the hardest session I have ever had to do. When Jeff said he had to twist my arm to do this, he didn't mean that figuratively."

Sarah's openness gives me the comfort I need to go forward. "We spent a full day yesterday doing Leveraging appointments, Sarah. Now that we've got these names we want to turn as many of them into appointments as we can, and we hear you are the expert."

Sarah's eyes light up. "How many names did you get?"

I can tell from her reaction that we aren't the first ones to do the one-day Leveraging Blitz. "I got fifty-six names. How many did you get?"

Her smile broadens. "Sixty... and from those sixty names I was able to book twenty-five initial interviews!"

Teddie and I swap glances, trying not to be too surprised at Sarah's success. To be honest, if I had been her I would have been sounding off to everyone in the office. And, I'm not sure Sarah could have said anything better to kick the meeting off. Certainly, booking appointments with almost half the referrals she received deserves serious attention.

"Both of you guys have been in sales longer than me, so why don't you tell me where you want to start."

Tenure hasn't served me well lately, I muse, and jump in. "Why don't you start right at the beginning, for my good friend Teddie?" Teddie smiles and says nothing, so I assume he agrees.

"Teddie, would you mind playing along with Bob's humour? It's good for his ego," Sarah says with a wink.

Then she passes us a handout and begins with, "The first thing you need to know is that getting appointments involves far more strategy than just picking up the phone and asking. Being effective on the telephone starts with controlling not only what you are saying, but more so: how you are saying it. After all, if it were strictly a case of having the right words, there would be a single perfect approach that we could all use."

Teddie grabs the paper with one hand, and with the other hand cupped around his ear starts reading an imaginary script as if he is a news anchor. Mechanically, he delivers each word phonetically perfect.

Sarah nods. "Exactly, Teddie. Prospects and clients make conclusions based on what they hear in your voice. The problem is, if you are not properly prepared all they will hear is how nervous you are. Although having a prepared approach is important, your success will be more impacted by the attitude you portray over the telephone. Let's make a list of words describing the attitude you want to portray when you call."

Instinctively, my hand shoots up and I feel like I am back in grade school.

"Bob, I have already told you that you are supposed to go to the washroom *before* class starts!" Sarah cries, trying to control her expression. "Sorry, Bob; I couldn't resist. What did you want to say?"

Short of a good comeback, I push to get the meeting back on track. "I think you need to come across as confident and knowledgeable."

Teddie decides to add his two cents worth and says, "I think you also should come across as friendly, but not like you are their best friend... you have to be both sincere and professional."

Sarah scribbles the words down on the easel as fast as we can throw them out. "You also have to demonstrate a conviction about your services," we say, "because after all, if *you* don't believe you have something valuable to offer, how do you expect *them* to?"

I decide to add my opinion. "I agree that if you are nervous or anxious on the phone, the question your prospect is probably asking himself is; "If this person has something so great to sell me, why are they so uptight?" So, Sarah... how do you relax when your breath is short and your palms are cold and sweaty?"

"Good question, Bob. I think it helps to know that everyone gets nervous when making calls, even us old and seasoned professionals. We have to remember, though, that it is *just a telephone call*! We've all seen salespeople put the weight of their whole career on the outcome of each call they make. With each "No" they get, the more they believe they can't be successful!"

Teddie starts giggling. "No kidding, Sarah. You remember that one guy who ended up breaking out with sores all over his body from the stress of making calls?"

"That's not funny, Teddie," Sarah grins, "but it is true. We have all got to remember that with every call we make, regardless of whether the prospect says "Yes" or "No", we are taking another small step towards our success."

"OK Sarah, but you still have not said how you get yourself relaxed when you are making calls."

Teddie jumps to a standing position, with an imaginary phone held to his ear. "I stand up and walk around when I am making a call... if I am nervous. I've heard if you can move around freely you sound much more relaxed... even if you're not."

"Good one, Teddie. I'll have to try that!" Sarah exclaims. "What I do to relax is I put a mirror on my desk and I look at myself to make sure I am smiling. It sounds strange, but I believe people can hear the smile in your voice."

"I tried that too," I tell her, "but about seven years ago it fell off my desk and broke. Do you think that was just a coincidence?" I scratch my head questioningly.

It isn't enough to throw us into hysterics, but we all have a good laugh - these two know my history as well as I do. It feels so good to have the three of us together laughing, talking, and most importantly: doing something about getting better.

When the moment drifts away I continue. "Do you know what works for me? I force myself to slow down. When most people get nervous on the phone they tend to talk faster - especially me. Speaking slower helps me to relax and I also think it helps the person I am talking to, to relax as well. Perhaps most important is that when I slow down my rate of speech it gives me more time to think about what I am going to say."

Sarah is quick to add in her opinion. "I realize how speaking slow helps to relax, Bob, but you have to be aware of the tone and tempo of the person you are talking to. If their tone is abrupt and they are speaking quickly, you might just frustrate them by speaking too slow. You think so?"

"You're right, Sarah... as usual. You need to slow down your rate of speech but it should be close to matching the pace of the individual you are talking to. I guess if I also have a well-prepared approach I will not need to slow down just so I can think of what to say next. Is that better?'

"Don't get me wrong, Bob; I agree that consciously slowing down when you are on the phone helps you to relax - there's just a few things you need to be careful of." Sarah turns and walks to the easel. "You should also keep these words in front of you while you are on the phone." She points to each of the words: *confident, friendly, sincere, knowledgeable, professional,* and then she underlines *speaks with conviction!* "Always staying conscious of these words will positively affect your tone and your message."

Sarah walks over and stands directly in front of us. "I've got an idea I want to share with you. One of the most common mistakes salespeople make is when they call their prospect and start talking without checking to see if they have called at a bad time: They act as though the person was sitting at their desk waiting for them to call. They don't understand why they get cut off with "No, I am not interested!", followed by a click and a dial tone. When salespeople get this response they assume the individual either is a poor prospect or else they don't have a need for what is being offered. More often, the reality is that the prospect was busy with something or perhaps they were right in the middle of the *crisis of the day*, and the last thing they cared about at that point and time is what this salesperson has to offer."

Teddie bursts into laughter with Sarah and I staring at him. "I got the name of this great prospect who had just been appointed controller of a large manufacturer here in town. Heck, I even got her cell phone number - although I didn't realize it at the time. Anyway, I was having trouble getting in touch with her; I was always getting her voicemail. I decided I would call her at the end of the day when everyone else was going home and 'Bingo!'; she answered. I wasn't going to let the opportunity pass so I jumped in and started telling her everything about our company and our great services. She didn't say a word, so naturally I thought she was listening. When I got around to taking a breath, I started hearing all of these announcements in the background. Well, I finally figured out that I had caught her at the grocery store."

By this point Teddie can hardly talk, he is laughing so hard. He takes a breath and then continues. "She didn't even hang up the phone - she just stuffed it in her purse with me blabbering all the while! I was so embarrassed I never called back again!"

We all share a good laugh. The story is funny, but what is funnier is that we have all been there before. Sarah gets back to her original message. "Great story, Teddie. You of all people will appreciate this next advice. On *every* call I make to either a prospective or an existing client, I always fully introduce my company and myself, briefly describe the purpose of my call, and then I ask the person, "Did I call you at a bad time?" Asking this question shows a respect for their time and their situation. If the time is right, I now have a receptive person to deliver my message to. If it isn't a convenient time, I ask them for a good time to call back. Then I make sure I call them back at the exact time they suggested - it demonstrates the type of person I am."

Both Teddie and I underline this idea in our notes while Sarah moves on to her next thought. "One last problem I want to talk about. When it comes time to ask for the appointment, too often salespeople ask for an initial appointment that is either too long or worse yet... has no defined timeframe. If you don't tell them how much time you will need, they might make their own assumptions and decline the appointment because they think the meeting will take too long. If you do need a longer timeframe - like one or two hours - make sure that the prospect knows this up front so that they can set aside the proper amount of time for you. Just remember, though; the more time you are requesting, the lower the chances of getting an appointment. Long appointments are tougher to fit into a busy person's schedule, plus there is the perceived risk of wasting valuable time if it ends up they are not interested in what you are offering."

Sarah sets her notes on the table and puts her hand on her chest. "I always ask for an initial meeting of twenty to thirty minutes and I commit to them on the phone that I will stick to that schedule. Twenty to thirty minutes is easy to schedule, easy to sell to my prospect, and is long enough for both of us to decide if there is any point in going forward."

I check my watch and I can't believe we have been in here an hour and we still haven't done a role-play... and then I look down at all the notes I have made. Although I contributed a few ideas, Sarah really deserves to be the one leading the pack.

Sarah flips the page on the easel to reveal the approaches I had been anticipating and I quickly read through them one by one; I am amazed at how short they are. "I can't imagine getting an appointment by saying so little. Where did you get those?"

With her hands fixed on her hips Sarah exclaims, "They're mine, and they work! I used these approaches to get appointments with all of my referrals!"

"OK, OK. Sorry I asked!"

"Bob, if your only objective is to get an initial meeting, you don't need to sell them the sun and the moon - just the appointment. Here's what your telephone approach should look like," and in a single swoop Sarah flips the page to reveal:

- Identify both yourself and your company.

- Mention the name of the person who referred you.

- Check to see if you have called at a bad time.

- <u>Briefly</u> describe your services.

- Get your prospect talking by asking good questions to better understand their needs and their situation.

- Ask for an initial interview, including the amount of time you need in the request.

- Close the call by summarizing the date, time, and place, and then thank them.

Sarah continues to reinforce her point. "Remember, you only want to meet them for twenty to thirty minutes. My motto is, *it's no big deal!* I am not going to twist their arm off to sign a contract; I only want to meet them to tell them a little about the great work we do and to learn about their situation. After that, we can both decide if there is any point in going forward." Sarah's eyes light up. "Come on, I'll show you."

Here comes the role-play, I think to myself. I close my eyes, needing a minute to mentally prepare for this. As I am psyching myself up, Sarah brushes by me on her way to the door. Over her shoulder she calls back, "Let's go!"

Teddie and I are a little confused as we jump up and follow Sarah out the door and down the hall. She walks into her office, goes behind her desk, and sits down. "Grab a seat," she orders, thumbing through some papers. In a second she is dialling the phone. Teddie and I swap looks of amazement at the thought that she would be calling a 'live' prospect as part of her demonstration. And we thought role-playing was tough!

Sarah taps her fingers lightly on the desk, waiting for the person to answer; and then she is off. Although I don't have her script in front of me, from what I can recall it sounds pretty close to what she had written down. I hold my breath when she asks for the appointment. Calmly and confidently she deals with a couple of objections. In the end, she doesn't get the appointment, but she does get them to agree to have her call back in a month. As she hangs up, we all break into laughter.

"Sarah, you were great!" I declare.

"Thanks, Bob. It's really nothing. Let them know who you are and why you want to meet them, ask your questions, and then ask for the appointment. It's really quite simple."

I shake my head. "Sarah, for years I thought that I needed a long-winded description of myself, my company, the services we offer, and so on and so on... thinking the person on the other end had to hear all this stuff before they would give me an appointment. Every time I got a new objection, I would add a little more information to my approach to avoid getting that objection the next time. It appears the opposite is true. The more you talk, the more objections you will likely face."

"Exactly!" Sarah stands up. "If you have a good prospect, give them enough information to grant you the appointment and leave all the details to the initial meeting, when you can talk to them face to face."

Teddie leans forward and says, "I noticed that when you were on the phone you mentioned something about the types of problems we solve. That was very good!"

"Actually Teddie, I got that idea from Jeff. Although clients may not identify with your solution right away, they definitely will recognize their own problems. For example, you might say, *we specialize in helping organizations that have these types of problems... Are any of those situations issues with your company?*"

"I like that, Sarah; that is good. Now I would really like to go back to the training room to see if Teddie and I can create our own approaches."

After several attempts we both settle on our own approaches that also incorporate the ideas we have picked up. With Sarah's coaxing we deliver our message over and over, getting more comfortable with each pass.

Just as we are getting rolling, Sarah checks her watch and cuts us off. "We should spend some time talking about objections. As we all know, if you are going to be successful getting appointments you need to be able to deal with objections. The first thing to understand is that most people have an immediate 'knee-jerk no' reaction to every sales call they receive. You need to get beyond this 'knee-jerk no' to see if there is an opportunity with the prospect or not.

Teddie sits there with a baffled look on his face. "Sarah, in the Leveraging training didn't we learn to tell our 'great' client that if their referral says "No", we will respect that?"

Sarah concedes with a smile. "You're right, Teddie: You have to be very careful that you don't jeopardize the relationship between your good client and their referral. If the referral has an objection, you have to really listen closely to determine if their objection is a 'knee-jerk no' or not. You have to remember too that you are not trying to sell them anything; you only want a short meeting to introduce yourself and to find out more about them - it's really no big deal!"

"Well, Sarah? How exactly do you handle these objections?"

"First and foremost, I don't take it personally. If I get a strong objection I know it has a lot more to do with the person I am talking to than it has to do with me. Second, when I get an objection I remember to relax and listen carefully. I want to hear exactly what the individual is saying, and I want to give him or her enough time to say it. If I don't fully understand the objection, I ask questions to get them to expand. Finally, I always allow a short pause after they are finished, to let them know I am listening and relaxed. Here is a formula for handling an objection," she says, and points out a page in the handout:

a) Listen closely to the objection. Make sure you are staying relaxed even if the prospect is not.

b) Let them know that you understand their objection. (For example, So Ms. Prospect, if I understand what you are saying, you are concerned about this... Is that right?)

c) Deal with the objection.

d) Always finish by asking for the appointment again.

"And what do you do if you can't deal with an objection to their satisfaction?" Teddie quizzes her.

"I move on to the next call; immediately. Analyzing or dwelling on an unsuccessful call cuts away at the momentum I am trying to build."

Sarah flips through the pages on the easel. "Guys, there are only a few different objections a referral will give you. Let's make a list of all of the objections we can think of, and develop responses based on the formula we learned."

By the end of the meeting we come to the conclusion that we could be far better at dealing with the objections we identified than our prospects could be at coming up with new ones. We all know through experience that overcoming objections is not like winning an arm wrestle: if a prospect has legitimate reasons for not meeting with you, you aren't likely to change their mind. Also, if you are getting too many objections it probably means it is not a prospect you should be dealing with anyway.

On the way back to my office I think of how much I have re-discovered concerning what it takes to be successful at turning prospects into appointments. However, I also realize that maybe the most important tip of all wasn't discussed: Success starts with overcoming the biggest challenge of all - making the first phone call!

On that note I sit down, open my portfolio, and with a cold chill running up my back dial the first number on the list and listen to the phone ring.

Throughout the day, I make call after call. Once I get going I actually find that making the calls is far easier than I first imagined. I laugh at myself, though; every time I book another appointment I have to do everything in my power to not jump up and go tell someone. In fact, I did skip down the hall the first couple of times, searching for someone - anyone - to share in my latest triumph. But, both times the only person I found was Bruce, and he doesn't seem like a guy who would give me the 'atta boy' I am looking for.

Even with the odd self-induced distraction, I have been able to build momentum: Now that I have the ball rolling I don't want to stop. After I hang up from each call, I make sure I am back on the phone within a couple of minutes. When I do get a "No" - and I obtain my fair share of them - I always try to end the call positively. If they say they are not interested I ask if it would be all right to call back in three to six months. There is something about getting the person to say "Yes" to something - anything - just before you hang up: It may not be a total victory but at least it's enough to give me the strength to get on to the next call.

Every time I pick up the phone to call another referral, I find it helps to picture them as my next great client. Even when they say "No", I realize I have taken another step towards the "Yes" I am looking for. Re-living all these once-popular strategies for maintaining a positive attitude on the phone takes me back to my early days, when I first got started in the business.

Since I was the 'flavour of the day', John had asked me to do some training on the telephone with a young woman who was just getting started. John believed in killing two birds with one stone: First, he knew I had good skills and that I could help her; second, he also knew asking me was an effective way to stroke my ego.

I remember sitting in the training room, walking the young woman through all of the different phone approaches I used. I told her about objections and my responses, and gave her endless examples of how good I really was. She was like a sponge; sucking up every detail. By that afternoon she was busy in her office, putting her newly acquired skills to the test.

A few days later she came up to me in the hall, smiling from ear to ear. "So how have you been doing on the phone?" I asked sincerely.

"It's going great; I booked three appointments!" she announced, shaking my hand. Her enthusiasm was infectious.

"Good for you!" Although I was congratulating her, I was also indirectly patting myself on the back for being such a great teacher. The young woman was just about to walk away when I asked the question that told the real story.

"By the way, how many calls did you make?"

She was still smiling when she said, "A hundred."

I stood there, dumbfounded, as she continued. "The first fifty, I didn't get one appointment. Then I changed my approach a little and got one appointment on the next twenty-five calls and two more on the last twenty-five!"

I walked away from that conversation realizing that her success had far more to do with her attitude and stamina than it did with my teachings: while some salespeople would look at the ninety-seven who said "No", she saw only the positive side: the three who said "Yes". Success, she learned that day, is all about picking up the phone to make the call, and not about the call's outcome.

Sitting there, reflecting back, it occurs to me; that young woman was Sarah! I laugh out loud, thinking; no wonder she is so good now - she was trained by the best!

Without a doubt, nobody wants to make one hundred calls to get three appointments, but with every call you make you achieve two things: First, there is only one way to learn how to become effective on the phone and that is by talking to real, live people. Second, and perhaps even more important, I know that with every call I make I am taking another small step towards the success I am striving for.

While some people get anxious at the thought of making calls, I know there is more anxiety that comes from not making them. For years I would go home at the end of the day with a knot in my stomach because

I knew I was avoiding the inevitable. I thought of it as my 'fear' scale: on one side of the scale was the fear of making calls and on the other side was the fear of failing. If I was having some successes selling, fear of making calls far outweighed the other side, and no calls were made. In time though, as the successes slipped away, fear of failing would begin to take on mass. Eventually, fear of failing would grow to the point where the scale had tipped decisively to that side. That was the point where I finally picked up the phone and started phoning again. It really was an emotional roller coaster ride.

Back in the present, I look through the open door and notice Karen walking by. It occurs to me at that moment that I have been making calls all afternoon with the door wide open. It seems like a small point, but for years I have had to keep the door closed when I was making calls for fear someone might hear me. Now I don't mind if someone hears me. In fact, there's a part of me that hopes they do.

With Karen out of sight I catch a glimpse of my golf garb poking out from behind the door. I look at my watch and notice it is almost 3:10: I have my golf lesson with Russ at 3:30! I spring to my feet wondering what to do next, and then I stand there and silently try to slow my thoughts so that I can make a plan. Within seconds my plan is made - make a run for it! With my golf attire in hand I race for the door.

"Tina," I announce, "I have an appointment at 3:30 so if anyone calls I'll be back in the morning." The fact that I am holding golf clothes instead of a briefcase tells her what my appointment really is about, and Tina grins when she sees me.

Once I am in the car, I strategically place my clothes on the seat, untie my shoes, remove them, and then begin to drive. I figure, what the heck? If women can apply all of their make-up in a rear view mirror while driving at high speed in bumper-to-bumper traffic, certainly I can change clothes on route. As I approach the traffic light I watch as it changes from green to yellow. I check my rear view mirror and brake hard for a quick stop. I check side to side for any vehicles with an eagle-eye vantage point and then off go my dress pants... and on with my golf pants! The light turns green and off *I* go.

By the next light I have both my shirt and tie off. Bare-chested, I try to convince myself that it's a nice day; this is no different than being at the beach! However, the expressions on the faces of people glancing at me tell me different. I'm not sure what's worse, though; having them see me getting dressed in the car or having them see me without a shirt. I decide the latter is worse and quickly slip my golf shirt over my head. As I pop my head through, the light changes again and I am off.

With my car parked in its favorite stall - at the back of the parking lot, of course - I tie up my golf shoes and check myself over in the mirror.

Just as I thought, I have transformed myself from looking like a scattered businessman to looking like a scattered golfer. I slip on my golf hat to top off the look, and I am on my way.

I make a beeline for the driving range, to meet Russ. This is going to be so good! I have worked hard at mastering the basics over the last few weeks, and I am confident Russ is going to see the difference: I can easily picture hitting great shot after great shot. Then I hear a whistle on my way down the path to the driving range, and I look back over my shoulder to see Russ sitting in a golf cart.

"You're late!" Russ shouts. "Come on, let's go!"

Walking briskly towards him, I wonder what he could possibly be up to. As I approach, I see that the basket behind him is loaded with balls, as well as a retriever.

"Throw your clubs on; I want to start your lesson," Russ says now looking straight ahead.

I jump dutifully into the seat beside him. "Hi, Russ. Sorry I'm late."

"Don't worry about it - I don't bill by the minute; only by the lesson." He stomps down the gas pedal and we're off. As we drive past the range I become even more confused.

"Where are we going, Russ?"

"We're going to hit balls, of course!"

Did he say "of course" or "off course"? I wonder to myself. This conversation is going nowhere; it's time for an 'atta boy': I pull the laminated card out of my pocket and wave it so Russ can see it. "Russ, I have been out practicing almost every morning since I last saw you. Pretty good, don't you think?" I speak with pride.

"Good for you, Bob... " Russ continues looking straight ahead, expressionless.

I wonder to myself if this is the same Russ I met a few weeks ago. A few moments of silence pass by awkwardly before he says, "Bob, do you remember why you wanted to take golf lessons?"

"I sure do."

"When you achieve those things, they will be your reward for practicing every day. I am here to help you develop the skills, but you are the one who is responsible for putting in time to turn what you learn into results."

I take in the scenery and Russ's message becomes clear. I smile to myself, thinking of how sweet it will be to consistently shoot in the eighties again, and to feel happy and confident about my game - oh yes, and to take money off of the Butcher and the Baker for a change... that will be reward enough!

With the warm breeze on my face and the smell of golf in the air, I think of a new way to make my next million. Besides my 'golf sounds' tape, I'll have a full line of 'golf smells' that can be used in the car, office, or home all year round. There will be the scent of 'Golfing in the Rain', 'Golfing in the Morning', or even 'Golfing with Friends', which will include a slight hint of cigar smoke!

About halfway down the fairway of one of the holes, Russ pulls the cart over and stops. "Bob, I checked the tee times and based on my estimates we have about twenty-five minutes before the next group comes," he says, getting off the cart.

As he is grabbing the balls I reach for my clubs. Finally I get it; we are sitting about 160 yards from the hole and he is going to help me practice my approach shots. Instinctively, I grab my six and seven irons and walk towards the center of the fairway.

"Where you going?" Russ calls. I look over to see Russ sprinkling balls through the bush and sand trap. "Come over here."

"Bob, I want you to picture in your mind that you are having a great game up until this point, but you have now landed your shot here. Maybe you are within a stroke or two of the competition and the outcome of this shot will likely mean the difference between winning and losing. Let's get started."

Unfortunately, this situation is all too real. I have a great game going and then on one hole I put the ball in the bush and *poof!* my great game disappears faster than Houdini in performance.

After warming up I begin hitting each ball, and I fully experience the predicament Russ has described. After ten or fifteen shots I realize that this is far closer to reality than what I would prefer and I do hit a few good shots, but most are bad.

Russ steps in to limit the bleeding. "Bob, now I want you to picture yourself hitting great shot after great shot. Your swing is fluid and natural: Each time you hit the ball you stand in the perfect finishing position, watching the ball land within feet of your desired target. You are confident and in control - you're unbeatable! With that picture in your mind, I want you to take a few practice swings and then try again. Remember... confident, controlled, relaxed. Unbeatable!"

I can picture this as well... almost too easily, I muse. There is that feeling that goes with hitting the perfect shot: You hold your club high at the finish of your swing and watch as the ball lands lightly, and then bounces down the center of the fairway. Oh, what a feeling! Fifteen balls later I consider myself the greatest golfer on the course.

Of course, maybe it could be argued that the second fifteen balls were significantly better because they were the second fifteen, but I know the difference came from a change in my perspective. I can feel the difference in my mind and body.

"Jump on, let's go!" Russ says, handing me the retriever. We drive along and pick up ball after ball, and it is easy to make out the pattern as we drive. I had a few really bad shots, quite a few good to very good shots, and finally... a few excellent shots.

With the last ball in hand Russ whisks off towards the clubhouse. "Bob, I can tell by your swing that you've been practicing. There is a dramatic improvement in the way you're hitting the ball."

"Thanks, Russ. I was hoping to go to the driving range to show you exactly what I have learned."

"We'll go back to the driving range now, Bob, but I have every confidence that you can hit the ball well when you are standing on perfectly level ground, with your ball perched on a tee. The reason I brought you out here is because I wanted to make a point. The greatest golfers become great because they have learned to deal with adversity. As good as they are, they still hit bad shots. What makes them great golfers, though, is that they know how to make the most of a bad situation. Dealing with adversity... that's what they practice.

In fact, most high handicappers could dramatically improve their scores by just learning to deal with adversity. Not only do they need to develop physical skills to hit the ball when they are in trouble, perhaps more importantly is that they need to learn how to mentally deal with their situation."

Before I can respond Russ turns to me and asks, "You said you were in sales, right?"

"Right."

"When I first started in sales they taught me all the right things to say, and being new I spent a lot of time learning the perfect approaches. What I found out, though, was that my prospects didn't know my lines... or theirs! Even though I did my part perfectly, they reacted in a variety of ways. What helped me to succeed in sales was I learned how to deal with adversity... I learned how to be good in the bush!" Russ says, adding his familiar chuckle.

Finally we pull up to the driving range and Russ stops the cart. Within a couple of minutes I am driving ball after ball while Russ takes a chair at his favorite table. One good shot, then two, three, four, and so on. Russ's approving nods and smiles are all the praise I need.

Halfway through the bucket Russ stops me. "Bob, you don't need me to tell you you're hitting the ball well; you already know it and that's what's most important. Come over here, I want to talk to you for a few minutes before we wrap up."

I slide into the seat across from him, anxious to hear what he has to say. "So Bob, you're ready to get out and start playing. But, I want you to do something: I want you to keep score."

Now I am confused. "You want me to keep score? I always keep score!"

Russ sits there, shaking his head. "Bob, do you keep track of how many times you hit the fairway on your drive? How many times you are on the green in regulation? How many one putt, two putt, three putt greens you have each round?"

I start, "Well, I don't exactly keep... "

He cuts me off. "Each of those statistics represents an opportunity to improve your game. The greatest golfers don't just track their score; they track their game. From now on, I want you to keep track of your *game* as well as your score. All right?"

Before I can answer Russ continues. "And, Bob... I want you to be honest when you mark your score down, OK?"

"What do mean? I'm honest!" In the back of my mind I can hear our threesome chanting, "If you're not cheating at golf, you're only cheating yourself!"

Russ reaches into his back pocket, pulls out a small booklet, and places it on the table. He looks me straight in the eye. "Do you ever take 'gimme's' on the green, or perhaps move your ball just a little to improve the lie?"

"Well, I..."

He cuts me short again. "This is a rule book. You need to know the rules of the game because when you cheat at golf, you're only cheating yourself. Bob, if you don't keep honest score you will never know if you are getting better or if you are just getting more creative with your scorekeeping. The greatest golfers are forced to play by every rule, in every game. There are some golfers who think they are great but end up being only mediocre when they are finally forced to play by the rules."

I feel a little embarrassed at being caught, but I know he is right. "OK Russ, I get your point. I'll play by the rules and I'll keep track of both my score and my game."

Russ smiles. "This is no different than being a successful salesperson, Bob. I learned if I wanted to be great in sales, I had to keep track of all my activities and not just the sales I was making. Most important, I learned I had to be honest. When I made phone calls I marked down exactly how many I made... not more or less." He pauses. "When I listen to myself I have to wonder why I ever gave up selling to teach golf - you don't have any sales jobs, do you?" Russ is sporting a smile that accentuates every wrinkle on his face.

"You can have my job, Russ. And I'll take yours - although I am pretty sure Canyon Meadows wouldn't want me teaching golf!"

"How are the sales going, Bob?" he asks sincerely.

"Great Russ... just great!"

"You salespeople are all alike, everything is always *coming up roses*! I have to get off to my next appointment. See you next time."

On my way to the car I think about Russ's comment -*coming up roses!* Sure, I think; things are turning around now. But had I not become re-focused when I did it would have been more like *pushing up daisies*!

Chapter 10
The Initial Interview —a Fine Filter!

When I arrive home the house is dim; it's nice to see the family is finally taking heed of my energy conservation speeches. Everything is unusually quiet when I step in the back door. "I'm home!" I yell as I stoop over to untie my shoes. But still no kids; I walk into the kitchen to see candles flickering. On the counter is an open bottle of wine and two glasses, beside a crystal vase. The sound of Sandy's 'I'm in the mood' music drifts through the house, and she appears from around the corner. I have always found Sandy to be a beautiful woman, but when I look at her at times like this I feel the same strong feelings inside that I felt back in the days when we first fell in love.

With a warm smile and a wink she asks, "So, Bob... how was your day?"

I try to piece the situation together. What have I forgotten? It's not Sandy's birthday or our anniversary... or Valentines Day. I stretch further; could it be the day we started going out? Or when we got engaged? Yeah, right, I think to myself, like I am going to remember that! "Sandy, I am a little confused. What's the occasion?"

In a sultry voice she says, "You tell me, Bob."

I may not be sure what the occasion is, but I'm willing to play along. "Where are the kids?" I ask on the realization that I still haven't seen or heard from either of them.

"They're at Mom's for the night," Sandy explains, sliding over and giving me a warm hug and a kiss. "So how was your day?" she asks again.

Although I don't want to spoil a good thing, I am totally baffled at this whole situation. I have ruled out any special occasions... at least any that I would be expected to remember. Then I think, what the heck? The kids are gone, the candles are lit, it smells like a great supper waiting... and best of all Sandy looks and feels great. "I had a great day, I... "

"Wait, Bob... " she cuts in as she pours two glasses of wine. "... let's go in the living room and you can tell me all about it."

Sitting on the couch, I raise my glass. "Sandy, I'd like to make a toast to the resurrection of my career," I announce, and we clink glasses.

"Did you sign a big contract today or something?"

"Not exactly, but today was a great day anyway." And I tell her about all the calls I made; we talk about the ones who said "Yes" and we laugh about the ones who said "No".

Over a beautiful supper we talk about old times as well as the times ahead. The only thing we don't talk about is why we are having this great evening together. I eventually come to the conclusion that Sandy just wants to be spontaneous.

Sandy is acting strange, though; she started the evening relaxed, open, and in love... but I did sense that she wanted me to tell her something. I didn't know what to say, and she wasn't giving me any clues, and now at the end of the night I am begging her to tell me but she won't. What started off as a great evening ends with Sandy going to bed early - without me! I straighten up the kitchen and finish my glass of wine while I wrestle with what has happened. Then, as I shut off the lights in the kitchen, I spot the empty crystal vase still sitting on the counter and I know then and there this clue has been calling out to me all evening... but as usual I wasn't listening. So I put the affair out of mind, slide quietly into bed beside Sandy, and drift off to sleep.

Although the wine was effective in getting me to sleep last night, it isn't helping me now as I lay in bed with my eyes wide open, at 6:00 in the morning. After fifteen minutes of tossing and turning I am resolved to the fact that I am not going back to sleep. I hope Sandy slept better than me, but I doubt it.

By 6:30 I am dressed, fed and watered, and heading for the door. I stop in my tracks and slip back into the bedroom to gently kiss Sandy on the cheek. "I love you, I'll call you later today," I whisper, but there is no response... no movement.

The morning fades into my golf practice; standing on the matt hitting ball after ball is usually a rewarding way to start the day, but today my mind is still on last night. While some people might take two sedatives to calm their nerves, I prefer two buckets of balls. By the end of the first bucket I am lucky to concentrate long enough to count to ten, let alone hit ten good balls in a row. During my second bucket the tension slips from both my mind and body and the results start to appear.

After that, on my way to the office, my focus changes to the day ahead: I know I have an initial interview at 11:00 and I am hoping to talk to someone who is familiar with the initial interview training before that meeting.

In the parking lot I see that Karen's car has already arrived. I ask myself; is she successful because she is here this early or is she here this early because she is successful? Kind of a 'chicken and the egg' argument, and it occurs to me that Karen would be the perfect one to talk to: not only is she doing a great job, but she has also taken training on the initial interview a number of times.

When I was first introduced to Karen I instantly had a grudge against her but I couldn't put my finger on it. The easy answer was that I was jealous, but I have figured out it's more than that. When Karen's success started to build, Jeff took every opportunity to show off what she was doing: she was featured in the divisional meetings, the bulletins, the emails... everything possible! I know Jeff was proud of her, but what some managers don't realize is that if they always highlight the same top performer it won't be long before the rest of the team will dislike that person, or at the very least will begrudge their success. I realize this and I decide that it is not her problem, so I am not going to let it affect my opinion of her.

When I walk up Karen is sitting with her back to me, studying the computer screen in front of her. "Good morning, Karen," I announce.

She lets out a scream and spins around to see me standing in her doorway. With her hand on her chest, she catches her breath before being able to get a word out. "You scared me! What are you doing here so early?"

"I'm sorry, I didn't mean to startle you." With the moment upon me, I suddenly question whether I am doing the right thing. "Karen, you look like you're busy. I'll catch you later."

With her composure now intact, she stops me. "What did you want?" Before I can answer, she continues and says, "I was just trying to get through my email before the day gets started. Come on in!"

"Karen," I start, "a while back I sat with you in a training meeting on the initial interview. Do you remember that?"

"Remember it? I've been through that class three times since I started!"

I push a laugh out to lighten the moment and Karen responds with a smile. "I have booked a bunch of initial interviews and my first one is today," I tell her, pausing for a second to muster my courage before continuing. "I know you're busy... but I would very much like to hear how you handle an initial interview."

"I'd love to, Bob; let me just finish up with these emails." As quickly as each email is highlighted Karen presses the delete key. Once she has the rhythm down pat she turns to me and with a wink says, "My motto is, if they're really important they will reappear another day."

I'm not sure if I agree or if she is serious, but I love her spunk all the same. Karen spins her chair back to face me. She leans forward, crosses her hands on her desktop, and looks me straight in the eye. "What did you want to know?"

I pull out the training notes Jeff gave us and I start flipping through them, looking for a place to start. "OK," I say, "please describe the initial interview for me, from your perspective."

Karen thinks for a moment, and then speaks. "I guess I see the initial interview as a filter: if you are doing a great job of Leveraging you cannot afford to have every prospect enter your sales funnel. You need the initial interview to quickly filter out all but the best prospects; if you do not filter them at this stage your sales funnel will soon get plugged with a bunch of prospects that will likely never buy from you. The time you save by filtering can be invested into high-probability prospects, where the paybacks are significant."

"How would you describe a high-probability prospect?" I ask.

Off the top of her head Karen recites, "High-probability prospects are those who are qualified buyers, recognize their own need for your services, and who can relate well with you. They are the ones you want to have in your sales funnel!"

"So what happens to the rest?"

"We operate under the Theory of Plenty, so we have the power to say "No" to those who do not fit the profile. We might choose to deal with them later, or we may choose to never approach them again. The most important thing to remember is that the initial interview puts us in control."

"So what does your initial interview look like, Karen?"

She reaches across her desk and flips through a couple of pages, drawing my attention to the words 'The Timeframe'. "On the phone I specifically ask for a timeframe of twenty-five minutes," Karen explains. "Setting a timeframe up front with a client and then sticking to it speaks volumes about the way I do business. Not only does it tell them I am a person of my word, it also tells them I am sensitive to their time constraints. When I walk into an initial interview I check the time with the client, get an agreement on when the appointment should end, and then I stick to it."

I think to myself that I have been guilty of either not setting a timeframe up front, or worse yet, not sticking to the one I first communicated. "So Karen, after you have set the timeframe, what do you do then?"

"After the initial chitchat I start by explaining the objectives of the meeting. Next, I take some time to introduce our company, and myself, in more detail. That usually takes about five to eight minutes at the most. Then I have the client answer questions that will pre-qualify them and most important, I help them discover their need for my services. At the end we wrap up by determining the best next steps."

"What are the objectives of the meeting?"

"Well, the objectives are to introduce myself and my services, learn more about their organization and their needs, and to determine the best next steps, if there are any. In other words, I want both of us to figure out if there is any point in meeting again."

I think back to the objective I have been striving for during initial interviews with my new prospects over the last few years: Sell them on our company and myself so that they agree to a second appointment. That usually meant long lunches with big bills, and certainly no tough qualifying questions. As I ponder Karen's approach I wonder how she can be so effective in such a short timeframe. "This sounds good, Karen, but how do you achieve all of that in twenty-five minutes?"

She smiles and reaches into her case to pull out a pocketsize booklet. "With my secret weapon!" she says, handing it to me. "Let me show you how I use this; let's do a quick role-play."

Karen starts by setting the timeframe up front. She gives me an overview of what we are going to cover in the meeting, which includes having me complete the form she is holding. I throw out the natural objection of, "You mean you want *me* to complete this?"

"That's right, Bob. This form allows us to maximize our time together, and it will only take you about five to seven minutes to complete. The form helps me get an overview of your situation, and your answers to the questions will help you see if you have a need for the services I am offering. Fair enough?" Karen asks confidently.

I nod my head in approval.

Karen opens the booklet to the inside cover. "Here are several points to help you understand a little more about our company and our services. I'm not going to go through each of these with you, but I feel these two particular advantages are most significant." Karen proceeds to expand on the points she identified, and then moves on to talk about her role and the value she believes she brings to her clients. "Any questions, Bob?"

"No Karen, it sounds good." I look down at my watch: By my estimate the introduction of the company - and herself - took seven or eight minutes. I think back to my initial interviews from the past... like Selectrum. Once I started talking I always found I had a hard time shutting up.

Karen flips the booklet around to me and hands me a pen. "Bob, this will take about five minutes to complete. While you're doing that I thought I might review some of the brochures from your company. Take your time, and when you're done let me know."

I read through each of the questions and do my best to answer them from a prospect's perspective. Most of the questions are based on the typical needs or problems a prospect might have that our services could solve, and the last page is a checklist of specific services I might be interested in getting more information on. I leave that page blank and hand the form back to her.

Calmly, Karen takes the booklet and goes directly to that page. "I see you haven't checked off any of the boxes requesting additional information on the services we offer. Would you mind reviewing that list once again, to see if there is anything you are interested in?" she asks with a smile, before handing me back the form.

"How did you know I didn't check off anything on that page?" I say, slightly amazed at her intuitiveness.

"That's easy, Bob; that's always the page I start with because that's where you tell me if you are interested in the services I offer. If you are not interested in anything then I want to know that up front."

"And what do you do if they don't check anything off the second time?"

Karen falls back into the role-play. "I assume you have no need for the services we offer at this point. Thank you very much for your time. Here is my card; give me a call if your situation changes." And she smiles and gets up.

"Would you really do that? It seems to me that you have a whole booklet of information you could use to point out needs for what we are offering. Why not flip through the answers, find a need, and then propose a service?"

"I believe the people we deal with know when they need our services and when they do not. Forcing them to see a need doesn't usually produce a great long-term client anyway, wouldn't you agree?" she asks, trying to conceal her 'I know I'm right' smile.

I concede the point, and then flip through the booklet looking at the questions I have just answered. "So what if I did indicate I was interested in getting information on your services?"

"Simple: I would go back through the questions at the beginning to make sure there are no 'red flag' answers; a red flag answer tells me you may not be a qualified buyer. If the red flag answers look OK, I would then review all of the other questions to understand your needs further. I would wrap up by suggesting we arrange another time to probe further on your needs; a time when I can describe my company's services in more detail as well."

I flip through the pages, wondering if I have the nerve to hand something like this off to a new prospect while I am sitting across from them. "Why can't I just ask the questions myself and write down the answers?"

Karen gives me a strange look as if to say, *why would you ever want to do that?* I guess I shouldn't be surprised by her reaction. After all, she has never known any other way of approaching a new client. She picks up the form and starts flipping through it, page by page. "Well, I guess you could use the form like an interview guide... that would allow you to personalize the approach for each prospect you met." She pauses for a moment, and then shakes her head and looks up at me. "But there would be drawbacks: First, some of the 'red flag' questions are easy for a prospect to answer in a booklet but would be difficult for you to ask directly. Second, it would be hard to keep the meeting on track and almost impossible for you to have all those questions answered within eight minutes."

She hesitates for a moment and then goes on. "Bob, I have never had a prospect who wouldn't complete the form for me. I guess it's a personal choice, but I like having the prospect complete the booklet because it's effective and also is a twist from what the client might expect - and that makes my approach unique from the competitors'."

"Good point, Karen. It is obvious this works for you."

"Bob, would you like to try a couple 'dry-runs'?" she asks with a wink.

"I thought you would never ask!" For the next half hour we go through each part of the process again and again, with Karen offering suggestions along the way.

"Bob, I'm really impressed; you really are as smooth as they say!"

"That's very kind of you, Karen... I learned a lot from you this morning." I check my watch. "Karen, I have already taken enough of your time. Thank you very much... I appreciate it."

"No problem, Bob. It's nice for me to give back to the people here in the office. Indeed, I have appreciated everyone's help since I got started."

During the walk back to my office I shudder a little. Maybe Sarah has been helping out with the new salespeople in the office, but I haven't.

In fact, it has been quite the opposite. I am determined to change that, however.

Sitting in my office, I flip through the training material for the initial interview as well as the booklet Karen gave me. On a piece a paper, I begin writing out my own notes:

- The objective is to determine if the prospect is a qualified buyer, if they have needs for our services that *they* have identified, and if there is a basis for a relationship. The objective of the initial interview is NOT to sell any services.

- The initial interview acts as a filter for the sales funnel; the goal is to filter out all but the best prospects!

- Roughly one-third of the meeting should be spent providing information on our company, our services, and myself. The remaining two-thirds should be spent finding out about the prospect and their needs.

- The structure of the meeting should be as follows:

a) Set the timeframe up front and stick to it.

b) Explain the objectives of the meeting.

c) Introduce the company, and myself.

d) Either have the prospect complete the booklet, or else have ready a list of questions that I can ask which will help the prospect see their need for our services.

e) Review the potential needs as well as any 'red flag' issues.

f) Determine the best next steps.

I pick up the booklet and flip through it, page by page. Even with Karen's conviction about this booklet, I can't help but think that prospects are going to resist filling this out with me sitting there in front of them. At that point, it occurs to me that I am falling into the trap again.

It's funny how salespeople will make up their mind on what they think their clients will or won't like. I remember one salesman who decided that his prospects and clients didn't like to get calls on Monday mornings, and so he stopped. Funny thing was, all the rest of us were having great success calling then. A few months later, this guy decided they didn't like getting a call until they had a letter in their hand, and as a result he wouldn't pick up the phone until a week after the letter had been dropped in a mailbox. By the time he was finished with us, this salesman had decided that clients didn't like getting calls - period - and so he stopped calling all together.

The truth of the matter was that it had nothing to do with his clients and everything to do with him and his preconceptions. I remember the 'Old Guard' labelling him as a WMI (Won't Make It), but the reality was… we all had our own preconceptions about what our clients liked and disliked that we stood by as well.

While I ponder my past Teddie comes bolting through my office door. "Bob, we need to talk… quick!" When I raise my head and see the look on his face I get a terrible feeling that my day is about to take a turn for the worse.

As Teddie and I head out of the office on our way to the coffee shop, there is one part of me that wants to push him to tell me what is so urgent wrestling with a bigger part of me that doesn't want to hear. Walking in silence isn't easy, and I finally give in to my curiosity.

"Teddie, what's up?" I ask, trying to act as casual as I can.

He glares at me and in a serious tone says, "I can't tell you here; wait 'till we get to the coffee shop." And he picks up his pace.

Oh, that makes me feel a whole lot better, I think to myself. I'm glad I asked!

Sitting at the table with our coffees in hand, Teddie looks at me and sneers. "I can't believe you did it, Bob!" he says, shaking his head.

"Did what?" I ask, confused at what I possibly could have done to get Teddie so upset.

He snaps back. "You know exactly what I mean! Why did you buy all those flowers for Sarah pretending as if you were Bruce? You really are cruel!"

I immediately feel sick, not really knowing how to respond. The questions race through my head; how did Teddie find out? And why is he so upset that I gave her flowers? My eyes look up, down, and side-to-side, but it is difficult to avoid Teddie's penetrating stare. I try to think of the best way to respond but there is no sense hiding the truth now. "I was just getting back at Sarah for…"

"What could Sarah possibly have done to you to deserve this?" he cries, his voice rising.

"Calm down, Teddie; let me finish. A while back Sarah went to Jeff and told him I came up with the handle 'Sparky' and…"

Teddie jumps in again. "You *did* come up with that name!"

"Look Teddie, did you want to hear this or not?" I am getting incensed at Teddie's brow beating; his silence tells me to go on. "OK, I realize I came up with the name but I didn't want Sarah opening her mouth and telling Jeff. Then, to top it off, she told Jeff I was Rocket-Man... "

"Oh Bob, when are you going to get over this 'Rocket-Man' thing? You are and always will be Rocket-Man, like it or not. You should consider yourself lucky to get a handle like that: I remember back to when we called you Rocket-Man more than we called you Bob. I really looked up to you, and so did Sarah and the other people in the office: you were the kind of salesman I wanted to be. When you walked around the office I remember you carried yourself like Rocket-Man. Heck, the way you threw your coat over your shoulders... you could have sworn it was a cape."

At that moment my thoughts of Sarah and my practical joke are gone; I am absorbed in Teddie's description of Rocket-Man. I never realized that Teddie, or any others for that matter, looked at me quite that way. I try to conceal my smile, thinking about Teddie's description of Rocket-Man's cape. The funny thing is; I actually remember putting my coat on as if it were a cape with each new high I attained. Here I thought I was being subtle, but obviously that wasn't the case. I realize now that maybe it was a little childish... but back in those days I really thought I was invincible! While most salespeople were succumbing to the obstacles of sales, I welcomed the challenges and overcame them - again and again!

Teddie's glare brings me back to the moment. "Teddie," I ask, "how did you find out that I was delivering the flowers?"

The emotion builds in his face and his voice. "Yesterday morning you left a whole bouquet of flowers, right?"

"That's right. I was going to talk to Sarah today and let her know all about Sparky, Rocket-Man, and my little practical joke."

"Well, Rocket-Man, you don't have to tell her: she already knows it was you! When I came in this morning I found her crying at her desk, and by the looks of it she had been crying for quite a while. When I asked her what was wrong, all she would say was that you had been giving her the flowers the whole time."

I sit there, lost for words. All I wanted to do was get back at Sarah for opening her mouth... I certainly didn't mean to hurt her. Now, her telling Jeff about Sparky and Rocket-Man seems so innocuous compared to what I have done in return.

I look down at my watch and see that it is 10:30. Panic immediately sets in as I remember my appointment at 11:00. Leaving now will compound the problem, but I don't have a choice. "Listen, Teddie; I know you're mad at me, but I really need you to do me a favour. Can you tell Sarah I want to apologize to her? I can't talk to her until after my appointment, unfortunately."

"You're not going to talk to her right now?" he says, disgust in his voice.

"I booked this initial interview a few days ago and I can't cancel on them now. You understand that, don't you?"

Teddie gives me a small nod of consent. "OK Bob, but you give me a call on your way back so that I can let her know you're on your way - I don't want her sitting there all day waiting for you."

"I will. I promise," I assure, checking my watch and seeing the minutes slip by.

Teddie offers to pick up the bill and tells me to get going. On the way back to my office I promise myself I will never call him cheap again... even if he is.

I grab the Initial Interview form Karen gave me, make my way out the door, and run for my car. On my way to the appointment I try to clear my mind of Sarah so that I can focus on the meeting ahead. I run through the approach in my mind: I need to set the timeframe up front, introduce the objectives of the meeting, highlight a couple of advantages of our company, and talk briefly about myself and the value I believe I bring to my clients. Pretty simple, I think.

It feels good to be going into this meeting holding a little form and nothing else. It's like raising my arms, waving my simple booklet in the air, and saying, *"Don't worry...I am unarmed!"* I have seen so many salespeople (including myself from time to time) walk into their client's office loaded up with a computer, a large portfolio, and even one of those oversized briefcases stuffed with paraphernalia. I'm sure in the client's eyes the salesperson comes off looking like Sylvester Stallone in a poster for *Rambo*.

Having only this simple booklet and a short, twenty to thirty minute meeting eliminates the possibility that you are there to sell them something - and they know it. On top of that, setting the timeframe and explaining the objectives of the meeting builds the trust and credibility you are striving for. The goal is to minimize the prospect's risk in meeting you, and to maximize the benefits: this initial interview structure appears to do just that.

I pull into the parking lot of 'my next great client', jump out of my car, and step in through the door. Within minutes I am in the meeting and we are exchanging friendly conversation about their company, the person who referred me, and myself. I check my watch, confirm the timeframe, and I am off. When I start moving through the new approach I have learned, it is like having an out of body experience. Then I ask the prospect if she would complete the form; I have to hold my breath as I watch her flip through the booklet in silence. She agrees and I go forward.

On the way to my car, I am taken back by the success of the meeting: I stayed within the timeframe, I gave a simple yet impressive description of our company, and most important; I learned a great deal about their overall needs. We booked a second meeting and outlined clearly what next steps we need to take care of before we meet again: all-in-all a home run!

The euphoria disappears when I see my cell phone sitting on the car seat. I pick it up and dial Teddie's extension. "Hi, Teddie; I'm on my way and I should be back at the office in about twenty minutes. Did you talk to Sarah?"

"I did, Bob... I'll tell her you are coming," Teddie says and hangs up.

Chapter 11
Discovering the Needs

I manoeuvre out of the parking lot and wind through the streets on my way back to the office. As I pull into my stall, a shiver runs up my spine when I realize that I have just driven across the city - through at least ten intersections - but I can't recall any portion of the trip. In fact, I'm not even sure which route I took! All I can think about is Sarah, what I am going to say, and how she will react. I still can't figure out why she is so upset - what's the big deal?

When I step lightly through the main office, it feels like everyone is watching my every move, as if they know exactly what is going on. Maybe they do, I think... I put my head down and pick up my pace.

My pace slows as I step up to Sarah's closed door. I take a deep breath and tap lightly on the door, but there is no answer, so I slowly turn the knob and open the door. Sarah is sitting there with her hands over her face, weeping quietly, and my heart sinks as I realize how difficult this is going to be. "Can I come in, Sarah?" I ask softly.

Sarah spins her chair around and with her back to me cries a little louder. On the desk, the flowers from yesterday are a reminder of this practical joke gone wrong. The door squeaks intermittently when I close it for privacy.

Sarah's voice comes to life. "Don't close the door Bob; I don't want to be in here alone with you!"

Pulling the door open again, I quietly start. "Look Sarah, I apologize for giving you the flowers... "

Sarah begins sobbing. "You jerk! You don't realize how hard it is for a divorced woman to find a man. After James left me, I became incredibly lonely. I did my best to keep positive - I started working out, buying new clothes, spending more money on haircuts. I thought nobody ever called because I was unattractive or too old or something!"

I jump in. "Sarah, you're a beautiful woman... "

She cuts me short. "Shut up and listen, Bob. One day Bruce started taking an interest in me, and eventually he worked up his nerve to ask me for a date. The first time we were together at that restaurant I started to fall for him. He was so gentle and understanding, but he was also shy. I didn't want to set myself up for a disappointment, so I just sat back and waited for him to make the next move. Then, a few days after our date, these roses started showing up - I let my guard down, and I really fell in love. I haven't had those feelings for years," and she starts crying again.

I stand there silently, knowing there is nothing I can say to make her feel better.

After a couple of long minutes, Sarah composes herself and says, "Well, I didn't say anything to Bruce, and he didn't say anything to me. With each flower and note, Bruce seemed more removed, and I couldn't figure it out - until this morning." I can see her shoulders shaking as she begins to bawl.

From behind, Teddie walks up and puts his hand on my shoulder. Embarrassed at the situation, I look down at the floor - well aware of what I am in for. After a moment, I open my eyes and slowly lift my head, turning to look at Teddie.

Shock and confusion spill over me: Teddie starts smiling, and soon enough his smile is accented with a giggle. I look at Sarah, who has now spun her chair back towards us and I see her holding her breath with her hands cupped over her mouth. When she pulls her hands away the floodgates open and out comes uncontrollable laughter.

I've been had! I realize. Sarah wasn't crying at all... she was faking it! I stand there, not quite sure what to do next, as I watch the two of them move to full-blown hysterics. I surely don't feel like joining in, considering I am the 'punch-line' of this joke.

Sarah moves around the desk to Teddie and they embrace to hold each other up. Just when they begin to gain control of themselves, they peer at me and lose it all over again. I turn to walk out of the office, knowing that this could go on for some time, but Sarah stops me. "Wait, Bob. I need to tell you something," and she attempts to compose herself. She elbows Teddie, who now appears to be forcing a laugh out, just to take her off track. Then, with her hand on her chest, Sarah takes a couple of deep breaths. "Bob, you really did have me at the beginning; everything I said was true - including how I felt. You see, when I found out that the flowers were from you, I decided I needed to give you a dose of your own medicine."

Teddie jumps in, "This morning when we went for coffee and I told you about Sarah, I had to do everything in my power to follow through with the plan. The expression on your face just about put me over the edge - you know what I have learned from you, though?"

I stare at him, not giving him the satisfaction of an answer.

"Role-play!" and he breaks out laughing again. "Sarah and I role-played the whole thing three or four times before you and I got together." They reach out and give each other a high-five.

Now I start to smile; it's hard to not get drawn in with these two goofs going on like they are. My smile changes to giggles and then to all-out hilarity as I start to recognize the humor in the situation. Between fits of laughter, I take a breath and force out, "So, Sarah... did Bruce finally 'fess up that he didn't give you the flowers?"

Sarah's tone becomes serious. "No. I still haven't talked to Bruce about this."

I stop dead in my tracks. "Well then, how did you figure out the flowers were from me?"

"Sandy called me this morning and asked about the flowers. I guess you left your credit card at the flower shop yesterday, and they called your house to let you know."

Now, suddenly, everything becomes clear: Sandy was expecting me to give *her* that beautiful bouquet of flowers! That's why she had the romantic evening planned and that's why she sent David and Amanda to stay with her mother and... that's also why the empty vase was sitting on the counter!

I make my way back to my office in a trance: I can't imagine how a practical joke could go so wrong! It doesn't end, however; Tina is walking down the hall toward me waving a piece of paper. "Bob," she says, "your wife called this morning... I told her you were tied up with Sarah."

Although a picture may be worth a thousand words, these particular words bring a thousand pictures to mind and my eyes roll back in my head. "Did you use those exact words?"

Tina gives me this look as if to say, 'Do you really think I am that stupid?' "No, Bob. I told her you were in a meeting with Sarah and that you would call her when you were in," Tina explains, slowly.

I feel a small sense of relief and breathe, "Thank you, Tina!" before I take the note and read it.

Tina turns to walk away, and then spins around. "Oh, yes, and Peter Most from Selectrum called back and asked for another meeting with you. I've checked your schedule and I booked a time for you this afternoon."

"I thought Selectrum had already made a decision to go with another company!"

Tina shrugs her shoulders. "I guess it didn't work out!" And she turns and walks down the hall.

Stepping into my office, the note in my hand is an unfriendly reminder of the call I need to make. A strong urge tells me to pick up the phone and call Sandy right now, but common sense tells me to think it out first. I rest my head in my hands, close my eyes, and try to think my way through this situation.

I am not sure how long I am in there like this before I hear a tap on the door. "Hi Bob... is Sandy going to be mad at you?" I hear Sarah ask, tentatively. I lift my head to see her looking back at me with a concerned expression.

"What do you think, Sarah?"

"Why will she be so mad, Bob? It was just a joke!"

"Last night Sandy planned a romantic evening because she thought I was bringing those flowers home for her. She didn't let me know that she knew about the flowers, and I wasn't smart enough to figure it out. When the bouquet didn't materialize, Sandy headed off to bed early... leaving me scratching my head."

I stop for a second and then go on. "Unfortunately, Sarah, part of the problem is that Sandy has never forgot about that night you and I were together."

"Nothing happened that night, Bob... " she pauses and continues in a less certain voice, "... right?"

"Nothing happened," I assure her. "What exactly did Sandy say, anyway?"

Sarah looks up to the ceiling, searching for the answer. "Well, she phoned me first thing this morning. When I answered, she said, *hi, it's Sandy Stephens calling...* " She hesitates as if the story is about to take a turn for the worse.

"Go on, Sarah; tell me what happened."

"Then she just said straight out, *"Bob bought some flowers yesterday and he didn't bring them home. Do you have any idea who he might have given them to?"* I immediately went into shock as I sat at my desk staring at the flowers in front of me. Without thinking, I told her that you gave them to me. Before I could say anything else, she said good-bye and hung up."

"This is worse than I thought... you made it sound like I gave *you* the flowers!" I accuse her.

"Actually Bob... you *did* give me the flowers."

"Hell, I know that... but you made it sound like it was some romantic gesture!"

Sarah's Irish temper flares. "I did not, Bob. All I said was that you gave me the flowers and before I could explain, your wife said good-bye and hung up! You seem to forget that this is your fault, not mine!"

Even before she is finished, I know she is right. "I'm sorry, Sarah. I know this isn't your fault."

Sarah's temper subsides. "Do you want me to call Sandy back and tell her the whole story?"

"Thanks, Sarah, but I think I need to solve this one myself. Would you mind pulling the door closed so that I can give her a call?" and I pick up the phone and dial. As the phone rings, I realize how this is tougher than any cold call that I have ever had to make.

"Hello," Sandy answers abruptly.

"Sandy, let me explain..."

"What are you doing buying flowers for Sarah?" she demands, her volume rising.

"It was a practical joke," I explain. "That's all."

"That's quite a sense of humor you have, Bob. I'm sure everyone must be rolling in the halls!"

"Let me explain..." I say, and I proceed to tell every detail. After re-explaining the situation several times over, I sense that Sandy is starting to sway my way. "Listen, Sandy, I understand why you're so upset; you should talk to Sarah directly if you don't believe me. Here, I'm going to transfer for you," I say and then wait in silence for her answer.

After what seems an eternity, Sandy concedes. "No, Bob, that's OK... I do believe you. That was supposed to be a joke? A practical joke? Anything involving flowers isn't really that funny, Bob."

"I know that now, honey. Thanks for understanding... I love you!"

Just before I am ready to hang up, Sandy cuts back in with a question. "What kind of flowers were they, Bob?"

I pause for a moment, wondering why it matters. "Roses, Sandy. I figured roses would work with the joke."

"You're lucky... When are you coming home?"

"Not too late... I promise."

"I'll see you then," Sandy says, and then we say our goodbyes and hang up. I think, why am I lucky that I gave Sarah roses?

After hearing a knock, I look up to see Sarah standing in my doorway. "Did everything work out OK with Sandy?"

"It worked out just fine... did you talk to Bruce?"

"I did talk to him," she says, breaking into a smile. "Bruce did think the flowers were from some other guy interested in me, and since we had only gone out the one time, he didn't want to intrude. When I told him that you had given them to me as a practical joke, he jumped up from his desk and gave me a kiss right there - we're going out for a date tonight!" she explains, and her voice's tone is musical.

I sit there shaking my head in disbelief; there is a certain irony about how this whole thing has worked out. Sarah betrays a trust and opens her mouth to Jeff. To get her back, I blow $50 on flowers and now she has a guy who loves her more than ever... and I have a wife who's probably in tears right now.

With Sarah on her way, I sit at my desk trying to put the day's events behind me; I have to meet Selectrum this afternoon and I need to come up with a plan. As excited as I am about my meeting with Peter, I know that I have to convince myself I operate under the Theory of Plenty.

With my strategy set, I pick up the phone and dial. "Hi Peter, it's Bob Stephens calling. Did I call you at a bad time? Great! Would you mind if we took fifteen minutes on the phone right now so that I can get a better understanding of your situation?" I check my watch and then begin asking prepared questions, and listen carefully while he responds. I learn that my competition has dropped the ball, and now Selectrum needs to re-consider their alternatives.

"Sounds good, Peter. I'll be there this afternoon at 2:00: I'd like an hour of your time if that's OK. Agreed... we'll see you then." After I set the phone down, I determine that first, Selectrum truly represents a 'high probability' prospect, and second, that if I am going to turn Selectrum from a prospect into a client, I will need to do a better job of helping both them and myself understand their needs. It's time to brush up on my fact-finding skills!

There is so much trouble that comes from not having good questioning skills. If you don't ask enough questions - or the right questions - you either miss possible problems you could solve or worse yet, you develop and present the wrong solutions.

Good fact-finding skills also help keep you on track when the prospect throws you a token buying signal: I remember so many occasions where my good intentions for asking the right questions evaporated at the first sign of a buying signal. Having good skills allows you to slow the process down and keeps you in control. Most important, the right questions will force everyone to look at needs and problems as opposed to premature solutions.

So, what's wrong with presenting a solution too early? The problem is, if you present before both you and the prospect have solidified the need, it is like walking through a minefield of objections: one step in the wrong direction and *kapow*, you're hit with an objection you didn't see coming. The other problem is that presenting too soon really damages your credibility.

A smile comes to my face as I remember John Andrew's story about his doctor. I sit back in my chair and I can vividly picture John's one-man role-play.

Doctor: "John, what's the problem?"
John: "Doctor, my shoulder is really hurting, I... "
Doctor: "I understand completely. Here's what your problem is.... Take these pills three times daily and call me back in two weeks."
John: "I don't think you do understand... the pain starts in my shoulder but then it shoots down my arm..."
Doctor: "Why didn't you say so? If that's the case, the problem is... Give me back that prescription."
John: "Well actually I also have pains that shoot across my chest and numbness in my fingertips."
Doctor: "Oh, that's different... let me call the ambulance!"

Then John would switch to a serious tone. "Don't laugh... the same can be said of some salespeople. They ask a question, identify a problem, and then right away they offer a solution. The solution gets rejected and so they ask *another* question, and propose a *different* solution. Every time they get a hint of a sales opportunity, they take off their 'fact-finding' hat and put on their 'sales' hat. The moral of the story is that you have to make sure you ask all of the questions and have identified a need that the prospect agrees to *before* you present your final solution - and if your prospect doesn't see or agree with the need you have identified, then pack up and go home."

I remember one salesperson asking, "Why couldn't you present your solution anyway; they might just buy it!"

John could have given him the obvious answer but instead he jumped back into his doctor example. "Good question, I want you to imagine you are visiting my doctor friend for a check-up. He takes you through all the regular routines, including asking questions about your general health. Your answers tell him you are healthy, but to your surprise, he pulls out his pad and writes a prescription while he sells you on this latest, greatest drug. How would you feel about that taking that drug? How would you feel about him as your doctor? It's no different for you as a professional salesperson. If the answers to your questions don't uncover a need, do yourself a favour and tell your prospect you can't help them. You will walk away from that meeting feeling better about yourself, and your prospect will feel better about you too!"

I pull out my pad and try to think of ways to sharpen my fact-finding skills. Looking to the ceiling for answers, I spot all the training binders that I have collected over the years on the top shelf of my wall unit; each binder is full of good intentions never put to practice. I drag my chair across, step up, and try to balance myself. One-by-one I pull them down in search of the one with the answers.

"Ah-ha!" I say as I carefully pull down a two-inch gold binder. With a mighty puff, a cloud of dust circles up in the air, and flipping through the pages is like flipping back in time. As I read through the pages, I highlight the jewels as I spot them.

Then, with my strategy set, I pull out my portfolio and start making my list of questions, using all the different techniques suggested in the book. It's funny; in the past few years, prior to meeting new clients, I would spend all my time trying to figure out what I was going to say as opposed to thinking of what I was going to ask. After reading through the material, I am convinced that maybe that was another part of the problem.

Over the years as my experience grew, instead of asking more questions, I asked fewer. I believed that I already knew the answers to most of the questions, so what was the point of asking them in the first place? After studying the material, I figure out that although I knew what the problems and needs were, many times my prospects didn't. Taking the time to ask the proper questions allows prospects to *discover* their own needs as opposed to me telling them what their needs are.

I check my watch and realize that it is time to head out for Selectrum. With my strategy set, I gather the pages of questions I have developed and place them neatly into my portfolio. Then I do what I have done so many times before - I flip through the assortment of colorful corporate brochures that I have relied on for so many years to sell our services.

It occurs to me that I don't need those brochures to sell our services. Once the need has been identified, agreed to, and I have presented the appropriate solutions, I can leave some brochures at that time. At this point in the sales process, those brochures only represent a crutch - a crutch that I don't need.

With my portfolio in hand, I close the door to expose both my coat and the mirror on the door and notice a refreshing confidence staring back at me. With a *bounce in my step, and a smile on my face*... I am on my way to Selectrum.

Driving back from Selectrum I triumphantly slam my hand on the steering wheel and reach over to crank up the tunes - what a great appointment! Peter Most knew he had a need for our services, but by the time I was finished asking him all of my questions, he felt that need so strongly I could tell he wanted to sign a contract right there and then - and to think I haven't even shown him our solution yet! It just proves people want to buy from someone who understands them and their problems, as opposed to someone who only knows about the solutions they are offering. Now, after asking all the questions I had prepared ahead of time, I know exactly what Selectrum's 'hot buttons' are, plus I know what possible objections I might face when I present the solution!

When I wrapped it up at the end, it felt so professional to summarize what I had learned in our meeting. The words jump to the front of my mind: "Peter, before I go back to the office to put together some new solutions for Selectrum, I want to make sure I completely understand your situation. Would you mind if I took a few minutes to confirm what I have learned about Selectrum and your needs?" As I confirmed my understanding of their situation, each answer to each question led him to a solution - my solution. I knew it and so did Peter.

Chapter 12
Presenting Solutions

I pull into my stall and walk briskly to my office with my portfolio under my arm. I have several more appointments to prepare for, and most important, I want to talk to Jeff to get some ideas on the best way to present my solution to Selectrum. Although presenting has always been a strength of mine, I now believe that every so often you need to take a lesson to keep your skills sharp - it's no different for sales than it is for golf.

Speaking of golf, this really is a great day; I've got a golf date later this afternoon with my buddies and I can't wait to take a little bread off the Baker and maybe have the Butcher cut me a steak or two. Since starting my practicing routine, I've only missed one day at the driving range, and now I've moved off the mats to work on improving other parts of my game... like my putting and approach shots.

On my way to Jeff's office, I stop at mine to drop off my portfolio and check out the events of the day. A few emails to read and a few client calls to return, but nothing I can't handle - especially today! While sitting at my desk, I glance up and see Jeff scooting by my office. "Hey, Jeff!"

Whipping back from around the corner, Jeff peers in. "Oh hi, Bob. How did things go at Selectrum?"

"How did you know about Selectrum?"

"A good manager has a pulse on all his salespeople... especially his good ones!"

I hold up the list of questions and notes that I scribbled down from the meeting. "Just great, Jeff! In fact, they want me to come back right away to present the solutions." Peter had also told me to make sure I bring along a contract ready to sign, but I decide to keep that piece of news to myself. I know that celebrating contracts yet to be signed is a waste of enthusiasm, and Jeff knows it too.

"I knew you would do a great job, and so did you!" Jeff looks down as his watch and winces slightly. "I'm on my way to an appointment, Bob - did you need me for something?"

"Don't worry about it, Jeff; I just wanted to brush up on my presenting skills before my next meeting with Selectrum and I was hoping to get some ideas from you; I'll figure something else out."

"Geez, Bob, I'm sorry. I've got appointments for the rest of the day. How about breakfast tomorrow?" Before I can answer, his face brightens and he points his index finger in the air. "I've got the answer! You get your laptop computer up and running and I'll be right back," He turns and disappears down the hall.

With a kick of my foot, I locate the laptop computer that is stuffed under my desk, out of sight and out of mind. Over the years, I have avoided the computer for the most part – with the exception of email, which I viewed as an essential ingredient to survival. For the longest time I thought if I did something wrong, I would wreck something or maybe end up looking stupid - mostly likely the latter.

I'll never forget the day I got my very first computer from the company. I had fumbled around enough to turn it on and to get one of the software programs up and running, and that's when I experienced my first crisis. So, I picked up the phone and called the Helpdesk: the number was printed on a bright orange sticker stuck to the side of the monitor. No one answered, so I left a detailed message describing my problem: "I don't know what's wrong with my computer. The pointer is in the center of the screen, but I need to get it over to the left side where the buttons are. I have already moved my mouse as far to the left as I can but I am now at the edge of my mouse pad. If I move my mouse any further to the left, it will come off the pad. What do I need to do?"

To make matters worse, when they didn't call me back right away, I searched around the office for someone to describe my dilemma to. I don't remember who I told it to... but the story went through my division like a fire through dry grass backed with wind. Every time it was repeated, the opening line was, "Do you want to hear something really stupid? Do you know Bob Stephens?" My warm welcome to technology!

It wasn't only me who had problems with the computer, though. I saw some of the older salespeople around here try to avoid the computer by making a mad dash for retirement - you would have sworn they thought this new gadget was an angry bull and they wanted no part of it.

Over the years I have learned one thing about computers - how to talk about them with my buddies at the coffee shop. I find the way people talk about their computers is hilarious. It reminds me of how the guys used to talk about their cars: "Oh yeah... mine has Holley four-barrel carburetor, an Edlebrock manifold, headers, and the engine has been balanced and blueprinted!" Over the years, the cars advanced but the guys didn't; now most of us are scared to open the hoods of our cars. Nowadays, everyone talks about their computers the same way: "I've got a six-gigabyte hard drive stacked with a 100 megabyte cache of RAM, a 56k modem, and dual Pentium processors... "

I better get this thing turned on, I think; Jeff's going to be back here any minute. I pick up the laptop looking for clues on how to open it. I find the secret button, open the lid, and push the power button... nothing. Push it again... nothing. This is why I hate computers! Jeff walks into my office, so I press the power button again and again, a little harder each time.

"You need to plug it in," Jeff explains politely.

"I thought it ran on batteries."

"It does... but you need to charge them first," Jeff says, trying to conceal his smile.

Another 'stupid' moment, I think to myself.

Jeff takes control to save me from further embarrassment. "These things are tricky... let me get it going for you."

Within seconds the screen is alive with color. "Bob, I've just got a set of training CDs from the company and there's one here on Presenting Solutions."

"You mean head office is going to have us trained by computers instead of people!" I say in disgust.

"Not at all, Bob. We still need to do training person-to-person, but these CDs will allow our salespeople to reinforce their sales skills whenever they want. I saw a demonstration of this particular CD and I was impressed - you can even role-play with it!"

"This I've got to see... " I say, thinking my computer might be a little kinder than what Teddie has been in some of our role-plays. After a couple of keystrokes, the host comes to life on my screen, introducing both herself and the training program.

"Do you still want to meet for breakfast, Bob?" Jeff asks, walking towards the door.

"Actually Jeff, I'll go through this, this afternoon, but I wouldn't mind having breakfast to get your ideas on closing the deal."

"I'll meet you at the restaurant on the main floor at 7:30," Jeff says as his voice fades down the hall.

My attention turns back to the computer, and I begin to flip from screen to screen as I listen, read, watch, and even record and playback my voice. The first time I activate the record button to practice a suggested approach, the bouncing sound waves across the box on the screen are enough to clam me up. With the door closed and a few more tries under my belt, my courage and comfort increases, and I start having fun. Not bad for a 'techno-nerd', I congratulate myself.

At one point I hear a familiar double rap on the door and look up to see Teddie. "Ready for a coffee, Bob?"

"Old habits die hard... " I mumble to myself.

"Pardon me?"

"I was just talking to my computer, Teddie. Jeff gave me a great CD on Presenting Solutions and I was just going through it. Can we do coffee another time?"

Teddie moves around the desk to get a closer look. "So what did you learn?"

"Seriously?"

"What, Bob? Do you think you're the only person presenting solutions around here?"

"OK Teddie, I get your point. Anyway, I'm not sure I learned anything new... but I did pick up some good ideas."

"Like what?" Teddie asks.

"Well, you should start the meeting by confirming that both your understanding and the prospect's understanding of their situation is still the same."

"Why's that?"

"Teddie, have a seat, and let me explain. You know how sometimes you have those great fact-finding meetings with prospects where you identify a 'huge' problem that's begging to be solved. They ask you to put together a solution so you scurry off to your office just knowing there is a sales opportunity. Then you come back a week or so later with your neatly-bundled solution and when you start presenting it, they go cold on you."

"I know exactly what you mean, Bob. Hey - I've even got the frostbite to prove it!"

"A lot of times what we don't realize is what happened to the prospect in the time that elapsed between the two meetings. Maybe they got a call from a competitor of ours... or maybe they talked to someone from their company who made them second-guess themselves. Maybe they just had a mental relapse."

"So what are you supposed to do?"

"It's really pretty simple. All you need to do is ask some general questions when you first get in the meeting. Questions like: "Have you thought about our discussion since our last meeting? Have you had a chance to talk to anyone about the problems we identified? Have you learned anything new about your situation or the problems we identified that I should know about?" Then, if their understanding of their problem is still the same, take that as a green light and move on. However, if new information has surfaced that either affects their problem or your solution, you can either take it as a yellow light and ask more questions to re-define their need, or else you take it as a red light, and perhaps start the whole sales process over again."

"That's funny, Bob. Where I come from yellow light means step on the gas!"

"Where you come from there is only one light... and it's always red!"

"Cute, Bob... so then what do you do if you get a green light?"

"Remember all the facts we collected in the meeting where we discovered their needs? You should review that information before you begin presenting your solution."

"And what does that achieve?"

"If you assume your prospect's desire to solve the problem is still at the crescendo you attained in the previous meeting, you may be disappointed with their reaction to your solution. Reviewing the data allows you to confirm the information you have collected, and more important, it helps to re-build the prospect's motivation to solve the problem - more specifically to solve it now!"

"Can we present our solutions now?"

"We can, Teddie, but an important rule to remember when presenting a solution is: *Weak arguments dilute strong!* We should focus on the features and benefits of our solution that relate to the most significant needs and problems that we have identified. If we describe in detail how our solution solves each and every problem regardless of how big or small, the unimportant features will end up diluting the important ones. Also, we need to not only discuss the merits of our solution, but also any potential pitfalls. Prospects appreciate and trust salespeople who aren't afraid to openly admit that their solution has shortcomings."

"This is really interesting, Bob, but remember... I just came to your office to ask you to go for a coffee."

"Relax, Teddie. It helps me to understand what I have learned by verbalizing it, and it doesn't hurt you to hear it either."

"OK. Go on," Teddie says, sitting back in his chair.

"Next lesson: Having a range of solutions to offer the prospect makes the buying decision far easier for them. If you walk in with only one solution to their problem, you force the prospect into a "Yes-No" decision. If possible, bring three solutions to the prospect so that they can choose between them - for example, a minimum solution, a total solution, and a middle solution. The minimum solution will solve only the most pressing problems identified, the total solution represents the fully-loaded Cadillac option, and the middle solution is somewhere in-between. After you have presented your options, you can simply ask, 'Based on your situation today, which of these three solutions do you feel best meets your needs?' It's an easier question for you to ask and more important, it is easier for them to answer."

Teddie starts to stand and begins, "I want to thank you for this today, Bob... "

"One last point, Teddie: Your challenge when presenting your solutions is to give your prospect the right amount of information to make a decision - no more, no less. If they don't have enough information, they will be unlikely to make a buying decision. On the other hand, if you give them too much information, you run the risk of confusing them; confused prospects do not usually make decisions to buy. To present the right amount of information, you need to be watching for 'buying signals' - buying signals like leaning forward, nodding, smiling, or perhaps questions about cost, delivery details, service guarantees, whatever's on their mind. So when you start seeing strong buying signals, wrap up your presentation and get ready to ask them to act!"

Teddie jumps to his feet in applause. "Now can we go for coffee?"

"Sure, Teddie. I'll meet you down there; you order the coffee and I'll pay for it!"

"It's a deal!" he says, making his way out the door. With a few points and clicks, I find my way out of the training - not bad for a 'neophyte' like me! Looking on the screen I see all the software programs I have been trained on, but have never used. Whenever anyone suggested that part of the problem for my lack of sales was that I didn't use these great software tools, I always had my handy dandy comeback to defend myself: *"It's a poor carpenter who blames his work on his tools!"* I smile as I relate my 'tools' excuse to the great golfers of the world. Can you imagine the professional golfers of today using golf equipment from 25 years ago? They would still be great golfers, but you can't help but think that their outdated tools would have a significant impact on their ability to win against the best.

If I have learned one thing over the past few months, it's that I need to re-think how I conduct business. I definitely need to invest more time taking advantage of the technology the company has invested in. Much like a golfer, I don't believe the tools will make me successful on their own, but if I could gain more time, be able to communicate more effectively with my clients, or even potentially find more clients... it would be worth it.

I close the lid on the laptop and check my watch, realizing I still have to get ready for golf. With my back propped against the door, I get changed at record speed. I turn my collar down, give myself a 'once over' in the mirror, open the door, and I am on my way to meet with Teddie.

As I am opening the door of the coffee shop, I can already hear Teddie calling out, "Bob, what took you so long? You didn't need to get changed just to have coffee with me!"

I take my seat, pick up and slurp the cup of coffee that is now lukewarm. "So Teddie, what have you been up to?"

"Not too much, Bob - same old, same old," Teddie says, unexcited.

"What about all those leads you got from the Leveraging Blitz?"

"I called most of them, but I didn't get too many appointments," Teddie explains and looks out the window.

"You mean you called all forty-five names and you didn't get any appointments?" I question.

"Well, I didn't call them all yet, and I did get a few appointments - so what time do you golf, Bob?" Teddie is shifting his eyes between the window and his empty cup of coffee.

I smell something fishy here. "Teddie, when you came to that restaurant with Jeff and me, did you really get two pages full of referrals from your clients?" I ask, trying to make eye contact.

"Well, maybe not quite... "

"You fudged those names... didn't you?" I accuse him.

"Look, Bob; after all the time we spent in the training room, I couldn't show up there without any names."

I say emphatically, "Teddie, when you cheat in sales you're only cheating yourself. It doesn't make a difference to me or Jeff; you need to be accountable to yourself and no one else."

"I know, I know - it's just that I'm not sure I can do this, Bob! Heck, I'm not even sure I want to! I make a decent living and I'm happy plodding along at my own pace. I may never be rich, but that's OK with me."

"Teddie, you have to ask yourself, is this career your passion... or is it your pastime?"

Teddie sits in silence not saying anything. His answer is obvious.

"Well, *you* can do better, Teddie. I know you can. Look, if you want me to help you, I'd be willing to go along on some appointments - maybe you can even come on some of mine!"

In a monotone voice, Teddie says, "That sounds good Bob, maybe I'll do that. I've got to get going - you said you were going to buy, right?"

"That's right, Teddie. I'll buy," I drop some money on the table and then I shake my head in disbelief and disappointment as I watch my friend shuffle out the door. I can't believe that Teddie didn't do the Leveraging appointments that he said he had. It was all a big sham - to think that he even went to the trouble of phoning Jeff to say that he had one last Leveraging appointment and that he was going to be late as a result. He was probably late because he had such a hard time making up all those names of fictitious referrals. No wonder he didn't want me to see the papers in his portfolio!

On the way to the golf club I am consumed with thoughts of Teddie. Offering to invite him on my appointments, or to join him on his, only represents a desperation move on my part. Teddie has got to get to the point where he *wants* to improve his results before anything is going to change... he needs to find the passion!

For a moment, I set aside my self-righteous attitude to re-think the situation from another perspective: perhaps if the shoe were on the other foot and it was Teddie who had become re-energized and re-focused with me still stuck in the doldrums, maybe I would feel the same way he does. I decide I need to give Teddie the time and space to figure this out. He's a smart guy - it won't take him long.

Standing on the driving range, I relax, pick my target, and execute shot after shot. A bucket of balls later, I am limber, focused, and most important, I'm ready for the Butcher and the Baker. I haven't even made it to the first tee when the chatter starts. "How many strokes do you want today, Candleman?" Butcher barks.

"Actually, guys... straight up would be just fine!" I say, attempting to conceal my cockiness.

"Oooooh," they both sing out in unison, followed by a handshake to mark the celebration of an anticipated victory yet to come.

Their pain starts slowly, but continues to mount hole-after-hole. As expected, not every shot of mine reaches its desired target - in fact, many flat-out don't. The difference today, though, is that I am prepared both mentally and physically to deal with adversity. Once the club makes contact with the ball, I accept the outcome, be it good or bad. I then walk up to the ball relaxed, ready to take on whatever challenge lays ahead of me.

Russ's comments about keeping an honest score ring in my ears, and I resist the temptation to improve my lie or to take the few 'gimme's' these guys are willing to throw out. On my card, besides tracking my score, I also keep track of my game by recording the number of times I was on the green in regulation, as well as each of my putting scores and anything else I think may help. Walking off the 18th green, I slip the card into my back pocket for future analysis.

With my golfing buddies, over the last couple years, I have had to learn to be a good loser. Naturally, becoming a gracious and modest winner is going to take some time and to try to start today would be just too taxing.

"I want to meet this 'Russ' dude who gave you the lessons," Baker whines as he pays out the cash. If these guys hadn't taken so much of my money over the years, I might even feel sorry for them... but not likely.

"Yeah, Candleman. He must have some secrets my golf pro isn't sharing with me," Butcher chirps.

I don't honor them with an answer; I just smile, fold their money, and stuff it in my shirt pocket as a friendly reminder of an *'oh so sweet'* win. Today, I achieved all my goals: I shot in the eighties (something I haven't done for some time), I was confident in myself and my game, and I had fun. And most important, I beat the Butcher and the Baker! Russ's comments about this being my reward for the lessons and the practice couldn't have been more accurate! The only thing sweeter than this will be the high-pitched whine of these guys begging me for strokes when we meet again!

"So Bob, is the selling game going as well as the golf game?" Baker asks.

"As a matter of fact, it is! Thanks for asking."

Butcher sits up. "Bob, what happened to you? It wasn't that long ago you were complaining about how difficult it was to get ahead."

"I figured out that being successful in sales is no different than being successful in golf," I explain. "You need to understand the basic process, you need to practice your approach until it becomes unconscious, you need to learn to deal with adversity, and you need to keep accurate score so that you can tell where your opportunities are for improving."

"You know what, Bob... I have to hand it to you. I could never be a salesman, out there in the cruel world peddling my products and services to unwilling clients... even if my life depended on it. Cheers to you!" Butcher raises his glass to clink with the Baker and then with me.

I have heard these underhanded insults before, and in the past, I have ignored them - but not this time. "You guys have no idea what sales is all about! A good salesperson works with his or her clients to understand and identify the types of problems that they can solve, and then presents the solution. How is that any different from what you do?" I ask, trying to control my emotion.

Butcher raises his two hands in defence. "Relax Bob... all I was saying is that I couldn't sell."

"You guys don't get it; you are both salespeople just as much as I am - it's just not written on your business card! Butcher, how do you get your clientele? Did they walk up banging on your front door begging you to provide your services? I don't think so."

Butcher attempts to defend himself. "You're right; I did sell those people on my services. But..."

"I rest my case!" I interrupt. Silence lingers as the conversation sinks in. "The two of you talked about increasing your clientele. How do you do that?" I ask, still feeling the sting of insult.

Baker steps lightly into the conversation. "Well, I think there are a couple of ways. The first thing you can do is to head back to the books to improve your knowledge and skills - people are always looking for accountants who are a cut above."

"You're right, Baker; and in a perfect world, an investment in being better skilled at your profession will attract more clients. How else can you build your clientele?"

"You can keep your eyes and ears open for opportunities and when you find one, drop a card in their lap - that's what I do!" Butcher says.

"My old manager used to call that 'cash register' eyeballs. He told me the good salespeople always have their eyes open to new opportunities, at work and at play."

Baker shakes his head. "I don't think I'd be comfortable running around handing out business cards at every cocktail party I go to."

I spot my chance to make my point. "I agree, Baker. And you know what - the two of you could really benefit from the some of the sales training I've taken. Remember, I told you about Leveraging last time - would you like to Leverage the successful relationships you have built with your clients into many more new clients the same way I have?"

"So who's going to give us the training?" Butcher jumps in.

"I would," I say, matter-of-factly.

"And why would you do that for us?" Baker asks with a puzzled look.

"Three reasons: First, because you guys are my friends. Second, because I know if I have to deliver the training it will force me to keep my skills sharp. And third, because I want to prove to the two of you that your sales skills are just as valuable to you as they are to me!"

Baker jumps in first. "I'm in! You just name a time!"

"What the heck! Maybe I can even wear my plaid suit; if I'm going to act like a salesperson, I might as well dress like one too!" Butcher throws his hands up in the air and breaks out in laughter before I can speak. "I'm kidding, I'm kidding! Just let me know when and I would be happy to learn about Leveraging - maybe I'll even bring a couple of the newer lawyers... if that's all right?"

On the way home, I re-play our conversation in my head again and again. That's so typical of Butcher to get his little digs in whenever he can. People like Butcher don't realize - or won't admit - that we are all salespeople in one form or another; we are all trying to sell something we have to offer, whether it is our abilities –physical or mental, our knowledge, our opinions, or even our looks… and we are selling those things every day! People have to remember that their expertise isn't worth a plugged nickel until it is sold to someone willing to pay for it. The people who have the expertise *and* the ability to market themselves are the ones who will be in most demand.

Maybe operating under the 'Theory of Scarcity' over the years made me feel more like a peddler as opposed to a professional sales person, and perhaps that's why the digs and comments stung a little more than they should have. Feeling good about my career and myself should start with re-defining what a professional salesperson is:

A professional salesperson is someone who proactively approaches potential customers, helps them identify their problems–needs– opportunities, develops appropriate solutions, and then motivates them to act.

I should have this printed on the back of my card as a reminder of what I do. Striving to be a 'Professional Sales Person' by this definition is something that I can be proud of.

Driving around the corner, my house comes into view. There, sitting on the edge of the lawn, is David with his elbows resting on his knees and his chin cupped in his hands. When our eyes meet, he launches to his feet waving his arms, and I remember that this kid is unconditionally proud of me; the only job title he cares about is 'Dad'.

As I pull into our driveway, I have my window rolled down, and David starts with the cries of, "Dad, Dad!" David knows me too well - probably through experience, I guess. A single "Dad" usually isn't enough to break my thought pattern.

"Hi, David. How was your day?"

"Dad, Dad…" he says again. This must be serious, I think to myself. "…I need you to help me with my chocolate sales - let's go right now."

"Can't we do that another night?" I sigh.

"Dad, we have to do it tonight!" David says, jumping up and down and hanging on to my door handle, shouting through the window.

I think to myself that tonight is a night during which I would like to have a nice supper and just relax. "David, I'm sorry… but we are not doing it tonight and that is that!" I say decisively.

Chapter 13

Asking for the Business

"*D*ad, hurry up!" David calls as he runs ahead.

"I would if I didn't have to carry all these chocolates," I mumble, trying to pick up my pace.

Yes, David and I are out selling chocolates. Kids can be so persistent; it's like they don't understand the word "*No*". They ask again and again, slowly breaking down your resistance until they get the answer they are looking for. David was tenacious: he worked me over from the car to the house and finally into the bedroom closet before I broke down and gave in.

Something happens to most kids as they mature into adults, though - they stop asking when they hear "No". There are a lot of experts who tell you that when you say "No" to your child, you should never, ever give in. My opinion is that that may be great advice for dealing with children, but how good is it for raising future adults? I wonder if our stubbornness doesn't teach our kids to give up asking as soon as they get a *no*, or worse yet, teaches them to stop asking all together. I know of so many adults who are afraid to ask the question for fear the answer might be *no*. How many opportunities do these people miss in life as a result?

It's funny, whenever you hear of these people who became *gazillionaires*, a common thread that runs through many of them is their unwillingness to accept *no* as the final answer. It's almost as if each *no*

179

they hear makes them a little stronger and a little more determined to ask again. Unfortunately, with most of us, it's just the opposite.

I can think of so many examples of salespeople who have left us because they didn't want to ask for the business for fear of being rejected. They would meet a great prospect, identify a need, and then they would start presenting their solution - and they would keep on presenting in the hopes that their prospect would eventually get down on their knees and beg to be sold. When you ask these salespeople why their prospect didn't buy, they usually tell you that the prospect wasn't interested in the solution, but the truth is they never bothered to ask them to buy.

"Dad, should I call on that house?" David says, looking up to me with a wide smile.

"Go ahead, David." As he runs up the sidewalk, bursting with innocence, I smile and wonder how many adults would be able to do what he is doing.

My thoughts come full circle: so how should we people deal with *no*. I believe that if people hear no, if they *really* believe in what they are asking for, by all means, they should ask again. It's even more important that people never assume the answer to their request will be *no*, and not ask for what they want because of that preconception. By having the courage to ask, they open the opportunity of hearing *yes* - something they will never get by staying silent!

As David comes running back down the sidewalk toward me, I have my fingers crossed behind my back, and I ask, "How did you make out?"

He shrugs his shoulders. "They didn't want any," he says, and hand in hand we walk down the sidewalk to the next house.

House after house, the answer is the same... again and again. Although the "No's" don't seem to be bothering him, they bother me. There is a temptation to dig into my pocket and buy the whole box, but what would that teach him? I wonder to myself, how else can I help? The answer hits me between the eyes!

I kneel down and look at my son eye to eye. "David, are you interested in learning a new way to sell those chocolates?"

"What do you think, Dad?" he says acknowledging his difficulties.

First things first: I pull a comb out of my pocket and do my best to fix up his hair. Then I put his ball cap back on straight and try to brush the wrinkles out of his jersey. "David, people like to buy from someone who looks and acts successful!"

We take a seat on the curb to begin the lesson. "OK, David. Why are you selling the chocolates?"

"You know that Dad... we're raising money for the team!"

"I know... but what are you going to use the money for?"

His face brightens. "If we raise enough money, we're going to take a bus trip and we get to play in a tournament!"

"Excellent, David." I open up one of the boxes of chocolates. "Now I want you to close your eyes and open your mouth," and I set the chocolate in his mouth. David tries to chew with his mouth closed, but the smile on his face makes it difficult. "Tell me how the chocolate tastes," I order.

While still enjoying the last morsels, Dave garbles, "Dad, these chocolates are sooooooo good!"

"Good, David. Now you're ready!" He opens his eyes and looks at me, wondering what he is ready for.

During the next ten minutes, we prepare a short presentation and practice it again and again. He is going to give his name, the name of his team, and ask if he has called at a bad time. He will then explain that the money that is raised from selling chocolates will be used to pay for the bus trip and the entry fee for a little league baseball tournament. Finally, he will describe how delicious the chocolates are, and most important, he will look them straight in the eye and ask them, "Would you be willing to help out our team by buying one box, or do you think you would like two?"

We talk about how some people will say "Yes" and how some will say "No", but regardless, David has to remember to thank them for their time. "... and remember, David; every time you hear a *no*, you are a step closer to the *yes* you are looking for!"

I stand there, watching in anticipation as he runs to the house, up the stairs, and around the corner out of sight. One minute goes by... then another, and another... A good sign, I try to convince myself.

Finally, David comes around the corner and takes the stairs, two at a time. He is holding up money in one hand and the boxes of chocolates in the other.

"What happened, David?" I ask as he approaches.

He stops in front of me, catching his breath. "I did it just like we practiced, Dad! When I asked her if she wanted one box or two, she took two... " he pauses to take a breath, "... and then she told me she was allergic to chocolate!"

As he runs off to the next house, my smile is so big my cheeks begin to ache. What a great kid! We tour our block and do a few more houses and then decide to call it a night.

David yells as we walk in the back door, "Mom... Dad and I sold almost all the chocolates!"

Sandy appears from around the corner. "Good for you, David."

"You sold all the chocolates, David. Not me!" I correct him. "Hey Sandy, you should have seen him... he's definitely a chip off the old block!"

"I don't need chocolate sales to tell me that," Sandy says. "David, you better run off and get after your homework," and she disappears back around the corner.

Watching Sandy disappear, I find myself thinking of the team effort that is going on here in this household, the team effort that is helping me bring my sales back up in more ways than Jeff Townes could hope for. I decide then and there that I want to do something nice for my wife, and I go to find my daughter. "Amanda, what are your Mom's favorite flowers?"

"Tulips, Dad... you know that!" she says, looking up from a book.

I think to myself, "That's right! Sandy loves tulips - fresh cut!" No wonder she said I was lucky to give roses to Sarah. I shudder to think of what would have happened had I used tulips! Then, I pull out a piece of paper and wrack my brain trying to think of all of the things Sandy has told me she loves -little things to me, big things to her!

By the time I go to bed, I have my list, I have made a couple of calls, and most important, I have put together a plan. Cuddling up to Sandy, I can tell she really is asleep and within a few minutes... so am I.

I awaken to the sun shining and the birds singing, and it suddenly occurs to me I have a breakfast meeting with Jeff this morning. I bolt out of bed and rush between the bathroom and bedroom getting ready. Every couple of minutes, I check my watch, which helps to maintain peak anxiety levels. On the way to the car, I slip on my jacket and adjust my tie. With the car started, I watch in the rear-view mirror waiting for the instant I can slip under the opening garage door... and then I am off.

Pulling into the parking lot of my office building, my anxiety fades when I spot Jeff getting out of his car. I whip into my stall and Jeff stands by his car, waiting for me to join him. Within minutes we are sitting at our table sipping on our first coffees of the day. "So you want to talk about asking for the business, do you?" Jeff asks.

I think to myself that 'asking for the business' sounds so much nicer than 'closing the sale'. 'Closing' sounds like the end of the sales process, when in fact, with our business, the relationship is just getting started when the contract is signed. "I do, Jeff; I want to learn all the tricks you used to get those clients of yours to sign contracts."

"Actually Bob, it's very simple: my only trick is that I *do* ask. I believe the only way salespeople can learn how to effectively ask for the business is by doing it - again and again. Some salespeople ask too soon and too often while others don't ask often enough. The difference is the ones who ask too often learn how and when to ask for the business through experience. It's difficult to learn this skill if you are not prepared to ask the client to buy."

As I listen to him speak about asking for the business, the situation with David from the night before comes to my mind and I begin to chuckle. "My son David has learned how to be an effective closer..." and I go on to recap the story.

"Excellent story, Bob. David is what we call a persistent closer. You see, there are two different ways to ask for the business; first, you can be persistent, like David, where you keep asking over and over again until you get the answer you are looking for. Or second, you can be blunt; you ask directly for what you want in no uncertain terms. You see, some people can be persistent but may not ask directly for what they want. On the other hand, there are others who might be blunt but then they're not persistent - they ask once and when they hear 'no', they don't ask again. Being great at asking for the business is really a combination of these two styles. Bob, how would you describe your closing style? And what do you think you need to do to get better?"

"I think I would probably lean more towards the persistent closing style. I guess I need to get better at asking directly for the business."

"Good, Bob. Half the battle begins with understanding where you need to improve. Let's switch gears now. When does the process of asking for the business start?

"Actually, I guess it is right after you have presented all of the information on your solution... ." I absorb what I have just said and then continue, "... but I think it's really more than that."

"What do you mean?"

"I think asking for the business is just a series of small sales. For example, when you conduct an initial interview properly, and you decide to book another appointment with them and they agree to meet again, you have just made your first small sale with that client. Next, when you ask all of your questions to discover their needs and get their agreement on the needs you identified together, you have made another small sale. The next small sale is when you have presented the solution and you get them to agree that your solution solves the problems that were identified. If these three small sales have been made, getting them to sign the contract is simply a matter of asking."

"So Bob, how do you know if the three smaller sales have been made?"

"I would say by asking specific questions at each stage in the sales process."

"You're right! You can and should do that all the way through the sales process, but sometimes they will give you 'soft' yes's all the way through the sales process only to give a 'hard' no when you ask them to sign the contract. Asking them to make a buying decision is when the rubber really hits the road - that's when you know the three smaller sales have been made!"

Sitting there, I silently reflect back over the years. I know from past experience, both good and bad, exactly what Jeff means: it's so easy to just keep on presenting more information, waiting for them to beg you to sell them your solution... but the reality is that doesn't happen. Assuming you have a trusting relationship and an agreed-upon need, when you have presented enough information for them to make a decision, you have to be prepared to ask them to act.

After a moment Jeff starts again. "So Bob, exactly how do you ask them to act?"

I think to myself and then begin. "There are a number of ways you can do it. You can cut straight to the chase and say, "Based on what we have learned about your situation, we both agree there is a problem as well as a solution. I would like to take the next steps to put that solution in place. Does that sound fair?" Or, if you have presented a couple of different solutions, you might say, "These are two possible solutions to your problem. Which solution do you feel best meets your needs today?" Another possible way to get them to act is to simply assume the sale is made. If they agree with their need, and understand how your solution solves their problem, you can assume you have made the sale and start by taking the appropriate steps - like completing the paperwork."

"Great ideas, Bob. After you have asked the question, what's next?"

I sit there, saying nothing. After a long and pregnant pause, a smile spreads across Jeff's face, and he is smiling when he says, "You're right Bob, silence is the most powerful closer of all. Once you have asked them to act, you have to shut up and wait for them to respond - the silence can be uncomfortable, but you have to hang in there. After all, if you have given them all the information they need to make a decision, there's nothing more that needs to be said."

"I have had to learn this through experience, Jeff. So often, I would ask a closing question and before the prospect could answer, I would jump in and start talking again. I've learned that when you ask a question for a buying decision, you have really reached a fork in the road with your prospect. The next words out of their mouth will tell you which road you are on - are they going to buy or do they need more information?"

"I learned those same lessons, Bob. If the prospect doesn't want to act on the solution, what do you do then?"

"If they won't sign the contract, then it is almost always one or more of these three problems. First, they don't feel comfortable with either our company or me. Second, they don't believe they have a need or a problem, and third, they don't believe I offer the best solution for their problem."

"Exactly, Bob. If they have unanswered questions or concerns about any of these things, they will either say "No" or they will avoid or defer making a commitment. So what do you do then?"

"If you are getting hesitation or a *no* decision, you need to go back and ask questions about each of the three potential areas to pinpoint the problem. For example, does my prospect have any questions or concerns about our company or me that I need to address? If that doesn't reveal any concerns, I have to move to the next area to confirm that they agree with the need. Finally, I need to check the solution I have offered. It is not only important that they believe I am offering a good solution, but more specifically, do they believe my solution will solve the need or problem we have identified?"

"And what if you don't uncover any concerns?" Jeff quizzes me.

"If there are no concerns in any of the three areas, then I need to ask them to act again."

"What if they are comfortable with you, agree with the need or problem that has been identified and understand the solution, but are uncomfortable with the price?" he comes back.

"It's not so much the price of your solution that matters; what's more important is how that price tag relates to the amount of pain they are feeling by not satisfying the need or solving the problem you have identified. In other words, if the pain of the problem is significant, they will pay a higher price for a solution. When the pain of paying for the solution is more significant than the problem they are solving, they won't buy it - it's that simple.

"Excellent perspective. Also Bob, when you ask questions to discover their needs, some of those questions should uncover how much they are prepared to spend to solve a potential problem. Your solution should either fit within that budget or you should have supporting evidence to justify why they should be spending more."

"One other thing, Jeff - if my prospect tells me they can't afford my solution, I simply ask, "So Ms. Prospect, what can you afford?" If they come back with a reasonable number, I might ask, "If I were to put together a solution at that price, would you be prepared to act on it?" The answers to these questions tell me whether I am dealing with someone who is prepared to act if the price is right. After I have those answers, I can either ask more questions to re-define the magnitude of the problem so that it exceeds the cost of the solution or I can adjust the solution to fit the dollar figure they have agreed to."

"Great idea, Bob, but I have one last challenge for you: The prospect likes your solution and they can afford it, but the problem is they don't want to do it right now. How do you deal with that?"

I sit there and reflect; I have heard these types of objections too many times before. With my thoughts organized, I say, "I believe you need to uncover what the benefits of making a decision today are versus the risks of postponing the decision to a later date. If the benefits outweigh the risks then you should ask them to act now. On the other hand, sometimes people do need time to think before they make a decision, and if that's the case, you have to respect that - after all, you've worked too hard at building a good relationship with your prospect to spoil it at the finish line by pushing too hard."

"Bob, the only thing I'm not clear on is why you wanted me to help you!" he exclaims.

"You gave me some great ideas, Jeff, but you also helped me to tap into some of those things I already knew about asking for the business but had forgotten over the years. Asking for the business is not about smoke and mirrors... or about using high-pressure closing tactics. If you have a prospect who is comfortable with you, who sees their problem, and who understands how your solution will solve it, it simply comes down to having the courage to ask."

As the waiter passes by, I hand off the cash and the bill. "How have things been going for you, Jeff?"

"Great Bob... just great," he says. His tone is unconvincing.

"It doesn't sound too great to me, Jeff. What's the problem?"

"I find, Bob, that I have to spend so much time coaxing some of the salespeople to do their jobs that I don't have time for the ones who have the potential to do really well - some days I feel like I'm a human bicycle pump. There are a few salespeople who show up in my office every other day with their self-esteem and self-confidence deflated; I pump them back up and then they're off again until the next time - it's like they're ego junkies and I'm their dealer."

I cringe at the thought that he may be describing his relationship with me; this tire pump analogy has 'atta boy' written all over it. "Jeff, am I one of the deflated people you are talking about?"

"Not at all, Bob; you have invested a lot of time and energy into improving your results - you're the kind of salesperson I want to have more time for."

"Thanks, Jeff. I really do appreciate the time you have given me. Do these people you pump up produce a lot of business?"

Jeff chuckles. "If that were the case, I wouldn't have so much trouble with it! Most of these salespeople are just doing enough to get by."

"So why don't you wean them and concentrate your time on those who are putting in the effort?"

His eyes go wide. "I can't do that; the good salespeople don't need me like these people do. Besides, I've looked at the numbers, and I've figured out that if I could just get the bottom half of our team to raise their sales numbers up to average, we could crush all of our targets for the division!"

It reminds me of the teacher who wanted all of his students to be above the class average. "Jeff, I told you I would be willing to help out. If there is anything I can do for you, you let me know."

"I appreciate that, Bob. And when I figure out how you can help, I'll be taking you up on your offer. Oh yes, and thanks for breakfast!" he says as we both get up. "So Bob, what do you have on today?"

"I'm going to be on the phone. I've got a few initial interviews to prepare for, and I have my final presentation with Selectrum this afternoon," I grin. "And tonight I've got a special evening planned with Sandy."

"Is it your anniversary?"

"No, she's been beyond patient with me, and she's helped me so much with turning my game around that I want to do something really nice for her."

Jeff checks his watch and starts off down the hall. Over his shoulder he calls back, "I think I hear the sound of escaping air. I had better get back to my office and get my pump ready. Have a good time tonight!"

The phone on my desk rings, and I walk over to pick it up and answer, "Good morning! Bob Stephens... " and my day is off.

By early afternoon, I am finished my appointment with Selectrum and I am racing off to the nearest shopping mall to get ingredients for the evening ahead. Shopping is a blur, but soon I have visited even more stores than I intended. With my arms burning from carrying the collection of bags and boxes, I race from one end of the shopping mall to the far opposite end, where my car is parked.

On the way home, I phone once again to confirm the coast is clear. Sandy had told me a few days ago that she had appointments all afternoon and that she wouldn't be home until late. I remember her saying... a number of times, "Bob, make sure you get home early so the kids are not alone too long." At first, I thought about my 'when it's work, it's work' speech, but with the number of days I have left early for work and come home late, I know this is one obligation I can't pass off.

In the garage, I reach into the back seat and grab all of the parcels with both hands and every finger to avoid making a second trip, and the house is still and quiet as I set my packages on the counter. I rummage through the linen closet to find one of the bib-style aprons I had been given for Father's Day in years gone by, slip it over my head, and tie it awkwardly behind my back.

Then, as I create my version of a gourmet meal, the dishes stack higher and higher. I ask myself, "How hard can it be?" as I glance between the recipes and the pictures of each chosen dish. In my mind, I attempt to picture the collage of dishes as the final meal. "It's going to be beautiful!" I say aloud, rubbing my hands with glee. I'm so lost in my cooking that I nearly jump out of my skin when David comes barreling through the back door screaming, "Hi Mom, I'm home!"

With my heart still pounding, I begin to rally the troops. "Hi, David! Your mom's going to be home later, and I need your help! Where's Amanda?"

Before he can answer, the door opens again. "Is that you, Amanda?" I call out cautiously.

"What are you doing home?" she asks, looking around in disbelief. Before I can answer she blurts out, "What have you done to the kitchen?"

"I'm making Mom supper. Can you help me out?" I beg her.

After a few explanations and bribes, everyone is feverishly running around the house with me leading the charge. Although I am confident Sandy will enjoy my attempts at cooking, she will appreciate a clean house even more.

An hour or so later I walk around the house for a final inspection. "OK, you kids pack some clothes; you're going to be spending the night with Grandma!" There's something about going to Grandma's that can't be beat... like no rules, lots of good food, and the topping of a generous sprinkle of treats. "Now, when Mom gets home, I want the two of you to... " and I proceed to fill them in on the balance of the plan.

In the back entry, I hear the door close, sounding the start of our evening. When Sandy walks into the kitchen, she looks around, confused... perhaps even dumbfounded. On the counter are dozens of freshly cut tulips arranged in a rainbow of colors. I stand there in a freshly cleaned and pressed black suit and white shirt, finished off with the tie she's told me she loves. With my white gloves, I hold up a small tray sporting a half glass of red wine, surrounded with bite-sized chocolates. "Tonight," I say to Sandy, "I will prove my love for you!"

As the smile grows, her eyes start to sparkle and shine. Balancing the tray, I hand her the glass of wine and lean across to hug her. The hug advances to a kiss without a word spoken. After a few moments, I move on to my surprises.

"The water is running in the bathtub, honey, and I've bought you a few special bath things. While you're enjoying your bath, I'm going to take the kids to your mom's place."

"Bob, this is so nice!" she says as I entice her towards the bathroom. The bathroom is gently lit with candlelight and an assortment of bath oils, soaps, and scents placed around the room. I set the tray of chocolates within arms' reach of the tub and back out through the door, pulling it closed as I go. Then I call out to the kids and realize that they are already waiting in the car, anxious to get their pampering from Grandma on the road as well.

When I get back home, I tiptoe around the house lighting candles and, of course, I put on Sandy's favorite 'I'm in the mood' music. As I come around the corner, I catch her standing in front of the mirror modeling her new outfit for the evening. As she swirls to face me I swear she looks more beautiful now than the day I first fell in love with her.

The evening unfolds with good food, good wine, good music, and great conversation. Then, at the perfect moment, I begin the part of the evening that I had practiced (role-played!) again and again: I drop down on one knee in front of her and out of my pocket, I pull a small blue velvet ring box. "Sandy, this box contains a special ring for you... a ring that represents all those times I have forgot to say how beautiful you are, what a great friend you are, how much I respect you, and most important, how much I love you. Whenever you look at this ring from this day forward, I want you to think of it as a symbol of everything you mean to me and how much I appreciate all your help over the past few months. I also bought the ring in this box for me, to always be a reminder to say those wonderful things that you deserve to hear and to do those things that show how much I appreciate you." I crack open the box, pull the ring out, and with both of our hands shaking, I slip the ring on her finger.

When the hugs, kisses, and the tears subside, I finish off the evening with a little icing for our cake to show her that all her patience, support and help has not been in vain. "By the way, Sandy, today Selectrum signed the largest contract our division has placed this year... and they signed it with me. Imagine that! One down... thirty-nine to go!"

Chapter 14
Protecting your most valuable asset!

$\mathcal{T}$he alarm sounds to start the day: "Ting, tong, ding... ting, tong, ding... ". Now that's how an alarm is supposed to sound, I think. My theory is that the alarm clock is one of the most important things you will ever purchase. After all, it signals the beginning of each new day. In fact, I muse, the only thing better than waking up to my new clock would be waking up to a warm ocean breeze!

Today is going to be a great day! This morning, I am speaking to the division, and I have decided my talk will be titled: *Protecting Your Most Valuable Asset*. It has now been four months since I turned my business around, and, in that time, Jeff has frequently asked me to talk to everyone. Then, after working with some of the new salespeople, I started seeing them fall into the same bad habits that almost led to my demise. I feel I am an expert on this topic, considering I have learned as much from my failures as I have from my successes.

I roll out of bed and bounce off to the shower. By the time I am out of the bathroom, the scent of fresh, strong coffee hangs in the air. I walk into the closet and pull out a brand new suit, shirt, and tie - Sandy bought them all a week or so ago, but I wanted to save them for today. After all, I've got to set a good example for the team!

I stand in front of the mirror admiring my new ensemble. The first thing that catches my eye is the gleam coming off my shoes –compliments of David, of course! I work my way up the sharp pleats of my pants to my crisp white shirt and an elegant tie, which finishes off the look. It occurs to me that a transformation has taken place in the person smiling back at me, over the last few months. I walk over and grab my coat off the bed and fling it over my shoulder on the way to the kitchen and catch a glimpse of a familiar friend on my way past the mirror.

When I walk in the kitchen, Sandy is hugging her cup of coffee. "Good morning, honey. I poured your coffee a few minutes ago, but it should still be hot." She pauses to look me over, and with a smile and wink, she says, "Speaking of hot - don't you look good today!"

"Thank you, Sandy! This new suit you bought me is very classy."

"A classy suit for a classy guy! I thought you said you were golfing today with Russ. Aren't you taking your golf clothes?"

"Actually, I'm not golfing with Russ; he invited me out to the club for lunch. I was a little surprised to hear from him - I am really curious as to why he would want to have lunch with me."

"Maybe he figures he owes you a lunch after all those golf lessons you took," Sandy says with a nudge. "The cereal and milk is on the counter and there's yogurt there, too," she says, pointing. The fact that I can fit into this suit makes eating breakfasts like this tolerable.

Over the next half hour, I give Sandy the high points of my chosen topic between spoonfuls of cereal and sips of coffee. With my confidence well intact, I make the loop through the kids' rooms for a kiss good-bye and then back through the kitchen on the way out the door. "I know you're going to do great, honey!" Sandy says, and then gives me a big kiss for good luck.

When I walk by the meeting room on the way to my office, I notice it is already half-full. Front and centre is my good buddy, Teddie, chatting it up with Sarah. I smile to see this; it has taken Teddie a while, but he has finally come around. At first, he would just ask me how it was going. I tried to be modest about my successes, but my sales numbers in the monthly bulletin told the whole story anyway. Later on, Teddie asked if I would be willing to listen to his various sales presentations, and then he asked to hear mine. Eventually the results started showing up, and now my friend is rising in the pack. I realize that Teddie had to do it his way, and he had to do it on his own schedule.

Sarah and a few others are still well ahead of me on the year-to-date results, but I am closing the gap. It seems that the better I get, the better Sarah gets as well. These days everything about Sarah radiates success and confidence - her results, the way she carries herself, the way she looks... even her love life. Sarah and Bruce dated for a while, but eventually Sarah decided to break it off... or so I understand from Teddie. Since then Sarah hasn't had any problems finding eligible men to date. From time to time, the flowers show up on her desk but now they are from legitimate love interests. I've undoubtedly learned my lesson.

When I walk into my office, I notice a few notes on the corner of my desk from Tina, and I flip through them looking for points of interest. It wasn't that long ago I thought my clients needed me at their beck and call, but now that my clients are used to dealing with Tina, they seem to want to talk to her even more. What's even better is they now look at me in a far more professional light - they know what my expertise is, and whenever they need me, they call me directly.

"Are you ready to go?" Jeff calls as he walks towards my office.

"I'm just gathering up my notes... I'll be right there," I reply. Jeff continues by.

Jeff has really made some strides as well over the last few months - my hat goes off to him. He hasn't been hiring as many new salespeople as when he first arrived, but the ones he has hired have been the kind of people I would be proud to introduce to my best clients. I still find Jeff's management style with them too 'hands-on' for me, but without a doubt, he teaches them the skills they need to become successful. At least with Jeff, he has that one characteristic that really matters - he deeply cares about his salespeople.

With my notes organized and my portfolio in hand, I head out; as I approach the open door of the meeting room, I can hear the rumble of the group. I tell myself the anxiety building inside me will make my talk more vibrant - or at least I hope so, and by the time I reach the front of the room, the noise has died to all but a few isolated conversations.

Jeff raises both hands in the air to draw everyone's attention. "This morning it is my pleasure to introduce Bob Stephens. Although you all know him, I wanted to tell you some things about Bob that maybe you didn't know." He goes on to talk about my background, including my education, a little about my family, and when I started with the company.

"How many of you have ever heard of Rocket-Man?" Jeff asks, and instantly, the hands in the room go up. My smile goes wide, and my face turns red; Jeff had asked me ahead of time if it would be all right if he introduced my alias... but I wasn't quite expecting this.

"I am not going to tell you about the origins of the nickname - you're going to have to ask Teddie and Sarah about that - but let me tell you something about Rocket-Man's past... "

For the next couple of minutes, Jeff talks about the sales achievements from my early days in sales. There were many years when I discounted those accomplishments because I didn't believe I could ever achieve them again. From my new perspective, those early successes now represent the summit on the climb towards new peaks I am striving for.

Then Jeff moves on to point out some of my less-flattering statistics, from the years when I really bottomed out. I knew that was coming too, but it's a little embarrassing nonetheless.

"We're not here today to focus on these numbers, though." In a single swoop, Jeff flips the page on the easel to reveal the sales numbers and charts that tell the story of my success over the last four months. "Today we are going to talk about..." and he flips the page once again and reads aloud, "Rocket-Man: The Resurrection!".

Jeff had told me everything he was going to say... except this. I stand there dumbfounded as I stare at Rocket-Man while everyone applauds, waiting for me to begin. Up until this moment, I knew exactly what I was going to say and now, not a single word comes to mind. I look down at my notes, trying to organize my thoughts and gain my composure. "Thank you, Jeff. I'm not sure I would describe my achievements as the *resurrection of Rocket-Man* - there are a lot of salespeople in this room who are doing better than I and deserve the recognition. I must admit though, I have been singing in my car a lot more these days." Everyone laughs politely - except for Sarah and Teddie, of course - they giggle the loudest of all.

"Today the title of my talk is *Protecting Your Most Valuable Asset.*" I pause to let that sink in, and then I continue with, "So what do you think your most valuable asset might be?"

Rudy's hand springs up. "Your time?"

"Good answer, Rudy. Having good time management is certainly a big contributor to success. But, that wasn't the asset I was thinking of."

Sarah's hand slowly rises and in a sarcastic tone she asks, "It wouldn't be your attitude, would it, Bob?"

I give her a wink of acknowledgement - we both know all too well how your attitude can lead to your success or your failure. "Yes, Sarah, that's right. The higher your attitude, the higher your altitude," I say, holding my hand high in the air. "What does a good attitude mean to you?" I ask the group.

The hands slowly start to pop up around the room. "Karen, what do you think?"

"I think having a good attitude means being able to deal with the ups and the downs you experience in sales," she answers.

"Excellent point, Karen. Having a good attitude does not mean that you are happy and positive all of the time - we all get down from time to time. I have days where I feel down and there is no real explanation for it... maybe I'm tired or maybe it is just a grey day. I have other days where I get depressed because the prospecting calls aren't going my way or perhaps I get a disappointing call from a client. But it's times like this where a good attitude can make the difference; a person with a good attitude remembers that feeling low from time to time is natural. Trying to think your way out of a down time only intensifies the mood."

Now Karen raises her hand. "Does that mean I should focus on happy thoughts or pretend I'm not feeling down?"

"I don't know for sure, but for me, I find that denying that I am feeling down or trying to offset the mood with the positive thoughts only masks the way I am feeling. My advice is when you get down, accept it, don't dwell on it, and don't try to think your way out of it - it will pass as quickly as it came."

Rudy stands up to make his point. "I'd like to get some advice on a situation I recently went through: I had a client who had agreed to the specifications and the pricing and was ready to sign the contract... all I needed was head office's approval. By the time they were finished changing what we had put together, the client decided not to go with us and placed the contract with the competition. I was so disappointed I was ready to quit."

"We're glad you didn't, Rudy. Tell us how you handled it?"

"I finally told myself I had done everything right and that this situation was beyond my control."

"Rudy, you learned a valuable lesson about control and how it affects a good attitude. There are steps in the sales process we have a great deal of control over, and there are others that we don't. For example, do we have control over the number of Leveraging interviews we ask for?" Everyone nods. "What about picking up the phone and calling the referrals we get to book appointments?"

Sarah speaks up. "Well, you have control over making the calls, but you don't have control over whether they book an appointment with you."

"So how do you control the number of appointments you book, Sarah?"

"By making more calls - you always have control over that."

"What about the number of initial interviews you book, or the number of meetings you arrange for discovering needs or presenting solutions? Do you have control over those?"

"The further you go down in the sales process, the less control you have," Sarah states.

"Precisely, Sarah!" I focus my attention back on Rudy and continue. "In the example you gave us, you and your client were right at the end of the sales process. The problem is both the client and head office had all the control over whether this deal went forward. Is that right?"

Three or four voices call out in unison. "Right!"

"For years, I rewarded and punished myself for things I couldn't control - things like results. When the results were there, I was the happiest person in the office... and when they weren't, I beat myself up. The ironic thing was that most of the time when I was celebrating the results that were coming in, I wasn't doing the important things that had led to the results - things like prospecting, making telephone calls, and so on. Later on, when the results dropped off, I punished myself - even though I was back to prospecting and making calls again. What I have learned is that you must always reward yourself for doing the things that you can control - those things that contribute directly to your long-term success. There's nothing wrong with celebrating when the results come in as long as you regularly reward yourself for the activities that make the results possible. What else can you do to protect your most valuable asset?"

Teddie pipes up. "Watch who you have coffee with?" Sarah looks at Teddie and me with a grin and begins nodding.

"Good point, Teddie. Everyone gets frustrated and needs someone to vent with periodically. The problem arises when talking about what's wrong becomes the only thing you have in common with the people around you, and we have learned that a bad attitude can be as contagious as the common cold if your defenses are not strong. So, here are a couple of simple rules to remember: first, if one of your peers is frustrated and wants to vent, hear them out - most times they are just looking for someone to listen. However, if the complaining becomes a pattern, you need to either help them look for a solution, or if the problem is beyond their control, help them to recognize that. Second, don't fuel their fire by volunteering more problems of your own even if you are being encouraged to do so; adding additional evidence to support *what's wrong* is only going to make both of you feel worse. And, if you happen to be the one who is feeling frustrated or down, by all means, look to your peers for support. Remember though, the more you complain about what is wrong, the more you draw on their enthusiasm and optimism. Think of optimism like a bank account, and then make sure your withdrawals never exceed your deposits!"

"I second that!" Teddie shouts.

"There is another point I'd like to make about having people to talk to," I continue. "I believe we all need a coach, and I'd like to introduce you to mine. Jeff, will you stand up, please?" With Jeff standing there awkwardly, I walk over beside him and put my hand on his shoulder. "I was at a point in my career where I knew I wanted to improve, but I wasn't sure how to do it. I needed a coach who could help me figure out what was wrong and the best way to fix it, but I also needed someone who could help me maintain a good attitude. Jeff Townes fit the job description perfectly... thank you Jeff!" Our eyes lock on one another, we smile from ear to ear, and we shake hands. The expression on Jeff's face tells the whole the story and without him saying so much as a word, I make my way to the front of the room again.

"Let's move on. To maintain a good attitude, you also need to manage something else - your thoughts. Does anyone know what I mean by managing your thoughts?"

All across the room there is a series of blank stares back at me, so I decide a more direct question might be more appropriate. "Does anyone here ever get stressed?" Around the room, the hands shoot up and the chatter begins. "So what kinds of things cause stress for you?"

The examples start flying: "Making telephone calls to new prospects," one person offers. "Dealing with unhappy clients," another person adds.

"Good examples, but let me describe another type of stress... let's say you have a great prospect who is close to signing a contract. They ask you to call them on Monday to arrange a time to get the contract signed. You call as promised, but they don't answer so you leave a voice message - no big deal. The afternoon passes, and they don't return your call - your thoughts begin to build. You go home, and that night, your thoughts periodically flip back to the situation; you try to figure out why they didn't return your call. The next morning when you get into the office, you find they still haven't phoned you back. You call again, and you leave another voicemail. Throughout the day, you wait for them to call back, but they don't. Your effectiveness dwindles as your thoughts take on mass - maybe they are unhappy about something, maybe they have changed their mind, maybe they are going to buy from someone else. That night you can hardly focus on anything else. You pick away at your supper because you have lost your appetite, and instead of enjoying the evening with your family, you isolate yourself because you want to be alone. You have gone from imagining what could be wrong to convincing yourself the deal is off. By the end of the evening, you have thought of all of the rippling ramifications - I am going to miss my sales targets, my income is going to drop, my career is in jeopardy, and on and on it goes.

The next morning you go in to work early - seeing as how you can't sleep anyway - and you phone them again. This time he does answer, and he explains he has been away sick and apologizes for not getting back to you. You book your appointment, hang up the phone, and kick yourself for being so silly."

Rudy pops his hand up and says, "I think the doctors call those anxiety attacks, Bob!" and the laughter starts.

"Maybe the doctors call them anxiety attacks, but I call them 'thought' attacks. Particularly in sales, thought attacks can be paralyzing. Here are some things to remember about thought attacks. Most important: thoughts are just thoughts. You see, thought attacks occur when your mind and body react as if each thought were fact. The example I gave was real... it happened to me. The stress was real, the loss of appetite was real, and the fact that I couldn't sleep was real. The only thing that wasn't real was my thoughts about the situation."

"So how do I control my thoughts?" Rudy asks.

"It begins with knowing that you can control them if you choose to. Thoughts are just thoughts, and you need to remind yourself of that, especially when your thoughts are getting away from you. You also need to remember that you are the creator of each of your thoughts, and therefore you have the control to think - or not think - about whatever you want. When you find yourself feeling stressed, ask yourself if you are suffering from the symptoms of a thought attack. Ask yourself: is the stress based on facts, or have you let your thoughts get away from you? If you do not control them, they will control you."

Everyone nods and smiles in approval.

"I am going to wrap up by telling you a valuable lesson I learned early in my career: I had just come back from an appointment, and I was on top of the world. This wasn't any appointment though... at this appointment, my new client had just signed the largest contract I had placed so far in my career. When I ran into my manager, John Andrews, I must have been floating about six inches off the floor. John spotted my excitement right away and quizzed me for details. After I told him the whole story, John looked me straight in eye and shook my hand enthusiastically, and said, "Welcome to sales!" and then he walked away down the hall. A couple of days later, I arrived at work to see my newest client featured on the front page of the business section. The article disclosed how they had lost their biggest customer to their competition, and now there was fear of layoffs and possibly even bankruptcy. Within an hour of reading the article, I got a call from the controller confirming my worst nightmare... they were cancelling the contract with me. In a heartbeat, my big sale had evaporated into thin air. Later that day, I was shuffling down the hallway with my head hung and my shoulders slumped in defeat when I ran into John again. I told him every painful detail and when I was done, he looked me straight in the eye, shook my hand enthusiastically, and said, "Welcome to sales!", and then he walked off down the hall. I stood there dumbfounded and confused, but late, the picture came clear. The highest highs and the lowest lows are familiar territory for salespeople; to survive, a good salesperson has to be able to live through both. Thank you for your time this morning."

After the applause fades, the training class transforms into a group therapy session. The room becomes abuzz with everyone opening up and sharing their own personal victories and challenges - some are exhilarating, some are depressing, and some are even funny... but all of them are real. In the end, we agree that a good attitude is in fact the most valuable asset we each have; with a good attitude, problems seem small and opportunities appear to be unlimited. And most important, everything seems a lot more fun.

I am no sooner back to my office when it is time to make my way to my lunch appointment with Russ. As I walk to my car, I think about everything I have learned from Russ. Not only has he had a dramatic impact on my golf game, indirectly he has helped me get my sales turned around. At first, Sandy was uptight about the cost of the lessons, but as my cheques got bigger, her concerns got smaller. Hopping into the car, a smile comes across my face as I mentally tabulate how many golf lessons Butcher and Baker have paid for over the last few months - success is so sweet!

After I pull into Canyon Meadows, I navigate through the parking lot looking for a premium spot to park. I notice an open stall close to the clubhouse with all of the BMWs, Mercedes, and Porches. This must be my lucky day, I think. After carefully maneuvering into the stall, I rub the dash of my car and give it a gentle pat - you're going to be so happy rubbing shoulders with all of your new friends, I tell it.

In the clubhouse, I spot Russ sitting at a table along the windows overlooking the eighteenth green. "Hi Russ, how are you doing?" I call.

He turns and gets up to shake hands. "Great, Bob. Thanks for joining me today."

Over the next twenty minutes, we talk about everything except why he has asked me here today. As each golfer walks off the 18th green, when they notice Russ sitting there, like clockwork, they acknowledge him with a wave, a tip of the hat, or a smile.

"Russ, you sure must keep busy with all of the golfers beating down your door for lessons."

"I am busy, but it's not because they are beating down my door," Russ replies with a smile. "Bob, there are a couple of reasons I invited you out here today. First, I want to give you your last lesson."

"Last lesson... what is that?" I ask, confused.

"When you talked about what you wanted to achieve by taking lessons, one of the things was that you wanted to have fun, is that right?"

"Yes, Russ, that's right. And I am having fun."

"I'm glad to hear that. Having fun is critically important to being a great golfer. Why do you think that is?"

"I guess if you're having fun, you have unlimited energy for practicing, playing, and improving your game. I know with myself that now, instead of staying in bed, I am up early almost every morning, hitting balls and loving it."

"Exactly! Great golfers become great because they have fun at practice and at play. When you enjoy doing something, you are able to tap into an energy source that lies deep within us all. It's true for golf, and it is definitely true for the career you are in. Wouldn't you agree?"

I sit there absorbing his comments. When I first started out selling, it was a blast - I was up early and in the office before everyone else. I worked hard all day long, and when everyone was heading out the door at quitting time, I stayed late to get ready for the next day - being at work was fun, and I loved my job. When the fun started drifting away though, so did the energy. For years I dragged myself to work, looked for every opportunity to do everything else but my job, and I always escaped the office early. Now that I have re-discovered the fun in my career, I have also been able to tap back into the energy source Russ described.

"I couldn't agree more, Russ; sales can either be the most fun job there is or it can be a job from hell. When you love your work, you find the energy to do those things that make you successful - the things that the unsuccessful salespeople hate to do and usually avoid."

"That's great, Bob. I guess you've already learned this lesson all too well. But there is another reason I invited you out here today. Before I get to that, though, I want to find out if you thought the lessons were valuable."

"Valuable? Are you kidding? Between your lessons and my commitment to practicing, I haven't shot over ninety since... in fact, I even broke eighty a couple of times. The only problem I have now is that Butcher and Baker keep harassing me for more strokes!"

"That's great, Bob. I'm glad to hear you have found the lessons worthwhile. That brings me to the second reason I wanted to talk to you today. Bob, I would like to describe the type of golfer I like to coach... "

My mouth drops open as he takes me down an all-too familiar road: Russ is going to ask me for referrals! Part way through his description of his ideal client, I cut him off. "Russ, I thought you were extremely busy because of your experience from teaching the professionals. How come you're asking for referrals?"

A smile comes across his face. "I learned some of my most valuable lessons from my days in sales, and one of the most important was asking for referrals from satisfied customers. When I first came to Canyon Meadows, nobody knew anything about me except for the people who hired me. So, for the first little while, I sat behind the counter waiting for people to find me... but that wasn't working. Sure I was getting some business, but I wanted to be busier, and, most important, I wanted to choose my clientele. So I decided that every time I got a really good client - like yourself - I would do what I am doing with you today - arrange a meeting to get their feedback on my services, and if they were impressed, work with them to identify others who they know fit the description of the type of person I want to work with. It's worked so well I am busier than I have ever been!" He gives me a wink and then continues. "I also do it because it's fun."

"That's excellent, Russ! Where I come from we call that Leveraging... leveraging the great clients you have into many more new clients."

Russ rubs his chin and nods. "Leveraging... I guess that makes sense. So Bob, are you willing to help me out?"

"Well, of course!"

For the next fifteen minutes, Russ jots down names as I rattle off all the people I can think of. I even give him Butcher and Baker - I hope I don't live to regret that! "Are you going to call all of these people and ask for an appointment, Russ?"

"Good question, Bob," Russ says as he reaches into a folder to pull out a colorful brochure with his picture on the front. "I had these made up to give people: a little information on me and my history. I am going to send this card to each of the people you gave me, and if they are interested in my services, they will call... if they are not, then they won't. I was wondering if you would sign the back or possibly jot down a quick note so that they know their name came from you."

I write down a few appropriate one-liners for some, serious comments for a few others, and the rest I simply sign.

"I've enjoyed being your coach, Bob," Russ says, and hands me a card. "Here is a free lesson as a small thank-you for your support."

"Well, thanks, Russ, I appreciate that. I don't want you to think you have seen the last of me, though; if you are going to be giving lessons to Butcher and Baker, I can't afford to let my game slip."

On that note, we part ways with a handshake. On the way home, all I can think about is Russ's request for referrals. It really is true; it's not only salespeople who need to continually find new clients - it's people like Butcher, Baker, and now Russ as well! When it comes right down to it, there are lots of people in a wide range of occupations who could be leveraging their existing successes with their clients into many more successes with new prospects - even the people who are out there looking for jobs. And why should it stop with Leveraging? A lot of people in different careers could benefit from improved skills to identify needs or present their solutions, or even ideas on how to motivate people to act on the solution they are recommending. It is just as I always thought - we are all in the sales game one way or another!

Chapter 15 **Reflections**

I look across to Amanda who is sleeping on her mom's shoulder as we wait for the boarding announcement. Trying to restrain another yawn, I think to myself how we have already been up for two hours, and it's still only 6:30 am.

Over my shoulder, I spot David bouncing through the jungle gym at breakneck speed. I am sure those contraptions are purchased and installed by the flight attendants' unions based on their experience dealing with rambunctious kids like David. It's hard to know if he is more wound-up about Disneyland or his first plane ride!

I sit back in my chair and reflect back over the last year and the events that brought us here today, and I decide it all started with my attitude. I think back to that day when I drove through that neighborhood where I spotted the old man raking the leaves. Instead of absorbing the beauty of the setting, I focused on 'what's wrong with this picture?' and that really represented how I looked at most things in both my professional and personal life at the time.

I've learned that happiness is a feeling you can only experience in the present moment; past happiness is only a fond memory, and future happiness is a nice dream. If you are always dwelling on your past or future, many happy 'here and now' moments will pass you by in life, and you won't even realize it. Whenever possible, I make my way back down that street to remind myself what I have learned about happiness as well as to maintain my good attitude.

I also have learned that, much like golf, if you don't stay brilliant at the basics in sales you can lose your skills - the skills that represent the tools of your trade. If you don't maintain, update, or even replace your skills regularly, you will eventually pay the price in performance. The problem is, your skills can slip away so slowly, you may not even notice until it is too late. I know now that I've got to take some lessons... and most important, I've got to practice if I want to stay sharp. I've also learned from golf that learning to deal with adversity and keeping accurate score all contribute to becoming great at the sales game.

The biggest discovery was that I figured out I was suffering from the Theory of Scarcity. It took the "scare" in scarcity to make me finally realize I needed to turn things around or else I would be looking for a new career. I was guilty of investing a huge amount of effort with too few prospects because of my discomfort with prospecting. In the end, I figured out that proper prospecting is far less uncomfortable than the fear and disappointment that comes with the Theory of Scarcity.

This turnaround started, I muse, by my becoming a TOP (Theory of Plenty) student; eventually I became a TOP star. The Theory of Plenty has given me self-confidence I haven't had in years, and I now know there are many, many, qualified buyers who are looking for people like me to help them... and Leveraging was the key!

I now strive to make every new client leverageable, right from the start. They know that if I do a great job, I will be looking for their help to identify others who they know can benefit from my services. I also make weekly goals to do Leveraging interviews, and when I do get referrals, I contact them right away to book an appointment.

Another great thing about the Theory of Plenty is that it has given *me* the power to say, *"No, I am not interested,"* when the prospects don't fit the criteria. For so many years, I tried force-fitting every prospect into my solution at the expense of my energy, self-esteem, and credibility. Having an ongoing pool of high-quality referrals allows me to 'cut bait' quickly from those prospects that don't fit the criteria before I waste both my valuable time and theirs.

Sure, over the last year, I have learned some great skills... but I didn't do it on my own. People like Russ convinced me of the value of having a coach. Not everyone needs a coach, but I needed someone to talk to who cared about me and whether I succeeded or failed. Jeff may not have been the perfect manager in the beginning, but he had one of the most essential ingredients required... he cared about his people. Time and experience have taught him many valuable lessons over the last year, and the increasing sales results for our division are proof of that.

I like to think I am making a contribution to the division's success as well. Teddie, Sarah, and myself have now expanded our title from the 'Old Guard' to the 'Old Guardian Angels', and we now make a concerted effort to recommend high-quality people to our team as well as making a point to get to know each of the new people coming aboard. We also give back to the team by conducting training sessions whenever we can. At first I thought I was being charitable, but in the end I realized I was learning as much - or more - than they each time I conducted another session.

Success didn't happen overnight, though. It took me a number of years to form the bad habits that led to my spiral down in sales; you don't just turn those kinds of things around overnight. I had to stop measuring my success based on results (something I couldn't control) and had to start measuring it based on effort towards the right activities (something I could). John Andrew's advice still stands as the single biggest influencer of my activities each day:

Throughout your day, you are taking small steps; some towards the success you are striving for, some towards your eventual failure.

The more I rewarded myself for doing the right activities, the more in touch I became with the 'best' boss –the boss that had faded away over the years. I've learned that some of the most rewarding 'atta boy's I get now are the ones I give myself for putting in the effort. The results started with Selectrum, but with increasing frequency, more new contracts came each month.

It didn't take David long to make the link between the announcement of another new contract and his increasing chances of going to Disneyland; getting the family involved in the goal made me more accountable and gave them a sense of ownership as well. Particularly in the last few months, David would meet me walking in the door each night to ask, "Dad, Dad, how was your day?" What he was really asking was, "Dad, Dad, did we get closer to Disneyland today?" I hardly had my shoes off my feet and he was off polishing them up for the next day!

Amanda took a more subtle approach by making a rainbow chart on her wall. At one end of the rainbow was our home and at the other was a collection of Disneyland pictures. She broke the goal up into levels, and each time I reached one, she would carefully color another band across the chart. The finished rainbow still hangs on her wall as a proud reminder of where we have come from.

Sandy helped in her own way as well. Besides having a keen interest in both my successes and challenges, she helped me stay focused at work and helped me keep the rest of my life in balance.

From behind me, I hear the familiar call of, "Dad, Dad, watch this!"

I turn to see David coming down the slide face first with his arms stretched out in front of him calling out, "Rocket-Man!" while skidding to an abrupt stop on his stomach on the rubber mat at the bottom. I blush, thinking of the day I wrote the last contract to reach the goal we had set. I raced into the house with my coat hung over my shoulders like a cape, calling out "Rocket-Man!" By the time I stopped to talk to Sandy, both kids were right behind me doing their own 'Rocket-Man' imitation... and David hasn't let me forget that ever since.

Finally, the boarding announcement we have been waiting for comes over the intercom. As Sandy stirs Amanda, I motion to David, and then I begin to gather up our carry-on luggage.

Walking down the passageway to the plane, I look out one of the porthole windows and notice that the low-hanging clouds we arrived in are still there. For David's sake, I was hoping the clouds would have broken up by now so that he could have a better view once we are up in the air. Knowing David though, clouds are the least of his concern.

I check my watch one last time as they roll the plane back from the gate. We are right on schedule; I knew we would be! I look at David sitting beside me with his nose pressed against the glass, periodically glancing at me with wide eyes and an indelible smile as the plane positions to take off. The pilot applies the throttle and when the whine of the engines reaches a peak, he releases the brakes. The plane begins to roll slowly, but within seconds we can feel ourselves being forced back in our seats as the plane accelerates from the thrust of the engines.

Out of the blue, David starts calling out, "Five, four, three, two, one... BLAST OFF!" and at that moment, the plane lifts off. There are a few claps, as well as laughter from the passengers within earshot of David.

I always find that while there is a thrill just after you lift off and begin gaining altitude, there is also a slight fear when you leave the security of solid ground. David looks at me, then his sister, and finally his mother, to see if we are as excited as he is. Any sign of excitement from one of us provides another springboard to take his excitement to a higher level.

As we enter the clouds, David's view becomes limited to the wing just outside his window. I watch him closely as he stares out, trying to see through the clouds.

After ten minutes of 'nothingness', the plane pops through the clouds like a buoyant cork. Up above is the bright sun and beautiful blue sky, while the clouds form a pillow-like landscape for as far as the eye can see. David turns to me with a puzzled look and says, "Dad, I never knew that there was sunshine and blue sky above the clouds!" Before I can explain, he turns his attention back to the window to catch every aspect of his new discovery.

I close my eyes, lay my head back in the seat, and reflect on the moment. David's countdown takes me back to a recent sales meeting: Jeff was standing at the front announcing the leaders of the division for the year. He started off slowly - he announced fifth place and then fourth. By the time he got to third place, the eyes in the room were starting to focus on me. "In second place, we have... " he called out and then paused, "Karen!" and the applause began. With all the eyes in the room locked on me, he continued, "... and the #1 sales person for the year is... Bob Stephens!"

As I walked down the aisle to the front of the room, it felt much like going down that runway today, the same acceleration as well as the same tingle of fear. For years, I was like David today... I thought there were only clouds because all 'blue sky and sunshine' had disappeared from my view.

By the time I reached the front of the room to shake hands with Jeff, I broke through the clouds that had been hanging over me, and I felt the warmth from the sunshine that had been there all along.

And, from the back of the room I could hear the mumbled tones of Teddie, Sarah, and the rest of my friends all humming the tune of an old familiar song.

The End

A special thanks to all of those people who contributed to the book either through their feedback along the way, or through their contribution of ideas for content. I would also like to thank Joel Semchuk for his editing talents, and Mediashaker for the graphics design and website.

There is an endless list of people who shaped my ideas over the years; however, I would like to specifically acknowledge John Anderson, Harold Norlin, Todd Townend, and George Kjenner who exemplify success in sales and sales management.

Rocket-Man:
The Resurrection!

If you know of someone who could benefit from reading Rocket-Man, why not order an additional copy for them! We will ship the book to them, compliments of you! All you need to do is find our website at:

www.rocket-man.com

Once you are there you can fill out a simple order form, and we'll take care of the rest!

Onward and upward!